INFLUENCE

INFLUENCE

UNDERSTAND IT, USE IT, RESIST IT

JUSTIN HEMPSON-JONES

WILLIAM
COLLINS

William Collins
An imprint of HarperCollins*Publishers*
1 London Bridge Street
London SE1 9GF

WilliamCollinsBooks.com

HarperCollins*Publishers*
Macken House
39/40 Mayor Street Upper
Dublin 1
D01 C9W8, Ireland

First published in Great Britain in 2024 by William Collins

1

Typeset in Minion Pro by Palimpsest Book Production Ltd, Falkirk, Stirlingshire

Printed and bound in the UK using 100% renewable electricity at CPI Group (UK) Ltd

This book contains FSC™ certified paper and other controlled sources
to ensure responsible forest management.

For more information visit: www.harpercollins.co.uk/green

For Pea,
with love

Contents

Introduction

Meet Ashkar Techy, a social media star. Techy splices together content from elsewhere on the internet, enhancing it with engaging commentary and boyish energy. In 'types of wedding video' a groom falls off backwards while sliding down the bannisters inside a sumptuous venue. Another captures the groom placing the Hindu marriage ceremony flower garland, the Varmala, around the neck of the bride. Techy talks us through as one groom takes the flower garland, and – to the mortification of the assembled guests – places it round the neck of a woman standing next to the bride. Another video is titled 'Chinese food' and features one girl eating a bowl full of small crabs and another eating snakes. If this were not enough, someone slurps up a live octopus, tentacles first, and a guy eats a bar of soap. Other videos range from 'make-up' to 'funny newspaper headlines'. Techy's easy-going format has gained his most popular video over a million views.

And here is Everson Zoio, another social media star: Zoio has 1.5 million friends on Facebook, 3 million followers on Instagram and a whopping 12.9 million subscribers on YouTube. In one YouTube post his brother trashes his studio (14 million views). In another, Zoio and his friends walk into a supermarket and are kicked out after they start partying with drinks and snacks (17 million views). But in his most-viewed video yet, the prankster sticks his hand into an ants' nest and talks us through the pain as his fingers and wrists welt up from hundreds of bites (20 million+ views).

One of these stars is based in India. The other, halfway round the world in Brazil. But these two 'influencers' are also linked in a more sinister way. In 2020 the SARS-COV-2 virus burst out of China and across the world. As public health systems were pushed towards collapse and death rates soared, governments and corporations raced to adapt effective vaccines. In record-breaking times these vaccines were tested and then rolled out in those countries that could afford to pay for them.

Yet in a context of fear, uncertainty and distrust, many across the world were anxious and hesitant about taking them. After all, even the scientists and medical professionals who were supposed to know about these sorts of things seemed to disagree about strategy: lockdown or not lockdown? Did masks work or not? Was it really so important to social-distance ourselves from our loved ones? Into the breach of this doubtful swirl came all sorts of information.

Ashkar Techy, for one, took a detour from his typical content to share data that seemed to have leaked from the European Medicines Agency: apparently they had uncovered a stupendous difference in the death rates between the Pfizer and AstraZeneca vaccines. This seemed to cast doubt over the legitimacy of the vaccine roll-out – and the appeals of the scientific and governmental authorities responsible for it. Over in Brazil Everson Zoio also deviated from playing with ants to build this concerning data into video content. Why not? After all, anxious followers might be hungry for any information they could get their hands on which might help them make better sense of the chaos.

Now meet Mirko Drotschmann, a YouTube star based in Germany specialising in social and political commentary (1.3 million subscribers). And, while we are at it, meet Léo Grasset from France: a social media star focused on popularising science (1.2 million YouTube subscribers). Each of these individuals independently contacted media organisations to share a curious tale.

'It started with an email,' claimed Drotschmann. An email from a marketing agency called Fazze. They were asking if he would be amenable to share information they had come across: data apparently leaked from the European Medicines Agency – data purporting to illustrate wildly divergent survival rates for those who had received different vaccines. Grasset received the same unsolicited request: the agency was offering 2,000 euros in exchange for sharing the content on behalf of their client, who wished to remain anonymous. The two influencers played along.

'Act like you have the passion and interest in this topic,' they were told, and they were not to tell their audiences that the content was sponsored. They were also asked to share an article from the French broadsheet newspaper *Le Monde*, about a genuine information leak from the European Medicines Agency. However – and crucially – the reported content of the leak was unrelated to the data that Fazze was asking these influencers to share. Upon investigation, the data about post-vaccine survival rates seemed to have been thrown together and taken out of context from an eclectic range of credible original sources. Drotschmann and Grasset were also sent a number of other links from sources of more dubious origin, and asked to direct their audiences to these also.

But why? For what purpose? By whom? Journalists puzzled by these questions took up the scent and soon identified Fazze as part of a larger company called 'AdNow' based in both the UK and Russia. But when they called the UK Director, Ewan Tolladay, he appeared to have no knowledge of Fazze's approaches to influencers, nor could he shed any light on the mysterious client providing the financing. Tolladay did state, however, that Fazze was a joint venture between his business partner, Stanislav Fesenko – a Russian national – and someone else, whose identity he knew nothing about. In any case, before long AdNow had liquidated itself – and with it, any chance of better understanding the origins of the whole murky affair.

Who had a strong motive to influence publics across the world – to cast doubt on the safety of vaccines created in Europe and the United States? Who had the means to pay for such activities? Fingers were quickly pointed at the Russian State. But there was no smoking gun. Just insinuation and circumstance. The motive and capability seemed to be there: part of a recent and historic habit of sowing disinformation as part of a toolkit of so-called 'active measures'.

As for Ashkar Techy and Everson Zoio? Journalists investigating Fazze noticed that these two influencers had – virtually line by line – posted the content the ad company had been pushing. They promptly deleted this content and ignored requests for comment from journalists. Techy and Zoio, perhaps typifying a new cast of messenger within the twenty-first-century media environment, were also playing a much older role: that of the 'useful idiot', the unwitting agent for someone else's cause. Idiots, perhaps you're thinking. But in our interconnected age, none of us are immune to idiocy. How easily could this story have involved your friend or relation – your child or sibling? Or perhaps even you?

This episode highlights a number of questions about how we are influenced – and specifically how we are influenced in the age of ubiquitous information. What might someone gain from spreading deceptive information? What impact can this have? Why? And what might this have to do with recruiting influencers, with interests ranging from science discussions to catchy compilations of curiosities and pranks? The answers are to be found in the dynamics of social influence – of how our actions affect those of others. These in turn depend on how the architecture of our individual and collective minds – the product of evolution – interacts with technology. This is a book about social influence. Specifically, it is a book that highlights how twenty-first-century technological and cultural trends push social influence to work against our interests, including those of the democratic societies we live in. It is also a book about how changing the way we think can contribute to what we can do about it.

Why is this the right moment to know about social influence? What is special about now? Let's rewind just over a century, to early-twentieth-century Europe. The First World War is under way and millions of soldiers have been drafted from across the world – from colonies in Africa, Asia and Australasia; from North America – all the way to the muddy, blood-soaked trenches of the Western Front. There these men lived and died, often just a few hundred metres from those they had been sent to fight. It is a distinctive mark of a social species that millions of individual humans could be motivated to adopt such a strong 'us' versus 'them' mentality: to work so cooperatively with their comrades-in-arms ('us'), in order to attack and attempt to destroy others they had never met, nor held any personal grudge against – others who represented another huge conglomerate of millions working together ('them').

That this phenomenon could unfold was in part down to the skill of powerful states in motivating the masses. This related to an ability to instil aligned attitudes (thoughts and feelings), beliefs (attitudes about what is true), values (attitudes about what is morally right) and norms of behaviour in the combatants. This resulted from the information diets these soldiers had ingested over time. In turn, these diets depended upon whom they trusted – as well as what they paid attention to, and what they had memorised. And the sense they made of these depended upon the sedimented layers of attitudes and beliefs they had built up across the course of their lives, within which any of this new information would be assimilated.

Of course, the enemy might attempt to influence these fundamentals via the machine gun and artillery barrage: a quick but indiscriminate way of affecting the physical and psychological make-up of people. They also aimed to change attitudes, beliefs and behaviours through other forms of information: such as the dropping of written propaganda from the sky in the hope of convincing soldiers to surrender. It was am imprecise affair, with unmanned hydrogen balloons flying over no-man's-land ready to burst above the enemy trenches with leaflets promising humane treatment, while ridiculing faraway leaders. It was also crude: the creators generally had little ability to understand those they were trying to influence – whose attitudes, beliefs and norms of behaviour were formed in close interaction with others in the small communities of friends and family from whence they came.

That world is no more. In the twenty-first century, our behavioural systems include not only our family, friends, colleagues and fellow travellers, but also machines, electronic devices and software agents. Systems of influence more clearly than ever include technology as well as people – we are embedded in *sociotechnical* systems, or *social machines*. Some of these technologies clustered as a network or networks – an *internet* – connect us to distant loved ones; and they place news and information within our grasp at any time in almost any place, because the variety and volume of content with which to stock our information environments has proliferated exponentially. We are forced to become ever more discriminatory as our information spaces are flooded with viral cat videos, five-star product reviews, the babble of countless competing ideas and ideologies. The interconnected world exposes us continuously not only to vast volumes of information but to the proliferation of culture – and potentially to a hugely diverse array of attitudes, beliefs and values: to the stories of others.

A thought experiment: could the citizen warriors of the Western Front in the First World War have been corralled there and motivated to fight in the age of social media? On 24 February 2022 the Russian military began its brutal attempt to subjugate Ukraine. The physical violence would occur most intensively at the battlefront and be bounded mostly by Ukraine's borders. But in the information battlespace, there were few such bounds. The Russians were soon busy telling Europe that if only they had not made themselves belligerents in a faraway land, they would have enjoyed gas and warm homes for the winter; in the Global South they claimed that the West was to blame for the shortage of grain caused by the war. Meanwhile, from Ukraine came heroic tales such as that of a 'Ghost of Kyiv' aircraft savaging Russian MiGs from the skies; and the defenders of Snake Island, called upon to surrender, responding: 'Russian warship, go fuck yourself.'

These might seem to be old stories of wartime propaganda. But the means of delivery was newer – because now much of the work was done by the audiences themselves, as they joined in, shared, created, memed. Citizens from Western democracies might drop anti-war messaging in the Google reviews of restaurants in Russia, on Russian-language online games or in the chatlogs of Russian gambling and porn sites. Websites such as 'Call Russia' popped up to put protestors in direct contact with Russians via a random number generator.

These activities were inseparable from cyber attacks making similar use of digital-age connectivity. An estimated 2,100 attacks were hurled by suspected Russian actors at Ukrainian organisations during 2022, targeting not just security and defence apparatus but energy, financial and telecommunications critical infrastructure – as well as civil society groups (these would be complemented later by missile and drone strikes).

The fightback in the other direction appeared to focus on the Russian information environment. A campaign ostensibly organised by the hacktivist group Anonymous drew keyboard warriors from around the world to attack websites and services in Russia and companies still doing business there, and to hack Russian-based printers to pump out censorship-evading messages – and news sites and TV channels to broadcast imagery and information banned by the regime.

Information about all this and far more swirled around societies and across borders through a single interconnected system; one that included and also impacted soldiers risking their lives on the front line and their loved ones. Things had surely changed since the days of balloons dropping leaflets on the enemy.

The question of whether the warriors of the First World War would have been motivated to fight under these conditions is now more strongly than ever linked to events back at what was once known as the 'home front'. In our age society can be undermined or attacked directly, often avoiding engagement with conventional military forces altogether; it is a struggle to influence thoughts and actions that has become increasingly confusing and fragmented, fought on many more fronts and by increasing numbers of actors.

This brings into sharp relief what it means to be influenced within our modern social machines. It is difficult to disaggregate the behaviours of hugely different actors. How do special interest groups and corporations and terrorists get us to do what they want? What is the difference between what foreign states and our own governments can do to reach out and shape our thoughts and feelings? Indeed, how do the methods of any of these actors really differ from the ways in which our nearest and dearest influence us and each other? It's all smudged together in one gigantic, messy web.

And why should we care? Well, in front of us lies a series of terrifying survival problems. Not just the lurking natural threat of super-volcanic eruption, asteroid impact or interstellar explosion – but also those that we have created for ourselves. A heating earth. Pandemics that leverage our interconnectedness to spread, well, like a plague. Machines that cast the masses into unemployment and precipitate social unrest – and that's before they surpass our level of 'general intelligence' and take control completely. If this was not enough on the collective 'to do' list, geopolitical tension has returned with a vengeance in the form of a new age of competition and conflict between nuclear-armed states.

These states are currently busy infiltrating one another's social and economic systems with cyber infrastructure: not only the type of devastating weaponry that can knock out power stations and communications networks, but also the tools with which to shape the minds of others. No longer does the adversary drop leaflets on our soldiers in faraway lands. They can be there, reaching right into your mind; nudging you as you scroll your phone – whether in the workplace, while you sit on the couch or lie in bed. They can target us increasingly precisely; after all, you may have given them the keys to manipulating your reality through all the information running off you into the mighty data rivers of the internet.

Zooming out, new battle lines are being drawn: on the one side are a set of seemingly confident, invigorated, authoritarian powers. Ranged against them lie a loose alliance of embattled liberal democracies. This is a new struggle measured by our thoughts, feelings and behaviours – one that will be determined, in large part, by our actions and how they change those of others: by our social influence.

We should care, because the answers to twenty-first-century human-made problems are to be found in our ability to put our collective minds together and move in wise directions. This starts with resisting the lure of charismatic strongmen whose wisdom and interest in collective wellbeing are rarely the equal of their will to power. In our time, many question the virtues of liberal democracy to cater to our needs, including those of survival. In some societies, trust between governments and the governed seems almost irrevocably degraded. Meanwhile, all those diverse, squabbling voices around us often appear to just create messes. Democracy looks tired, like yesterday's form of political organisation. Instead we may have the impression that the future belongs to visionary autocrats like Xi Jinping in China and the butcher Vladimir Putin in Russia. Certainly, that's what they spend a great deal of effort trying to persuade us. But we have, of course, heard all this before. In the 1930s the fascists and their sympathisers claimed the mantle of vigorous, virile modernity and predicted the imminent demise of decadent democracy. We all know how that went.

Our liberal democratic systems still produce the wealthiest, healthiest, most creative societies ever known. They are still overwhelmingly the best at problem-solving on the frontiers of knowledge – or as Winston Churchill observed, 'Many forms of Government have been tried, and will be tried in this world of sin and woe. No one pretends that democracy is perfect or all-wise. Indeed it has been said that democracy is the worst form of Government except for all those other forms that have been tried from time to time . . .'

In a struggle for the survival of democracy – and, indeed, our wider futures – we are all now, more than ever, on the front lines: you, me and everyone we know. We must step up: learn how to think better in the information age, and act to preserve our collective interests. How does influence work? How can we harness it and use it ourselves? But, more importantly, how do we recognise when it is at work? How do we protect ourselves from it when it threatens our interests? How can we arm ourselves, our friends and loved ones, our societies, so we can not only survive in the decades ahead but, perhaps, flourish too?

We will investigate all these questions. But first, this book – like any form of communication – is an attempt to influence. As we will see, the content is often only as influential as the communicator delivering it. So who am I? Why should you let me be your guide? Perhaps you shouldn't. Any half-decent influencer will attempt to gain your trust in order to change or reinforce your attitudes and behaviours. I'll surely aim to make the most of this opportunity to alter the make-up and structure of the associations in your mind.

I worked for almost every part of the UK government that has to care about the dynamics of influence in twenty-first-century security and defence environments. I am an applied behavioural scientist, and my job is to help identify and understand how these dynamics work in the most extreme conditions of cooperation, competition and conflict. How can support abroad for violent extremist groups be reduced? How can we defend ourselves against cyber attack? What can be done about foreign states pumping propaganda and disinformation into open societies? In short: how can we change human behaviours? Applied behavioural science provides toolkits that can support solutions to these problems, drawing insight and method from the various disciplines that focus on the processes and outcomes of human behaviour – psychology, behavioural economics, anthropology and sociology.

What might you take away from this perspective? How can we think better in the information age? The first part of the book explores how influence works through the following elements:

Judgement. Evolution honed our judgement and decision-making processes to help us survive and prosper. This helps explain how influence impacts our attention – the focusing of our senses to collect information about threats and opportunities; our memory – stores of previously collected information that enable us to remember concepts that might be important to future survival (and reproduction); our pattern identification – comparing and contrasting information that we ingest and store; our emotion – our feelings, which set the context for action; and our ego – the self-protective drive to interpret our actions positively.

Trust. We are a social species, and many of our basic needs – to engage, communicate and belong; to compete and seek status – are directly linked to this way of being. Many of the cues we act on come from others. But which others? When? We are prone to copying those around us when in doubt. And we are generally especially responsive to those we find authoritative and those we find attractive. We are influenced by those we trust, and trust is often based on rules of thumb such as warmth or reciprocation. But these rules of thumb are also easily exploited by deceivers and other influencers who may not have our best interests at heart.

Culture guides how we behave, what we believe and whom we listen to. It influences who we are and what we want, by telling us who we should be and what we are supposed to crave. It provides references regarding who else belongs to our social groups and who does not – it directs us as to what we should think about both 'us' and 'them'. Drawing on culture is crucial for influence: not least because, being saturated in it, we may overlook when it is used to manipulate us.

Identity is a story about who we are, and therefore who is similar – and who is different. Identity informs how we think and how we act – including how we think about, and act towards, our fellows. Identity can be shaped and manipulated to the ends of others. Through shared identity, diverse minds can be brought together to great positive effect. But these same minds can also be abused by others to help sow fear and division, thus degrading the fabric of our societies and jeopardising our survival and prosperity.

Power. To achieve our goals we must mould our social environments – control them, to some degree. Power enables us to do this. Every time we interact with our family, friends, acquaintances and adversaries we negotiate our goals within webs of power. The manifestation of power has altered over time as culture and technology have changed. Power can be overwhelming, even devastating. But we do not have to submit to it: we can resist.

The second part of the book shows how the nature of influence is changing in the digital age, with the result that dangerous adversaries are empowered and our societies imperilled; it provides guidance about what we must do to protect them.

The Stage. Just as our physical bodies are the food we eat, our minds are the information we consume. Our information diets influence how we think and feel: they mould our attitudes, our beliefs and our behaviours – often without our being aware. In the internet age, powerful actors can reach us more easily than ever, seeking ways to gain our attention, memory and emotion, to harness our ego, to leverage our capacity for recognising patterns; they are enabled to entangle our thoughts and feelings in schemes far removed from our best interests. We must better *control our information diets.*

The Cast. Much of the information we share is with our trusted networks of family and friends – our social networks. These networks are augmented on the internet as mass-media communications that were once the preserve of elites but are now available to all. But, just as our access to the minds of others has increased, so they can access ours – bringing new opportunities for the mischievous and the malign. We must *become expert deception detectors.*

Who Are We? As our information environments change, extremists are empowered to radicalise large sections of the population, turning people against each other. These conditions are stoked by a host of predators, some hidden in the shadows, others in broad daylight. The result is a shared perception of degraded democracy; and since perception drives reality at least as much as vice versa, it is small wonder that this dynamic is further manipulated by democracy's enemies. We must *role-model and reach out with humility.*

Who Am I? The internet has revolutionised *which* others know *what* about us. Information about who we are and what we do, what we like and what we want; information that we might once have shared only with intimates is now freely exploited by interests far beyond these trusted networks. We give such information unwittingly, but often wittingly too, through our increasingly public performances;

these show what we do and who we are – they too can be exploited by others. We should *become a privacy watchkeeper*.

The Play. The digital age has wrought fundamental change to the nature of power – and specifically the exercise of informational power. On the one hand, the huge expansion of access to the minds of others potentially increases everyone's informational power. Yet on the other, those best placed to exploit such power are those who are already powerful. There are winners, like the Silicon Valley-based tech platforms and those who own them, and apparent losers – not least liberal democracies, which are now vulnerable to a range of authoritarian competitors; the consequences for our social and political hierarchies are uncertain, but potentially radical. We must *use our informational power wisely* – with the aim, first and foremost, of *taking back control of our information environments*.

Our future is not predetermined. Whether liberal democracies fracture and disintegrate, are 'rescued' by authoritarian strongmen, or renew themselves and survive to help us solve the problems of our age is down to us.

PART ONE:

HOW INFLUENCE WORKS

1. Judgement

We may live on the edge of survival, in the shadow of rising seas and nuclear holocaust. But in terms of daily subsistence our distant ancestor, the archaic human species *Homo habilis*, had it far worse. At the dawn of the tool-making era, this 5-foot-tall human with a brain around half the size of our own was preyed upon by crocodiles, bears and eagles, as well as hyenas, sabre-tooth tigers and other big cats. That *Homo habilis* existed was in itself the product of countless generations of organisms evolving and successfully reproducing: it was adapted for survival.

It was through adaptation that the mechanisms underpinning our judgement and decision-making began to develop across evolutionary time: mechanisms including attention, memory, the ability to identify and recognise patterns in information collected, the impact of emotion and ego. And it is through these elements of cognition that we still target one another for influence.

It is a key feature of our species that we can use our advanced reflective, conscious abilities to make sense of things. We can establish facts, apply logic and adapt our beliefs (thoughts or feelings about what is true) and behaviours in the light of new information – like when we complete a puzzle or fill in our tax returns. Sometimes we may even seem to act rationally: behaving in ways that align with our reasoning. In this case, doesn't influence simply boil down to persuasion – the use of reason and argument to change the attitudes, beliefs and behaviours of others?

Reason and rationality are closely linked to an ability to reflect. But much of our cognition is not reflective, but automatic: a system of

thought that is fast, frequent, emotional, stereotypical and uncon-
scious.[1] Imagine that you're taking a walk in a part of the world
inhabited by venomous snakes. Suddenly you spot a long object in
the undergrowth. Is it a stick? Or is it a snake? By now your adrenal
glands are pumping hormones into your blood vessels. This triggers
an increase in breathing rate, blood pressure and heart rate – boosting
your body's ability to fight or take flight. In this circumstance, unless
you are a seasoned snake hunter, you are probably already running
off, screaming wildly.

It is a windy day, though, which means rustling leaves, and it turns
out that what you thought was a snake is in fact a stick (it's all a bit
embarrassing, but hopefully there were not many witnesses). Having
a cognitive apparatus – a mind – that is tuned to (mistakenly) perceive
harmless objects as dangerous ones can aid your survival. These mis-
identifications – or *false positives* – confer a useful advantage in a
hostile world. Mistaking a stick for a snake is embarrassing. But
mistaking a snake for a stick may be deadly. And since the impact of
making *false negative* judgements like the latter may remove you from
the gene pool, natural selection means that most of us will be attuned
to identify more sticks as snakes than vice versa. Much of our cognition is driven not by a logic of reason or rationality, but one of survival
and reproduction – itself the product of evolution. By extension, it is
also this logic that we are targeting when we influence one another.

The ways we think often involve following rules of thumb, or *heuristics*. Heuristics have been helpful for humans and other animals in
solving core problems of existence – how to live to fight another day,
perhaps even long enough to reproduce and raise offspring to mat-
urity. But these modes of thinking can also lead us astray. Not least,
because others can manipulate them against our interest.

Remember the events that led to you identify a stick in the undergrowth. There was a potentially large amount of information around
you in the environment, but you homed in on a small portion of it.
Our tools for collecting this information are sight, hearing, touch,
taste and smell: our senses. They are limited portals: a tiny portion of
the available electromagnetic spectrum reaches your eyes – unless you
have special powers, you do not see in ultraviolet or infra-red. Your
ears can pick out only a small range of air pressure changes (sounds),

and you detect only proximate chemical and pressure changes via smell, taste and touch. And there is an almost infinite amount of information to ingest out there. So how can we best apply our senses? How can we separate what is important from everything else? And just how was it that you first spotted that stick in the bushes? You did this by focusing your five senses to collect specific information from the environment: by directing *attention*.

What you pay attention to not only decides what information in the environment you focus on, but how you will act. Attention is highly selective. By default, this means it tends to overlook what is not assessed to be important, as illustrated in a now-famous experiment by the psychologists Daniel Simons and Christopher Chabris. Here participants viewed a video in which a group of people threw a basketball to one another, and were asked to count how many times the ball was passed. Dutifully they performed the task and were then asked to watch the video again. This time, without the cognitive burden of having to count, they became immediately aware of one of the experimental team dressed in a gorilla suit strolling straight through the middle of the exercise.[2]

Part of the reason you may have identified an interesting object in the bushes earlier was because it stood out – was different – from its surroundings. Any animal that wishes to survive or prosper may benefit from having a mechanism of this kind that directs their attention towards things that stand out. *Homo habilis* hears a strange animal call. What does it represent: a meal? Or that they are about to become one? A colourful plant – is it asking to be eaten? Or warning predators not to? Attention is drawn to the novel. This is the isolation effect in operation. It has always made sense for an animal to pay attention to previously unencountered information: what does the novel stimulus represent – threat, or opportunity?

We can draw on this isolation effect to direct attention. A guy walks confidently into a crowded bar wearing gold platform shoes. Why? This is the journalist (and formerly self-styled profiler of 'pick-up artists') Neil Strauss, demonstrating a technique he describes as 'peacocking' to attract the attention of others by standing out.[3] As the name suggests, it is not a terribly novel innovation. Indeed, similar mechanisms determine why we wear jewellery, make-up and body art.

As well as directing attention, the isolation effect can be used to misdirect. We see this as a magician pulls an audience member on stage. 'Look at their hands,' they say, placing a distinctive object in this volunteer's hand (while also placing another version of the object on their shoulder). 'Now were you paying attention?' they ask. Because, sure enough, they are now drawing attention to the object on the shoulder – which seems to have miraculously migrated there. And while they do this, well, naturally they remove the volunteer's watch from their wrist . . .

Politicians are often especially adept at harnessing the effect in a format described by the Australian political strategist Lynton Crosby as 'throwing a dead cat on the table' or 'deadcatting' – so called because, in the words of former British prime minister Boris Johnson, 'everyone will shout "Jeez, mate, there's a dead cat on the table!"'. In other words, they will be talking about the dead cat – the thing you want them to talk about – and they will not be talking about the issue that has been causing you so much grief'.[4]

What we attend to – what is salient to us – regulates which specific items of information we ingest. At least as importantly, this process also helps determine what we overlook: we will tend to place too much weight on what we have attended to – and judge this informa-tion to be more causal than it is. In the experiments of social psychologist Daniel Lassiter, participants watched a suspect provide a confession during criminal interrogation. They assigned greater culpability to the criminal suspect when the camera was focused on the suspect, and less when the camera angle included the interrogator as well. The bias is completely reversed when the camera is sited over the suspect's shoulder, trained on the interrogator.[5] This is called a focusing effect. This type of effect can enable us to deliberately mislead others by putting before them factual, but cherry-picked, information: such as presenting a prospective client with authentic positive reviews of your organisation's amazing new service (though later, if they check online, they will see these outweighed by the many more authentic negative reviews).

Taking command of others' attention is to guide and determine which subset of information they will consume – to shape their infor-mation diet. But attention also links strongly to memory. Here is a task:

do not think about pink elephants. How is this working out for you, this not thinking about pink elephants? Difficult, isn't it? Impossible, perhaps. Because as you read these words you scan your memory for precisely the pink elephants you are supposed not to be thinking about. Such a mechanism can be used to get you thinking about virtually any idea: that Jews have been kidnapping and eating the children of Christians perhaps (a medieval classic). Or that maybe 5G mobile phone masts are responsible for causing COVID-19.

Where people are uncommitted to an attitude or belief, managing attention in this manner may directly change what they think. But more than this. After all, you may have entirely different, deeply held views to me concerning, for instance, should people be required to wear masks in the middle of a pandemic? By merely raising the issue, we can set the terms of debate and frame what is important: are masks the key issue in relation to pandemic management? Or is it underfunded healthcare services? And why focus on the pandemic: what about how to cut down on your fossil fuel consumption, reduce uncontrolled immigration, or manage the clutter of street signs in our cities and wind turbines littering our countryside? Even when people are already committed to opposing sets of attitudes and beliefs, we can still direct their attention to influence what topics they think about.

Let's explore the attention-memory link a bit further. New information we attend to becomes encoded within existing memories. We do indeed revise our attitudes towards someone or something in the light of new information – such as that pleasant colleague you say 'Hi' to in the corridor, but who you just saw abusing the delivery driver. However, once encoded, associations can be hard to erase – even when the evidence for holding them is contradicted by further information. This explains the enduring wisdom behind the advice 'make a good first impression': once we form an initial attitude towards someone, it can be hard to shift.

Memory can also be manipulated by message repetition. The same idea is raised again and again: no matter how hard you try, the idea imposes itself upon your memory. This strengthens both the encoding of information (as it transfers from short- to long-term memory) and the subsequent recall of these associations. It's especially effective when using simple, catchy content – an advertising jingle or political slogans like 'Finger Lickin' Good', 'Hope and Change', 'Take Back Control', or 'Make America Great Again!' On the other hand, too much repetition may prove counterproductive – and can bore the audience. If we initially judge something negatively, the repeated exposure of it may amplify our negative feelings towards it – as may be the case for some when they are exposed to soundbites from a well-known political figure.[6]

And yet, repeated exposure to information can also cause us to think that even something demonstrably false is true. The claim that childhood vaccinations are associated with a higher risk of developing autism, perhaps. We may once have believed this claim to be false, especially as others helpfully explained why. But then we encountered the assertion again and again. Finally, we were able to recall the details of the information, but not so much the reasons why we initially judged it to be false: now we fear those vaccinations as we would like to prevent our child from contracting any neural-atypical condition such as autism. Here the illusory truth effect is at work. Indeed, the strength of encoding in our memories may sometimes be so great that even after we have later acknowledged the falsity of information, it can still generate illusory truth.

The way in which associations form in our memory strongly influences what is recalled – and, in circular fashion, what we attend to. Depending upon our cultural experiences (more on this later), we may read the word 'chair' and more easily recall the word 'table'. We see 'butter' and think 'bread'; or a roaring fire and think 'food'. The way in which one stimulus quickly directs us to another is called priming, and it is associated more with our fast, automatic and subconscious thinking processes. The impact of priming is aided by the tendency of people to confuse the information they have been primed with for their own thoughts and feelings: they may feel as if an idea they were primed with 'just came to me'.

One study suggests that priming individuals with the words 'win', 'attain' or 'succeed' may help them do just that (although to muddy the water, another study failed to replicate this result).[7] Would we like to help employees live more actively? There is evidence that priming them with athletic words such as 'lean', 'fit' and 'active' can make them more likely to take the stairs rather than the lift.[8] Or how about being more cooperative? That could be good for business: words such as 'teamwork', 'united' and 'collective' are shown to have increased subsequent cooperation in experiments.[9] On the other hand, priming people with concepts of money can make them more selfish;[10] words associated with impoliteness can make people behave more rudely;[11] and words of violence such as 'he hit them' may lead them to behave more aggressively.[12] Meanwhile dieters primed with words like 'pizza', 'chocolate' and 'tasty' seem more likely to give up.[13] Suggesting associated words and concepts may activate the memory to alter judgements, decisions and behaviour.

What our attention is drawn to affects what we remember. And in turn, what we remember affects what information we attend to – as well as how we make sense of it to arrive at judgements and decisions. We tend to rely on what easily comes to mind – what is easy to recall – when making judgements. This is the availability heuristic. Do more people die from shark attacks or aeroplane parts falling from the sky? Many more people die from aeroplane parts falling out of the sky. But you may not know this for all the attention paid to shark attacks.

The availability heuristic has significant impact on how we assess risk. We worry about shark attacks off the Cornish coast. We fear terrorist attacks rather than car crashes, despite it being about 450 times more likely we will die or be seriously injured in a road accident. It might also explain a few of those domestic grumbles we have: have you ever thought that maybe you do a bit more around the home than your partner? Or perhaps you seem somehow to be pulling more than your fair share of weight with the childcare? We tend to overestimate how much we have contributed; not least because in making such evaluations it is easier to remember those times that we did something rather than all those other times when someone else did something.

The availability heuristic demonstrates the influence of attention and memory on how we sense and act; and the power of techniques that play on this. It is a combination that provides great opportunities for influence. As the Russian military began to surround and threaten Ukraine in late 2021 and after the collapse of diplomatic talks, the Western allies began utilising a technique known as 'prebuttal'. In January 2022 Pentagon spokesman John Kirby told reporters that

Russia had 'pre-positioned a group of operatives to conduct what we call a false-flag operation, an operation designed to look like an attack on them or Russian-speaking people in Ukraine as an excuse to go in'. This would involve operatives trained in urban warfare using explosives to carry out acts of sabotage against pro-Russian rebels, US officials continued. Ukraine's Defence Ministry claimed that similar acts were being prepared against Russian troops stationed in the breakaway Transnistria region of Moldova. The Kremlin protested that these reports were unsubstantiated and 'confirmed by nothing'.[14] But the fact that this information was now available may have affected how audiences interpreted new information, potentially inoculating them against Russian claims that, for example, without provocation Ukrainian rockets had just blown up a bridge or demolished a school.

The link between memory and attention can run deep. Imagine you visited a fortune teller (I don't know what impelled you to do so). They looked you over, fixed you with a mysterious stare and said: 'I can see that you are fond of animals', followed by 'You're clearly a very kind individual' and 'You're very loyal to the people you care about.' The truth is, you didn't much care for animals (I'm sorry to say), nor did you think of yourself as particularly kind (you were young and foolish back then). But your ears really pricked up when you heard the third statement because it was true, you were certain of it: you did indeed pride yourself on your loyalty. At the time, you were sure that this fortune teller held some sort of magical power. But now you are older and wiser, you realise the old charlatan merely wanted to impress you with their apparent foresight by using a series of gener-alised assertions – *Barnum statements*.

Here our selective attention is at work homing in on the informa-tion that seems to be of interest, potentially discarding the rest. As the mind processes what it attends to, it is not always deploying reasoned analysis in a systematic fashion. Rather we conduct *motivated reasoning* – placing more weight on information that will confirm and validate the existing attitudes and beliefs we retain in our memories. This also helps explain why we may be inclined to think a referee's decision is biased against a sports team we support, or why we are sure that the really expensive outfit we want to buy is actually good value for money. It is also part of the reason why, when polled, large numbers of Americans still believe that ex-US president Barack Obama was not born in that country, despite all the available evidence confirming the contrary.

In some circumstances – such as our preference for which traditional media sources to consume (print news, radio, television) – we may actively gravitate towards (pay attention to) those sources of information which will help validate our prior beliefs; this is known as *selective exposure*. Good scientists often seek to *disconfirm* their hypotheses. Our human default judgement and decision-making processes often involve the complete opposite. And the outcome of selective exposure and motivated reasoning is *confirmation bias*. We may attend to information that confirms our views; process and make judgements upon this information in ways that validate these views; and in turn we may become even further motivated to pay attention to this kind of information (at the expense of attending to alternative information). Over time this type of process can harden and polarise our attitudes.[15]

Attitudes may become so entrenched that there can sometimes be a *backfire effect* when people are presented with factual evidence that disputes their beliefs. Here, rather than being persuaded and modifying our thinking in light of new information, we may experience *cognitive dissonance* – a disjoint in our view of the world which potentially disrupts our ability to function coherently. The easiest way to reduce this cognitive dissonance is to discard the disruptive information and recommit to our beliefs. That news about a doctor falsifying results linking autism to vaccines? We thought about it briefly and felt distinctly uneasy. Then we realised: we already believe that vaccines cause autism – so there must be another reason for encountering this information . . . perhaps linked to the underhand motivations of those pushing it. If feeling sufficiently pressured, we may develop reactance and act even more vigorously on these recently threatened beliefs.

What underpins confirmation bias and its associated effects? Achieving our goals relies upon us having some reasonably coherent theories of the world. There may be a potentially hefty social cost to us too, in revising theories that bind us to our social groups. Where we already hold strong beliefs, we may prefer to be exposed to one-sided arguments that reinforce these views.

And yet motivated reasoning is not always at work. We are of course capable of reflection, which means that we can be open to persuasion. Where we are less committed in our attitudes and beliefs, we will favour hearing several perspectives – or being presented with choices. Indeed, those who are undecided in their attitudes prefer to hear more than one perspective and will likely identify one-sided arguments as polemical. But this does not necessarily lead to rational analysis either. Acceptance of a given argument may depend on the coverage principle: how much of the evidence seems to be accounted for? Or on the coherence principle: does a particular perspective seem consistent, plausible and complete?

When we are uncommitted in our beliefs, it is also easy to place too much weight on what is presented to us without thinking about what is not. We may be inclined to accept information and arguments based on how they are framed. Classically, is that glass half empty or half full? Advertisers may tell us that their tasty snack is low in fat. But they did not tell us that it was high in calories. This classic tactic is known as card-stacking, in which often wholly true information shared with us is only part of the picture: the part selectively chosen to benefit the communicator. Those with a political agenda often use this trick – again, often deploying wholly correct information to build a picture so divorced from a more complex wider context that it amounts to falsehood. The English racist Stephen Yaxley-Lennon has mastered this tactic, drawing on entirely true and highly emotive stories, such as gangs of Asian males grooming white teenagers, to make wider racist claims that British citizens of Asian heritage are unable or unwilling to integrate into society.

False balance arguments, meanwhile, present different perspectives as equally valid despite there being significantly more evidence to support one than another. When one of a handful of climate change-denying experts is wheeled out to debate with a climate scientist on TV, this misrepresents the fact that the overwhelming scientific consensus is that climate change is real, human-caused and likely – if unchecked – to lead to catastrophic damage to our lives and livelihoods.

But there are more specific ways in which our minds are susceptible to framing. A quick thought experiment: are you good with money? If you are offered (A) a certain gain of £3,000 or (B) an 80 per cent chance of gaining £4,000 or otherwise nothing, what will you choose? Or how about: (A) 50 per cent chance of losing £1,000, otherwise nothing, or (B) losing £500 for certain?

If you are like most people, you will have chosen (A) in the first situation. You will be risk-averse. But what did you choose in the second situation? Most will choose (A), taking a risk in order to preserve what they have! Why the difference? These were the choices offered in a classic experiment by the psychologists Amos Tversky and Daniel Kahneman, the results of which helped them develop prospect theory.[16] In simple form, this predicts that we will tend to take higher risks to attempt avoiding losses than we will to secure gains: a prudent bias to guide our ancestors' survival in harsh environments in which maintaining scarce resources could make all the difference. It helps explain why increases in prices are twice as likely to make customers jump overboard and switch utility provider than price decreases are likely to entice new customers from other providers.[17] Would we rather receive a £5 cash discount or avoid a £5 surcharge? Most prefer to receive a £5 cash discount.[18] We will be readily influenced when choices are framed for us along these lines.

More generally, human minds are poor at assessing probability. We tend to focus on payoff, but not likelihood – we suffer from neglect of probability. Improbable but highly attractive incentives strongly motivate us. Together, confirmation bias and neglect of probability make us poor assessors of risk – and enable others to entice us: that wildly exciting opportunity to invest in Brazilian mango-farming you've just received a letter about, for example. This is part of the reason why lotteries are so popular, even though we have less chance of winning the typical national lottery jackpot than being designated a saint by the Catholic Church or crushed by a meteor. It also explains in part why leaders tend to blunder into costly and unwinnable wars.[19]

More generally, our human minds are intuitive pattern identifiers. We see animals such as the great bear, tools like the plough and mythical heroes such as the hunter Orion in the stars, which may help us memorise them and better navigate. We see shapes in clouds. We see leopards in the trees – as well as sticks that look like snakes in the bushes. We draw a great deal of relationships, or *illusory correlations*,[20] between things that do not really exist. We base judgements on prior associations we have made, regardless of how accurate these might be. For instance, you're asked how much you might pay to save birds caught in an oil slick. People, it turns out, are willing to pay around $80 to save 200 birds, $78 to save 20,000 or $82 to save 200,000.[21] This seems odd. Why are they kind enough to offer payment, yet too tight to pay proportionately more to save more? It is because we use stereotypes to make judgements – we use a *representativeness heuristic*. We may tend to base our judgement here primarily on an instinctive, potentially emotional response to the representative proto-type of a single bird – we are not distinguishing quantity, which typically requires reflection.

Similarly, a given individual is introverted and likes reading books. Obviously, this individual must be a librarian! Or consider Linda. She is thirty-one years old, single, speaks her mind and is very smart. She has a degree in philosophy. As a student she cared deeply about issues of discrimination and social justice, and often went on anti-nuclear demonstrations. Back in 1982 Daniel Kahneman and Amos Tversky asked participants: do you think Linda is *more likely to be* (A) a bank cashier, or (B) a bank cashier who is active in the feminist movement?[22] The majority thought Linda was more likely to be (B). What about you? This cannot be an accurate judge-ment, for *probability theory* tells us that the chances of any two features being present (bank cashier/active in the feminist move-ment) are going to be less likely than a single one (bank cashier). Instead, people seem to reach for the representations they have stored in memory – then use these to make simplified judgements. Linda may really have looked, sounded and felt like a representation many people typically held.

The representativeness heuristic leads us to make choices that seem-ingly make the information we collect from our environment and our judgements align (an *illusion of validity*). This can be exploited all too easily, including by politicians who claim to represent 'the people' against the corruption and malice of elites – those who talk of a 'swamp' that must be drained, a 'blob' that must be purged, or a 'cathedral' that must be destroyed; no matter that with their Ivy League or Oxbridge educations, their trust funds and banking careers, they are not closely representative of the masses. Part of the erroneous judgement here is because there seems to be an initial good fit between outcome and input. This means that to influence a given audience we may only need to provide the information that helps them join the dots they already store in their memories: the stereotypes or any other beliefs we think they hold. Who needs real evidence when our minds are so good at identifying patterns in information in order to make rapid (but often inaccurate) judgements?

Faulty pattern recognition judgements don't just occur when we compare new information against our existing knowledge and beliefs. Have you ever negotiated for something in a foreign marketplace? How do you know what a 'good' deal might look like? You really want that cliché Moroccan lantern you saw in the bazaar. It's the highest quality in town, says the seller, smiling charmingly. After a bit of back and forth, you bargain them down to half the initial asking price. Success! That is, until you realise that the price you have negotiated reflects the starting point for the very same type of lantern at the next stall. This kind of bargaining strategy is known as door in the face, since you ask. It works because we will often place too much weight on the first information we gather in any new context: this is known as anchoring.

We often anchor ourselves to seemingly arbitrary fragments of information: what should we think about someone or something? Is another individual unreliable because they are lazy, or because they are conscientious and are trying to discharge one too many responsibilities? Will you change that first impression of someone now you have a memory by which to anchor your attitude towards them? It may be difficult unless you have a motivated reason to. Anchoring also explains the finding that many will apparently drive twenty minutes away to save $5 on a cheap calculator but not the same distance to save $5 on an expensive jacket (surely a saving of $5 is a saving of $5?).[23] Priming someone with an anchor can influence their subsequent judgements, decisions and behaviours.

We may spot patterns in information anywhere and everywhere. But we are generally happy to make judgements on the information we have to hand, without making particular efforts to seek out new information: we are terrible at accounting for what we might not know. This general mode of making judgements can be summarised as *What You See Is All There Is* (or, for short, *WYSIATI*). But more than this, we are not only typically happy to make judgements and decisions without thinking about how new information may have radically altered our assessments; we are happy to act on this basis too.

There is another key force influencing our ability to make sense of the world that we have not yet explored. All the processes we have explored so far are strongly influenced by something that can change how any of them work. This is *emotion*. We all know how emotion feels. But what is it? The Scottish philosopher David Hume claimed that 'reason is, and ought only be, the slave to the passions'.[24] The German philosopher Friedrich Nietzsche reckoned that 'Thoughts are the shadows of our feelings – always darker, emptier, simpler'.[25] The current consensus is that emotion is a key feature of our ability to reason. The neuroscientist Alain Berthoz describes emotion as a 'drive that prepares us for action':[26] in other words it establishes a context in which we act. After all, it's a complex world out there. Emotion helps us simplify context, allowing us to make an intuitive assessment of the whole. This enables us to react rapidly. For example, your response to the stick you mistook for a snake aroused the emotion of fear. This led to the release of hormones, and soon enough you were running away without needing to engage in any reflection. Fear, anger, guilt, sadness, disgust, pride, compassion, relief and hope: all are emotions that can be influenced to incite action.

Evoking emotion may be particularly influential in driving the behaviour of others. Emotion can be so powerful that according to the ancient Greek philosopher Aristotle, it 'may give rise to beliefs where none existed, or change existing beliefs'.[27] Intense emotion can also lead to increased suggestibility; to make us more inclined to accept and act on the beliefs, suggestions and directions of others. Complementing confirmation bias, emotion can also lead us to ignore or fail to pay attention to discomforting information (the *ostrich effect bias*); discard it as it arrives via the senses (*selective perception*); or later even drop it from memory (the *fading effect bias*).

Shrewd influencers (including demagogic leaders) have long known that appeals to emotion can be significantly more persuasive than reasoned argument. As the psychiatrist Drew Westen states, 'when reason and emotion collide, emotion invariably wins'.[28] Appeals to emotion can target:

Fear

> *'Tidy your room or you'll
> lose your pocket money.'*

Guilt or shame

> *'I can't believe you didn't tidy your room
> after all I've done for you.'*

Anger

> *'Why can't you just tidy your room!'*

Flattery

> *'Smart people like you always keep their rooms tidy.'*

Pity

> *'Poor you: unable to tidy your room.'*

Ridicule

> *'It's pretty pathetic that you're
> not able to tidy your room.'*

Wishful thinking

> *'If you tidy your room, I'll buy you
> that trip to Mars you've always wanted.'*

Information received visually tends to be particularly impactful, as it is parsed more directly through instinctive – rather than reflective – mental circuits. This helps explain the enduring motivational power of images of starving children or cute animals. The International Organization for Migration estimated that in 2015, almost 4,000 refugees – including hundreds of children – died attempting to cross the Mediterranean in search of a better life in Europe.[29] One of these children was the three-year-old Syrian boy Alan Kurdi. The tragic image of his lifeless body face down in the sand provoked front-page news stories and an outcry of moral disgust across Europe. This example illustrates the emotion-based *identifiable victim bias*: a form of the same representativeness heuristic identified earlier in the study investigating how much people would pay to save birds caught in an oil slick.

In the case of refugee deaths, we may also face a *collapse of compassion* as all those individual tragedies disasters add up – we rein in our emotion in order to cope. Together, identifiable victim bias and collapse of compassion seem to validate the apparent words of Soviet dictator Josef Stalin: 'if only one man dies of hunger, that is a tragedy. If millions die, that is statistics.' These factors are understood by effective campaigners, who sensibly tend to tell stories about the plight of specific individuals rather than focus on data about the numbers of people who may be affected by war or natural disaster. Indeed, adding statistics to buttress arguments centred around identified individuals appears to actually reduce willingness to help.[30] Targeting emotion, then, can allow others to bypass our reflective abilities – influencing us quickly and powerfully.

Finally, our judgement is also influenced by self-perception, and specifically what the psychoanalyst Sigmund Freud called *ego* – the drive to see ourselves and our actions in a positive light. Freud believed that ego served as a regulatory mechanism mediating the impact of our wilder instincts, desires and emotions on our goals and ambitions. This did not mean the ego enabled objective analysis, rather it 'refuses to be distressed by the provocations of reality'. The ego instead drove rationalisations and self-serving arguments, because we are highly self-centric in much of our cognition and judgement. Information about ourselves tends to be encoded more strongly in memory and is subsequently more available – or better recalled (the *self-reference* effect). Information that has personal significance is more likely to be believed (this is called *subjective validation*). Ego was also influencing which of those Barnum statements you picked up on earlier, because ego helps drive motivated reasoning and confirmation bias. Ego may influence us to believe we are better at something than we are; that someone else's different view of the context is wrong compared with ours; and that our love rival is a truly awful human being (the *horns effect*).

Ego helps us to integrate behaviours with positive effects as stable and central aspects of our identities. Actions we take which we are not proud of may be classed as fleeting and unrepresentative. Ego partly accounts too for some of the other features of our thinking we came across earlier such as cognitive dissonance, in which we tend to disregard information that might make us re-evaluate ourselves negatively (after all, it's not me, it's you!), and the backfire effect (I cannot be wrong in my positive self-beliefs). It may also help us have more confidence in our judgements than is merited by their objective accuracy (the *overconfidence effect*). Finally, ego explains the useful bias known as *naïve cynicism* whereby you may believe others are more likely to be affected by these egocentric biases than you are.

Self-deceit is baked into our mental processes. Because if we are able to evaluate ourselves positively, we may be more able to persuade others to evaluate us positively: we may deceive ourselves partly to better deceive others. This is illustrated by egocentric biases like the *superiority bias*. This is the phenomenon by which the majority of us believe we are better than others. In more individualistic cultures such as those prevalent in the United Kingdom or the United States, most people think they are smarter than the median average: happier, healthier and more popular; better at driving, better at telling jokes. They also, inaccurately, think that they are less susceptible to bias than others. In more collectivist cultures such as those of Japan or South Korea these biases may be partly reversed: people think they are less smart, happy and popular than others – a series of biases that may help signal humility, a character trait which is valued particularly highly in these countries.[31] Overall, ego mediates many of the key pathways by which we are influenced.

Few of the features by which our minds reach judgements conform to models in which we think rationally. Because, in summary, our thinking is often heuristic and *systematically* non-rational: human cognition is shaped not by the logic of reason or rationality, but by the logic of evolution by natural selection. These rules enable rapid assessments and decisions relating to where we direct attention; encode and retrieve information from memory; make sense of – and identify – patterns in data; set the context for action through emotion; and – via ego – protect our self-interests in the social world through understanding our own actions in the most positive light. These are generalised rules that have served our species well in the struggle to survive and reproduce. But, like the moth that is burned by flame, these rules, which help us in general, may fail us in specific contexts – including when they are exploited by others in ways that may not benefit us. Still, humans are social animals whose success has depended upon a remarkable degree of cooperation between individuals and groups – a feature that is crucial to understanding how influence works.

2. Trust

We live on a cold ball of rock, marooned in infinite space. That would be desperately lonely, if it wasn't for the crucial fact that we have each other. As we've noted already, we are a social species, and many of our basic needs – to engage, communicate and belong; to compete and seek status – are directly linked to us being so. Our cognition evolved to support us as we navigate the complexities of social life. Many of the cues we act on come from others. Sometimes from pretty much any others we sense. Sometimes from particular others. But which others? When? Here too we are hugely influenced by rules of thumb (heuristics), such as a propensity to respond to authority and attractiveness (whether we want to believe this or not); and indicators of potential trustworthiness, such as warmth and reciprocation. These types of heuristic enable us to seek out ways to come together, build relationships and find our home in the social world. But they are far from foolproof, because they can also be manipulated by deceivers and other influencers who may not have our best interests at heart.

Think about an important stranger you once met – a new boss, or your mother-in-law. What happened? Perhaps you gave some thought to what you might say or do beforehand? If so, you were using a skill called *mental time travel*, which enables you to plan and strategise in support of your goals. It seems to be a distinctive skill of our species, one based on our ability to theorise about the minds of ourselves and others. Because we typically recognise that others also think – that there are intentions behind their behaviour. And we instinctively model what may be going on in other minds – we *mentalise* them – based on social information that we collect over time: from observations of behaviour, from the gossip of others, from our own interactions with people.

Other species of Great Ape have some abilities to mentalise. Chimpanzees, for instance, can identify when others have spotted hidden food, and avoid going near this to prevent any conflict, instead preferring to look for other sources.[1] But the human ability to mentalise is spectacular. Young children treat toys as though they have personality and will – dolls and Lego people operate as conscious agents with personal histories and desires – and they are also able to judge the intent of others, such as whether an adult handling toys wants to play with them or merely tidy them up. Even children as young as two seem motivated to share theories of mind about what is going on with both objects and people, viewing both intuitively as sentient beings with whom they can share knowledge and beliefs.[2]

This ability to mentalise enables us to make judgements on the motivations and goals of others; to assess possibilities for conflict or cooperation. For instance, if we notice that other people are paying attention to something, we may automatically infer that it must be worthy of attention. A wily street entertainer takes the time to entice and build up the numbers of an audience, calling out invitations, encouraging applause and feedback. They know that nothing attracts a crowd quite like a crowd. They are aiming to benefit from precipitating an *attention cascade*, in which the objects of attention may gain exaggerated significance.

Our memory, too, is subject to similar impacts – and as we discuss and share information, we are more likely to remember it and raise it again later; this is called an *availability cascade*. Attention and availability cascades amplify one another. These can be harnessed to great effect – as the terrorist group Al-Qaeda discovered through their catastrophically successful attack on the twin towers of the New York World Trade Center on 11 September 2001. With effects lasting well over a decade, the event ensured the prevalence of terrorism discourses – even though by 2006 and onwards, terrorist attacks killed fewer people on American soil per annum (10) than parachuting accidents (19), being buried alive (29), or choking on food (1,086).[3]

Our interest in what others are doing can strongly influence our behaviour. Examples range from the mundane – a wave of coughing spreading across the audience in the cinema to the extreme – school-children fainting en masse in the Tokyo subway, or fits of crying and exposing of genitalia in the nunneries of medieval Europe.[4] And when a fire alarm goes off in a public space, we may become especially alert to what others are doing: do they ignore it and sit tight or rush towards the exits screaming uncontrollably? Whatever it is, we may decide to do the same. This heuristic is known, generally, as *social proof*.

On the edge of survival, it paid dividends to our ancestors to attend to social information – enabling them to gravitate towards opportunities and avoid risks they may not have completely understood. When social proof represents accurate information, the heuristic can be useful: aggregated data from others could help our ancestors find the best foraging grounds or run from a sabretooth tiger without having to see it. But on the other side of the ledger, social proof can have negative effects – stock market bubbles in today's world, for example, or a stampede towards specific motorway lanes as traffic slows. Worse: some of our behaviour may be motivated by a need to avoid punishment by others for failing to conform.

A famed experiment: social psychologist Solomon Asch presented individuals in groups with a card on which a line was drawn. Then he shared a further three cards on which three parallel lines were drawn, and asked which of the those lines was the same as that on the first card. These new cards would include one length that was quite obviously the same as that in the first, as well as two which were very obviously not. Asch employed several confederates posing as members within these groups. Their role was to make incorrect statements about which line from the second set of cards matched the line in the first. Under this kind of social pressure, only a quarter of the participants made correct judgements all the time. The remaining three-quarters conformed to the incorrect prompts from the confederates at least part of the time, suggesting that our need to conform with others is often a greater influence on our behaviour than our own beliefs about what is true.[5]

Drawing attention to apparent threats can stimulate cascading social proof. This makes a useful survival mechanism when a group needs to band together in the face of an existential threat to pursue common survival goals – to share scarce resources such as food, or fend off attack from neighbours bent on aggression. It can also be useful, though, to create threat perceptions using social proof for other reasons, especially if you are a cult leader, a dictator, a rising demagogue – or a propagandist for any of these actors. The Putin regime in Russia and its propagandists spent years telling the population that powers in Europe and the United States wanted to cow and weaken Russia. The regime, it maintained, was all that stood in the way as it made Russia great again, talking up unfairness and the threat from aggressors from without and traitors within. By generating high levels of threat perception, conformity can be incentivised and group members kept in line.

Then the Russian military invaded Ukraine, and contrary views among ordinary Russians and the last remaining independent news media outlets were shut down. Under social pressure, individuals can express different public attitudes to the opinions they hold in private in order to avoid the reputational damage and ostracism that they believe may follow from publicly disagreeing with others. This can create an illusion of agreement or consensus in a group, a *reputation cascade*, making it increasingly harder for dissenting voices to speak out – or for the private attitudes of group members to become known. It is a dynamic that helps explain why polling in authoritarian societies – even if done using reputable methods – is likely to be particularly inaccurate.

In combination, these cascade effects – of attention, availability, social proof and social pressure – can amplify and reinforce one another. Sometimes, too, they enable transformative change. In early 1989 in then East Germany, protests in Leipzig began with just a few activists challenging the Communist government. But then cascade effects started to kick in, and the numbers grew over the weeks until by October 1989 100,000 were on the streets, and by the start of November 400,000. By the 9th of that same month, the Berlin Wall had been dismantled.[6]

Why should we jump a red light while cycling in the city, watch a film or buy and read this book? Well, partly because of social proof. Trust represents the confidence we place in our knowledge, attitudes and expectations about someone or something. But it also relates to how much we are willing to rely on, share control with, or in any other way make ourselves vulnerable to, anyone else – in both thought and action. And whom should we trust in the absence of any other information? Maybe those whom other people seem to trust. Because of this, by drawing on social proof we may help others to trust us more quickly – if we seem like the most popular or respected colleague in our workplace, in the absence of any other information, it may help new employees to gravitate towards us. Social proof also drives client testimonials that businesses use when trying to convince you that you do need that new bathroom or garden shed.

Social proof is not the only heuristic to impact our social cognition. We tend to be more easily persuaded by those whose *authority* we perceive, who wield legitimate power because they seem to hold an office that commands our respect. For example, we park outside a restaurant. Someone in a uniform comes over and asks if we have a few pennies to help another motorist who needs to park but is short on change. What do we do? In social psychologist Leonard Bickman's study, 94 per cent of those asked would help out. This dropped to under half (42 per cent) if the requestor wore civilian clothes.[7] The uniform, it appears, conveyed authority – and led to an increase in conformist responses. Even the vehicles we drive can present authority signals. Researchers Anthony Doob and Alan Gross directed members of their experimental team to drive cars up to intersections and stay put when the traffic lights turned green. They drove either luxury (high-authority-reflecting) and budget (low-authority-reflecting) vehicles. It turned out that frustrated drivers behind them were significantly more likely to honk at the drivers driving budget cars.[8]

Our willingness to conform to authority can have harrowing effects in the real world. The Nazi Otto Eichmann managed the grim logistics for deporting Jews and others to be murdered in the death camps of the Holocaust. At trial, Eichmann later claimed that he was 'just following orders'. It was a claim that the trial judges rejected: he was found guilty and executed. But the social psychologist Stanley Milgram became haunted by this defence of 'following orders'. How could such a mundanely normal-seeming citizen such as Eichmann – like many others – have ended up becoming complicit in murder and genocide?

Milgram ran a number of now-classic obedience experiments. These involved participants being directed to administer electric shocks to actors, pretending to be a volunteers, when the latter guessed word association questions wrongly. Participants were encouraged to dial up the voltage as the task progressed, with the actors convincingly pretending to be in ever greater pain as they were increasingly 'shocked'. The participants, who did not know that this was all an act, often looked to the experimenters for guidance as the situation become more extreme. Concerns were rationalised away by the authorities, and participants were encouraged to keep administering the shocks; 65 per cent of them continued to do so right up to the highest voltages.[9]

All the studies of authority mentioned so far date from the 1960s and 1970s. Are their conclusions still relevant? Recent studies have produced similar findings – one using not only fake electric shocks but economic fines too as punishment.[10] Results from another study suggest that we are much more likely to open and read emails – as well as to act on requests contained within – when we perceive the sender's authority.[11] A further study suggests that the effects of authority in virtual reality settings even *increase* the likelihood of compliant behaviour (and we will discuss why this may occur later).[12]

It is not simply that we park our critical faculties and unquestioningly obey. We are more than happy to disobey and resist when we have something to lose. Some of our responsiveness to authority relates to compliance: we do as dominant individuals suggest or direct to avoid being punished even though we may not see their power as legitimate. But we often cooperate with authority because we believe that it is right to do so: it often represents wider systems of cultural expectations that can be harnessed to incentivise our obedience and conformity – when we ask questions like 'How am I supposed to behave in this situation?', as we will later see. It should be noted, too, that simulating the appearance of authority can be useful for deceptive ends – as attested by the continued proliferation of local news stories about con artists who deceive their victims by posing as police officers.

Across human societies, conforming to authority has some relation to physical bearing: we are influenced by size, and we pay more attention to taller (typically male) communicators.[13] This can make us defer to them – by moving out of their way on a busy pavement, for example.[14] Like the other great apes, (mostly male) humans also signal dominance with expansive postures – sitting with legs and arms outstretched instead of closed and hunched. But at least in our current age, this only goes so far (and later we will investigate why). After all, overt displays of dominance can also be mocked and belittled by others: take the concept of 'manspreading', applied to a man on the train whose knees have escaped their designated seat space.

Many signals of dominance tend to be associated with men – tone of voice, for example. High-pitched or shaky voices provide the tell: too much of the stress hormone cortisol produces that effect, suggesting someone well down the pecking order. Dominant males talk – like Barry White – in lower tones. Less gender-specific may be walking slowly and surely to convey confidence. The dominant also tend to speak more slowly – as though they are used to being listened to (because they are). In fact, as we implicitly know, it is not so much what we say as *how* we say it that determines the extent to which others listen to us. The communications psychologist Albert Mehrabian reckoned that the approximate formula for message impact relied 55 per cent on the communicator's body language, 38 per cent on vocal indicators and a measly 7 per cent on the actual content of the message (just 7 per cent!).[15]

Psychologist Robert Cialdini suggests three further types of authority signal that are immediately obvious to us: *titles*, *clothes* and *trappings*. Titles are the formal descriptions societies give to authorities – 'pharaoh', 'queen', 'baronet', 'senator', 'tribune', 'doctor', 'professor', 'reverend', 'general', 'director', 'shaman', 'chief', etc. Clothes, too, have always signalled authority – from the robes of emperors to the uniforms of the military and law enforcement. This is not only confined to formal authority, as is attested by the outlandish outfits of pop stars, not to mention the bow ties some professors wear to signal the eccentricity that can accompany genius; then there are trappings – police badges, rosaries, jewellery (although these all represent very different types of authority, as we will later see). How do we recognise authority? Partly because we observe that others do – social proof is at work. And why should we behave like everyone else? Partly because authorities guide us to. When you speak, do the eyes of others gravitate towards you? Does anyone who was previously talking pick up the cue and stop? It could be that other people perceive your authority, in which case you may find it easier to influence them.

We are also strongly influenced by communicators we perceive as sexually desirable: we are more likely to vote for them, or treat them leniently when they are on trial in court – and, if they are convicted, give them smaller punishments.[16] Part of what benefits individuals we judge to be physically attractive is a so-called *halo effect*, in that we also assume them to be more intelligent, more trustworthy, even kinder than others – on the basis of *absolutely no supporting evidence*. We may want to think well of attractive individuals, and this provides them with a gateway to influence. And even when we don't consciously or unconsciously find a particular communicator attractive, others may; in which case we can instead be influenced by the resultant effects of social proof.

What do we find attractive? With so much at stake, this area is full of academic and practical controversy. Still, some features have so far transcended space and time. We typically have a preference for symmetrical faces, which may signal some freedom from the ravages of disease and poor health. Heterosexual males across cultures tend to prefer younger women with high hip-to-waist ratios – a signal of potential fecundity. The picture seems more confused when it comes to heterosexual women. In industrialised societies, tall men are found to be attractive. And there may be some truth in the cliché of masculine attractiveness: a square jaw, and a triangular body that tapers from shoulders to waist – a sign of high testosterone levels, of dominance. However, there is also some evidence of preference for highly feminised male faces – these may partly reflect the interplay of different motives: do the underlying signals imply attractiveness as a biological father? Or of a cooperative mate for child-rearing?

Most signals of physical attractiveness are formed by the complex interplay of the biological and the cultural. The venerated female figures of Renaissance paintings are often plump – possibly the depiction of fertility machines glorified by patriarchal societies. In Arabian society in the Middle Ages, the ideal female face was round, like a full moon. In medieval Japan, women with long, narrow oval faces were celebrated. Around the same time in Chinese literature, it is claimed (our sources here are males from the literati) that beautiful male lovers should look weak, vulnerable, feminine and pedantic. In Middle English literature the ideal man had broad shoulders, a muscular back, large hands and arms and legs with huge muscles – all the better for driving the oxen behind the heavy village plough. Among the Bodi tribespeople of twenty-first-century Ethiopia, meanwhile, unmarried men compete for potential brides by seeing who can put on the most weight drinking only cow's blood and milk.

Being perceived as physically attractive can help us build our halo effects, increasing the propensity of others to trust us. But what is seen as attractive is part universal and part specific to culture and individual preference – and it can change too, quite quickly: one study set in rural Nicaragua observed an increasing preference for slimmer, curvier female bodies as more individuals consumed television produced by urban elites.[17] And it is well established that mass-media exposure can change the body ideals of those who consume it.[18] In this light, it may be important to make the most of our appearance while remembering that beauty – at least in part – really is in the eye of the beholder.

So far, all the social heuristics we have explored are inferred indirectly from others, or through direct observation. We also obtain information and make further heuristic judgements as we interact with others. For starters, we are often more willing to be influenced by people we like. This seems obvious. But the real question is, what makes us like someone? Why do you like the people you like?

One very basic aspect of whether we like others is simply the level of exposure we have had to them. We only need to have briefly seen someone's face in order to report that we like them more than someone whose face we have not seen: which is why, if we are looking to build rapport, it may be better to keep our camera on during online business meetings. We prefer those things with which we are more familiar; and this includes people. In a world full of risk, the unfamiliar typically generates a *fear and avoid* response. Exposure reduces our fear and avoidance response to others, increasing our positivity towards them.

Liking also relates to that reciprocal feeling we get when a communicator seems to *like us*. Discriminate and sincere use of flattery emphasising the positive aspects of others strokes their ego, playing into the desire we typically have to see ourselves in the most positive light. As the philosopher Desiderius Erasmus claimed, flattery 'raises downcast spirits, comforts the sad, rouses the apathetic, stirs up the stolid, cheers the sick, restrains the headstrong, brings lovers together and keeps them united'.[19] But the quality most typically associated with the feeling that others like us is *warmth*: signals of good intention, openness and willingness to develop trusting, beneficial relations – which help people overcome their natural fear and avoidance inclinations.

Solomon Asch asked participants to read descriptions of imaginary individuals, and they were then asked whom they liked the most. The single most important determinant was whether these individuals were described as *warm* or *cold* – with warm individuals being far better liked regardless of other qualities such as intelligence, skilfulness and industriousness.[20] Many features considered warm are shared with our ape cousins: open-hand gestures as an invitation to engage; smiling to convey happiness – as in *really* smiling with that crease in the eyes. The opposite is closed body language, that of defence (such as crossing the arms). Culturally appropriate tactile contact can also convey warmth, that very physical feeling of *being connected* – a pat on the back, a hand on the shoulder, a great bear hug.

Imagine. You walk into a new social setting – a business meeting, a neonatal support group or a birdwatching club, perhaps. You're not immediately displaying any signals of warmth. After all, the others don't know you yet, and until they have established your value such signals may create an unfortunate impression. After all, we may also find it easy to view those whom we perceive as warm to be incompetent, their ingratiating behaviours as appeasing and weak. We often find warm and attentive demonstrations towards us as *charming*. And as you later go for lunch with the same group – queuing for sandwiches and coffee – you start to express your charm as one inattentive conversation partner gives you a lengthy discursion on their travails with an ingrowing toenail, and you simply smile and respond sincerely, 'Please tell me more!'

If you are a reasonably smooth conversationalist, you may find your interactions with new others tend to start with *small talk* about neutral subjects, which is used by rapport-builders to initially tease out areas of common interest and unity – and to avoid awkward punts into divisive terrain. We may *actively listen* to our conversational partners by making verbal affirmations and sometimes paraphrasing key points back to them. In some European and North American cultures this same respect is demonstrated by direct eye contact. Altogether our body and verbal language is used not only to engage the other, but also to overtly signal our deep engagement.

Let's return to that new social group you joined. In the more informal setting of lunchtime, you gravitate towards the group leader. Soon you are both sharing – reciprocating – equal amounts of personal information. They ask about where you grew up. You ask after their family. This supports symmetrical trust-building. Through these iterations of information-sharing, you are building a more consistent theory of one another. As you do so you make yourselves increasingly vulnerable – because others can use the information you share to better compete with you or to exploit you. But you can use vulnerability to your advantage here. Because although you don't want to seem naïve, by demonstrating your own vulnerability – seeking advice, unafraid to signal an asymmetry of knowledge – you are also signalling your willingness to trust and be trusted.

More generally, you have initiated the principle of *direct reciprocity* that is especially important in guiding relationships beyond the family or immediate clan. Reciprocity implies willingness to enter a mutually beneficial relationship, and one act of generosity usually begs another: an act of giving to create obligation on the part of the receiver. We tend to leave higher tips when the waiter provides a mint with the bill,[21] and even send Christmas cards to strangers, if first they send one to us.[22] It is why we may experience resentment when an acquaintance donates to us their old clothes or children's toys out of the blue, because here we may feel they are placing us in their debt without having sought our consent – not least by potentially endowing us with something we neither wanted nor needed. Appropriate reciprocity usually starts small – and once the cycle of reciprocating begins, it can be difficult for someone to turn down a request. It's a feature that is exploited by wily negotiators in the *foot in the door* technique, which depends upon requests that start out innocuously but which then escalate rapidly in terms of the demands made of the giver.

Reciprocity not only applies to positive interaction that leads to trust-building. It also works negatively. Someone applies a cost to us – we repay them in kind. In places with weaker formal law enforcement mechanisms, reciprocal violence may be particularly prevalent. An insult here or a casual slur there can swiftly degenerate into a long-running vendetta or blood feud. This kind of negative reciprocity serves as a form of 'self-help' deterrence for those who participate: an advertisement that defections and insults will carry heavy costs.

Often we may be guided by a simple rule: if you cooperate with me, I will cooperate with you. If you compete with, cheat or punish me, I will repay you in kind – *an eye for an eye, a tooth for a tooth*. Reciprocation is baked into our behaviours across cultures.[23] The ancient Chinese sage Confucius chose reciprocity as the single most important prescription for life, because reciprocity is also embedded in our *values* – our beliefs about what constitutes morally correct ways to think and behave.

Back again in your social group's lunchtime recess; you and the group's leader are now so deep in conversation that you are turned slightly towards each other, mirroring, matching and mimicking one another's body movements, posture, language, tone of voice, volume and speed of speech . . . even the rate of your breathing – which induces a sense of togetherness and unity as you act in synchrony (although people who know each other well may dispense with all this). We are prolific copying machines too, remember. Imitation also supports liking (within reason: if we perceive that we are being consciously imitated, we may find it invasive and creepy).

Social learning theory claims that the ability to mentalise enables teacher and learner to communicate the meaning of actions, the better to transfer knowledge and skills between peers and from one generation to the next; this is facilitated by our propensity to imitate others. We copy those we like, those we trust and those with authority. We are more likely to catch a yawn from a family member than from a stranger.[24] Smiling, itching and emotional reactions are all spread contagiously to others by authority figures. We tend to find our interactions with those who imitate us more enjoyable, and we will subsequently be more ready to help them. We also tend to find individuals who have imitated us more persuasive.

At the next meeting of your new social group you find yourself talking with the leader again. Before long you're both joking about times each of you got stuck in a lift. Then you're sharing plans for making handmade pasta, starting Japanese flower-arranging or fixing up a classic car together. You're bonding, *resonating*. And when there is finally a lull in the conversation, what may recently have felt like an awkward silence has evolved into a long, comfortable enjoyment of the moment. Because now another component of liking is at work. This is similarity, the feeling that *we are like each other*. We prefer those who look the same way, whose faces are similar to ours: we will more easily trust them, help them or – if they are a political candidate – vote for them.[25] We like those who share our interests, backgrounds and life stories: they give us the feeling that we 'click' – which is what the protagonists in the hit movie *Frozen* are doing as they sing to one another, 'I never met someone who thinks so much like me'. With similar individuals we may judge that our goals are more likely to be aligned – that we can find commonality of interest and motivation. More than this, we can be increasingly confident in how similar others are building their mental models – our ability to mentalise them is enhanced.[26] Mostly, opposites do not attract.

Similarity can be key to creating an impactful messenger effect. In one successful sexual health intervention in Zimbabwe, women from low-income areas who braided hair for a living were trained to teach women from similar backgrounds in their localities how to use condoms, as well as where to find them and how to introduce them into a relationship. These were the communicators that the key audience had in common – making it easier for them to connect.[27] For similar reasons, the use of peers to help demonstrate more efficient farming practices during separate trials in Malawi and rural India seems to have significantly increased uptake of these methods.[28]

Having enjoyed a fabulous interaction with the social group leader, you say your goodbyes to one another. You hope your exchanges over the past day will spark a positive, reciprocal cycle of trust, one that leads to further interaction, more reduction in uncertainty, greater exchange. In future you imagine it will be easier to make trusted deals with this individual. Maybe you will vouch for each other in pressurised, high-stakes negotiations. Still, perhaps part of you should remain wary. Most of all, perhaps you should fear deception. After all, humans are not always honest. No two individuals – not even children and their parents, or identical twins – ever had completely aligned goals.

In this context the human capacity for deceit has flourished. So maybe you won't be completely surprised when it turns out that the group leader just made up all the information they shared with you for the lulz or something . . . no matter: you didn't want to spend your time in the company of such a psychopath anyway.

Deception is noted in the earliest of historical records: it is celebrated as a tactic in the writings of ancient strategists – in China, Sun Tzu in *The Art of War*; in India, Kautilya in *The Arthashastra*. In the Jewish Torah, even God's favourite, King David, is a systematic deceiver. Spotting the beautiful Bathsheba bathing on a rooftop, David seduces her, and she falls pregnant with his daughter. David has Bathsheba's soldier husband Uriah recalled from battle with the aim that Uriah will sleep with his wife and believe the child is his. Deception is common. We lie, knowingly tell untruths, and *palter* – knowingly leave out key pieces of information – to prompt others to reach misleading conclusions. Sometimes the truth may be irrelevant: we may say what we need to or *bullshit*, heedless of whether what we say is true or not. Research on deceit suggests that it is prolific, regardless of the injunctions against it we tell in our cultural stories. In a typical day many of us may lie at least once.[29] Apparently we even lie in a third of all interactions with our lovers and mothers, which rises to half between university students and their mothers.[30] Though some are much more so than others, we are accomplished liars.

Many of our deceits carry insignificant consequences, like white lies ('Your meatloaf is truly delicious!') or protective lies ('I really wanted to come to your party, but I have an essential family commitment'). Mostly these fibs grease the wheels of social life by flattering others – they are essential, even, to maintaining or developing our cooperative relations. We lie to be polite, to create a positive impression or to avoid social engagements. Sometimes we lie for no particular reason at all.[31] But many lies and deceits carry significant negative consequences for others, which gives rise to the fear you may feel when you start sticking your neck out for your new friend, the group leader.

In the end we are far more easily influenced by those we trust. But developing trust is intensive both cognitively and in terms of time, which limits the number of deeply trusting relationships we can sustain. Before the advent of social media made us question this, a scientific view had started to form that there was an upper limit in the low hundreds to the number of relationships our brains can sustain.[32] These are the people in whom we invest our social energy, those with whom we build one-to-one relationships and work with towards common goals; they are also the people best positioned to influence us.

But we can still use trust to influence without knowing others this deeply. Even as little as ten minutes of rapport-building can be effective. In one recent study, transgender rights activists knocked on doors in California. They then spent ten minutes getting to know an individual, soliciting their views. This could be enough to completely reverse the views of those they talked with. The effects of this *deep canvassing* lasted even in the face of anti-transgender rights advertising – the focus on rapport-building had effectively inoculated many individuals against further changes in attitudes and beliefs.[33] Before we are open to messages, we must typically be open to the communicator – not an easy problem to solve in a dangerous world. In order to influence, the communicator must have created a positive association with the audience. Then, through interaction, they must reduce the uncertainty that the audience experiences about whether they can be trusted. Only at that point can we be more easily motivated to change our attitudes, beliefs and behaviours.

We make many of our judgements and decisions based on social heuristics, which help us de-risk interactions with our physical and social environments as we identify opportunities to cooperate – a hallmark of our species and its success. If in doubt we do what others are doing (social proof). We tend to cooperate with/obey those we perceive as authorities. We have a propensity to trust people we like; and we like those we are familiar with, who are warm towards us, who flatter us, who are similar to us. Over time we reciprocate, allowing us to reduce uncertainty about the other as we enact our desires and goals. This feeds our amazing human ability to mentalise other people, potentially generating trust – that willingness to be vulnerable which represents the gateway to influence.

We are born cooperators. Yet we are also born deceivers, who regularly cheat and lie to glean benefits and advantages from those who can be persuaded to trust us and cooperate with us. Because while most of us want to get along with others, we often want to get ahead of them too. Social heuristics enable cooperation partly by offering some protection from these kinds of predations. However, many of these heuristic processes of rapport and trust-building can also be exploited by others: by effective salespeople; by police detectives leading up to, and during, interrogation; by terrorists aiming to radicalise new initiates and by paedophiles to groom children. And more: the relationships that are thus created and maintained can also be exploited by influencers, because these processes also plug us into wider social networks of trust and bonding, an ideal transmission route along which attitudes, beliefs and behaviours can potentially be disseminated and spread by us and to us – whether to our advantage or not. Social heuristics, then, are general rules which do not always work in our favour. In these circumstances, trust is precarious and can easily be undermined. Fortunately, there are wider influences that can help us build trust and cooperate – those related to culture. Unfortunately, these can also be used to undermine and divide us too.

3. Culture

We are all naïve realists at heart. We experience our own thoughts and feelings with such intensity that it can be difficult to believe that these experiences may not objectively reflect reality. Even if we can admit this, in the moment we will often still act as though what we think and feel is true. Reason too has objective limits in guiding action, running only as deeply as the prevailing knowledge allows. The philosopher Plato is often associated with the use of reason and logic, but even he acknowledged the limits of reason as a guide to action. Plato himself was open to some of the stranger-seeming influences in Classical Greece – which included decision-making by examining animal entrails or diviners bearing messages from the gods. Trace reason all the way down and its foundations are rooted in the sands of other factors, including – importantly – *culture*, that whole package of knowledge and schemes which groups of people have for making sense of the world together and with which we are all indoctrinated from birth.[1] Paradoxically, this culture, which so strongly influences our individual thoughts and feelings, in many ways represents our collective mind.

Culture is central to human social life: it changes the way we process information from our environments; what information we attend to and remember; how we make sense of this data and recognise patterns in it; even how we feel. Culture guides how we behave, what we believe and whom we listen to. It influences who we are and what we want, by telling us who we should be and what we are supposed to want. It provides references for who else belongs to our social groups, and who does not – it directs us on what we should think about both 'us' and 'them'. In this way, culture mediates the shape of our attitudes, beliefs and behaviours – and harnessing it is utterly critical for influence, not least because, being saturated in it, we are often oblivious to when it is being used to manipulate us.

There is no consensual definition of culture among those who study it. Anthropologists have tended to focus on the 'symbolic forms' – abstract mental representations – for communicating, perpetuating and developing knowledge, which is what we appear to specialise in. But many primatologists and evolutionary scientists have noted that other animals – including other great apes – can behave proto-culturally, which means they can transfer learning between themselves. Chimps copy one another in performing smart tricks, such as using sticks to pull ants out of their nests in search of a nutritious meal, demonstrating tool use, a key artefact of culture. But not only useful tricks: in one chimp troop a dominant female was observed wearing a blade of grass hanging from inside her ear. The others soon copied this fashionista's example, and before long many of the troop were doing so.[2] As much as anything, this hints that culture does not have to be directly practical in order to add value.

Culture is socially learned: drummed into us – through both accident and design – by our parents, our families, our social networks, media sources and institutions like schools and universities which marinate us in culture. The results can vary widely. Using tools to make labour more efficient may seem universally helpful. But if you are Amish, you may reject many modern tools as the work of the devil and carry out all your farm labour by hand. Sometimes culture diverges spectacularly, such as the ideology that venerated brother-sister incest specifically for the co-monarchy of ancient Egypt (which helped consolidate family power in turbulent times, even as it corrupted the health of the lineage); or the idea that certain roles required the mutilation and removal of genitals – the fate of boys due to be supplied as eunuchs to the imperial courts of Rome, China and the Ottoman Empire (and still the fate of young girls in parts of Africa, the Middle East and Asia).

But we share much in common. According to cultural anthropologist Donald Brown, there are more than 370 categories of cultural features that are common to all human societies. These 'cultural universals' include baby talk, having beliefs about death, definitions of the colour black and the colour white, coalitions, collective identities, mediation of conflict, cooking, cooperation, crying, dance, death rituals, dream interpretation, envy, ethnocentrism, feasting, food-sharing, gift-giving, government, the taboo of incest between mother and son, leadership, magic, medicine, music, oligarchy, property, reciprocity, sanctions, sexual regulation, tools, trade, weapons . . . and so on.[3]

How might culture directly influence our behaviour? One crucial way is through adherence to *social norms*. What are these? Why would we adhere to them? Let's start with a game called 'Stag Hunt'. This comes from the canon of *game theory*, an area of study that helps reduce complex situations down to their simplest components, producing clear models – or games – of how people may be incentivised to behave in a given situation. In this game, a group hunt deer which, being speedy and alert, are difficult to catch. It takes a whole hunting party to make a kill. Yet a single deer is packed full of nourishing protein, and if the hunt is successful the group eats for days on end. It takes only one individual to let the side down, though. Should a delicious-looking rabbit cross a hunter's path, then the temptation to defect from the hunting party is strong: after all, a rabbit requires only one hunter and much less effort to kill – even if the proceeds only feed a single family for a single day. Under these circumstances, the potential rewards from cooperation might be high. Yet the more defections that take place, the more likely the deer hunt will fail; the group can kiss goodbye to venison steak.

Given that each member of the hunting party understands this perfectly well, the chance of any single defection gets higher the larger the group becomes; it doesn't take long before the nakedly rational decision may be to cut short those future losses and hunt rabbit. Why not be the first to defect in such a precarious game? The stag hunt can be used to think about trust and cooperation among larger groups – or *indirect reciprocity*. So what devices may help groups of humans cooperate, and not defect from the stag hunt?

Classical economics assumed that we made decisions based upon cost/benefit analyses in pursuit of our goals – that we maximise utility. Yet there is often another driving question behind decision-making which is: *how am I supposed to behave in this situation?* Economics students may respond: *you are supposed to behave as a utility maxim-iser* – which may explain why they are more likely than others to defect in cooperation games.[4] And yet, more often than not, we coop-erate far beyond what might be expected of rational actors.[5] We do this instinctively, because in almost any situation there is a *right* way in which *we* are supposed to behave if we are to belong to our social groups. We know how we are *supposed* to behave according to the standards of those around us – and how the roles we are supposed to play should be acted out. This is because the cultural influences around us indoctrinate us with correct, or preferred, ways in which to behave: we copy the behaviour of influential others around us (social proof) and internalise the social norms we learn from them.

Members of any human group are typically expected to *conform* to social norms. But individuals may also be incentivised to defect from group goals, to free-ride on others for selfish gain if they think they can get away with it. Because of this, norms are enforced by commu-nities too, but not all are applied equally. They may be enforced more strictly (they are *tight*) or less (they are *loose*).[6] In most cultures, you should not have sexual intercourse with those who are not your main partner. However, in some looser cultures this is not always frowned upon as long as the main partner has consented. In much of Europe and North America, people caught cheating on a partner may be punished with a bit of gossip behind their back – and maybe some shunning by some of those they used to interact with. In some other parts of the world, cheating is not only illegal but may even lead to death by stoning. It is not quite this simple, however, because we are also endlessly innovative, creating new labels and meanings that make it easier to navigate normative systems. In Iran, being caught having sex outside marriage carries the punishment of 100 lashes. On the other hand, such behaviour is perfectly legal if one obtains a *Nikah Muh'ta* – temporary 'pleasure marriage' – which comes with a contract in advance. To Western ears, for whom unmarried sexual intercourse is typically the business only of those conducting it, the Iranian pleasure marriage may sound similar to prostitution – activity which is not only socially frowned upon in various ways across Western countries but often illegal too. Do these examples sound too strict? Too lenient? Too complicated? Our attitude here may tell us quite a bit, not only about our personal dispositions but also about the cultural influences that have helped shape the way we think and feel over time.

Norms are ubiquitous. They strongly regulate how we behave across social life. They help guide how we relate to strangers, colleagues, friends, parents and siblings, partners and children. What should we do when we enter someone else's home? What is an acceptable gift at a wedding? Is it appropriate to propose to our cousin? And what are the rules around teamwork on a stag hunt? Norms have evolved to provide communities with the means by which to coordinate. They facilitate cooperation at scale, creating the building blocks of trust beyond the kinship ties of family and our immediate interpersonal social networks.[7] How?

Another game. This one is called the Ultimatum Game. Here two participants must split a pot of money. One player – the proposer – chooses how to do so, then suggests this to the other player – the responder – who then gets to decide whether to accept or not. If the responder rejects the offer, both players receive nothing. In such games we tend to reject offers the further they move away from an equal share in the direction of the proposer's favour. The more unequal the proposal, the more our emotions are activated; the offer feels *unfair*.[8] Perhaps this makes intuitive sense to you. Why would anyone accept an offer that is unfair? A rational responder might choose to accept whatever is on offer. After all, something is often better than nothing.

Participants across cultures will punish those who put forward a low-ball offer, or more generally those who have been unfair to us. And unfairness is relative to what we expect. What do we expect? Behaviour along the lines of what the norms prescribe, of course. In a community in which you are supposed to act as a team to fulfil a customer order, till the soil or catch a deer, defection is unfair. Those who do not conform with the prevailing community norms we consider anti-social. And societies punish anti-social behaviour.

Those who defect from a group's norms may suffer reputational damage as people gossip about them. Although if we gossip too much we may also violate those norms, which could lead to being branded the reputationally damaging label, *a gossip*. Chronic or acute norm violation may result in an individual being ostracised from the group. Beyond this there may be sanctioned violence or confiscation of property – and in the final instance, forfeit of life (execution). Culture can be highly coercive. On the other hand, cultivating a reputation for upholding community norms (*pro-social* behaviour) can *enhance* an individual's standing. Failing to pull your weight at harvest time is heavily punished; but being first out of the door and toiling the hardest gains you credit.

Enforcement of norms has selected us for what Harvard evolutionary scientist Joseph Heinrich calls 'norm psychology'.[9] Norms train our minds to make judgements, including what and whom we should pay attention to, the content we should store in our memory, what patterns we should care about – even what shapes our emotions and drives our ego. Children as young as three are aware that there is a 'right' way to behave. At the Max Planck Institute, toddlers scold puppets that act differently from adults who have previously modelled a behaviour, protesting and issuing commands such as 'No it doesn't go like this!' or 'No don't put it there!' The toddlers do this even when the puppet's behaviour appears more focused and it completes activities more efficiently.[10] It seems there is a 'right' way to behave in many situations, whatever that may be. In your village there is a powerful norm promoting most agricultural work as a cooperative pursuit; it is taboo to defect. This means it becomes far less likely that someone will sneak off for a barley beer before the day's work is done, no matter how tempting that might seem.

Norms are a product (as well as a driver) of social learning. And social learning is enabled by our ability to theorise the minds of others – including those who follow different norms from us. We can say that someone who is good at recognising, representing and adopting local norms is *culturally intelligent* – which may be crucial for rapidly building trust with others in a novel environment. Looking to build rapport and trust across culture? Time to do some research and become an excellent mimic. How does small talk work? We're in India, so feel free to ask upfront: who are your parents? What do they do? Where do you work? In China it really is fine for someone to ask straight from the off: 'How much do you earn?' On the other hand, topics such as politics and religion may be rapport-building minefields almost anywhere, not least because they are quick pathways to identifying difference rather than similarity.

Norms around the use of small talk to build rapport can vary. In the Middle East, hours of small talk may preface a business meeting. Yet in Scandinavia, many prefer to get straight down to business. Here we see the potential set-up for a culture clash. The Middle Easterner negotiating the big deal in Norway may run the risk of seeming like a time-waster ('Get on with it why don't you!). But when the Norwegians turn up in Beirut for the next round, they are brusque to the point of offensiveness ('How can we trust someone who can't be bothered to get to know us?').

What about body language? That firm handshake we've honed can signal confidence in much of Europe and North America, while in Turkey or parts of Africa we're just being aggressive. Well-maintained eye contact with a conversational partner may signal respect and engagement in Europe, but across Asia, Africa and parts of Latin America we're simply making things awkward. How should we express gratitude? For speakers of Lao (South-east Asia) or Siwu (West Africa), such expressions may be made so rarely that they can easily seem out of place – even bizarre.[11] What gift should we bring when invited to someone's house for a meal? In Thailand, perhaps a pack of dried squid we can pick up en route. Social interaction is governed by endless variation in norms from one locality to the next. Negotiating local norms is usually critical for building interpersonal relationships and smoothing the path of influence.

Norms are also important in influencing others at scale – potentially placing us within the service of their objectives, for better or worse. Those who do this must respond to the question: *how does this population behave and how should I adapt?* The impact that Lawrence of Arabia had as he persuaded the Arabs to rise up against the Ottoman Empire appears to have been connected to his intuitive understanding of norms, his Arabian attire, his deference to traditional authorities in public, his careful observance of local norms around honour. On one occasion when the murder of a Bedouin threatened to generate a blood feud and derail his alliance-building, he took out a pistol and shot the accused man himself.

Changing people's behaviour can depend on signposting what norms everyone else is following (social proof again) – for example, in drawing out voters on polling day: 'Millions of people vote, so you should too'; or for hotels looking to reduce water use (and labour costs): '80 per cent of guests choose to help the environment and reuse their towels';[12] or in improving hygiene at university: 'Four out of five college students wash their hands EVERY time they use the bathroom'.[13] On the other hand, it may be counterproductive to highlight the undesirable behaviour of others – such as that sign in the national park that states: 'Over the years many people have stolen from the petrified wood.'[14]

Again, it is the appeal of a particular norm to a particular audience that is important.[15] 'Most people in your community are finding ways to conserve energy' (i.e. the norm for your group is to try and conserve energy) turns out to be a more powerful appeal than self-interest ('Save money on your energy bills') or environmental responsibility ('The time is right for reducing greenhouse gases'). This localised norm is also more powerful than generalised appeals to social responsibility such as 'We need to work together to save energy.'[16] The UK Behavioural Insights Team – popularly known as the 'nudge unit' – experimented with tax compliance messaging: appeals drawing comparisons to others within a community ('Nine out of ten people in this area have already paid their tax') turned out to be significantly more effective than highlighting the penalties for non-compliance.[17]

But we also weigh new information against what we already believe.[18] In a community in which most people think others are fiddling their taxes, would the normative message 'Nine out of ten people in this area have already paid their tax' still work? Unlikely. It might just seem like a cack-handed attempt to fool us; and few of us want to be a mug.[19]

Credible messaging must negotiate a culture's belief systems. This is because culture not only tells us how to *act* through behavioural norms, it also tells us what is *true* by insisting on the beliefs that we should share together. What are beliefs, again? They are attitudes – thoughts and feelings – about what is true. Effective messaging relating to attitudes or behaviour usually has to match the pre-existing beliefs of an audience. The ancient teacher Mouzi apparently intuitively understood this as he explained Buddhist ideas to the civil servants of ancient China drawing on terms that they recognised: 'It is because you know the [Confucian] classics that I quote them,' he said; 'if I should speak about the words of the Buddhist sutras and explain the essential meaning of Nirvana it would be like speaking about the five colours to the blind or playing the five tones to the deaf.'

Culture contains and propagates many of these *intersubjective* beliefs – beliefs that are true in as far as they are held by many, regardless of factual accuracy. Take money: the belief that the paper in our hands or the balance in a bank's data centre has some transactional value. We can, of course, decide to stop believing in fiat currencies – although if we do so, we probably ought to have some wilderness survival training in place. But if everyone stops believing, then there *is* a problem. Suddenly those numbers on our screens become worthless.

Money might be a useful social reality for a community to construct. Other intersubjective beliefs only make sense on establishing the adaptive benefits. Among some indigenous populations of South America, married women engage in extramarital sex in the belief that multiple fathers will bring their multiple traits to bear on the character of the offspring. But by encouraging the investment of additional fathers, the chances of children living beyond the age of fifteen are improved, providing an adaptive benefit.[20] It may seem less easy to understand the advantages of other intersubjective beliefs, such as the conviction that witches were prevalent across medieval Europe; and perhaps still less child sacrifice, which was practised across pre-Columbian America. But no matter how strange or crazy some intersubjective beliefs may seem to outsiders, many shared ideas prove highly resistant to change.

In the mid-nineteenth century a Hungarian doctor, Ignaz Semmelweis, discovered that mortality rates for new mothers with childbed fever – a bacterial infection following childbirth or miscarriage – declined tenfold when doctors disinfected their hands with chlorine before moving from one patient to another. He provided overwhelming empirical evidence for his finding but, remarkably, his fellow doctors rejected his recommendations. At the time even doctors believed strange injunctions, such as that a gentleman's hands could never pass on disease.

If questioning firmly held beliefs appears to challenge authority, then the result can be particularly severe. Famously, Galileo faced an Inquisition by the medieval Italian Church. His sin? Claiming that the sun did not, in fact, revolve around the earth. We seek evidence to confirm the beliefs we share with others and ignore that which might lead us to question them (motivated reasoning – remember?). And again, efforts to persuade us to the contrary may sometimes serve to validate and reinforce our shared beliefs (the backfire effect), shielding those beliefs against anyone who seeks to change them. Named after our Hungarian doctor, this is called the *Semmelweis Reflex*.

Even when there is a motivation to integrate new information, prevailing intersubjective belief systems can make this tricky. Take the 'cargo cults' of post-Second World War South Pacific islanders. These called upon the heavens to deliver to them the 'cargo' – the military and civil technology, food and other staples, gifts from the sky – that the islanders had seen arriving to help American soldiers prosecute their wars. How could they engage such generous gods? The islanders knew it had something to do with the odd constructions Americans built wherever they went, which they called *airstrips*. Once the Americans had left, the islanders attempted to reconstruct these useful-seeming places themselves, hacking landing sites out of the jungle; carefully adding control towers, communications equipment and even aeroplanes made from wood and vine, they used these in attempts to call upon the gods. The cultists drew on their existing intersubjective beliefs to understand anything new. How could it have been any other way? These groups could only make sense of new information from that already held within their *epistemic bubbles*, the complete understanding individuals and groups make of the world over time, which cannot include what is not yet known.

Intersubjective beliefs help guide our lives; by adopting them we instinctively signal to ourselves and others our allegiance to the groups we belong to. These can seem like reality because they *are* our social reality. But more objectively, as a whole package they are a mixture of facts and fictions – some useful, some . . . less so. How can we judge which is which? With reference to our beliefs and values of course. In the end, our intersubjective beliefs are the substance of our own epistemic bubbles, which makes us all members of one cargo cult or another – this seems to be an unavoidable feature of our existence.

The influence of a culture's intersubjective beliefs on an individual can be so strong that changing them often only occurs following severe pressure: when an individual has experienced sustained marginalisation, for instance; or the kind of sudden, dislocating trauma represented by the conversion of the Jewish pharisee Saul in the Christian Bible. Saul had been a committed persecutor of Christians. Then one day, upon travelling the road to Damascus, he was 'blinded by light'. 'The scales fell from his eyes' and the Jewish Saul was reborn (and renamed) as the Christian evangelist Paul. Similar processes may occur with the beliefs of those who end up as corporate or government defectors, whistleblowers or cult escapees.

Far easier than trying to change group beliefs is framing message content so that behaviour modification is achieved by working *with* the prevailing belief systems of a target audience – and this is the route often taken by canny influencers. In 2015 the Ebola virus raged through West Africa. Many in these communities believed that disease was the result of witchcraft, or punishment from God for breaking taboos – making it difficult to institute preventative measures.[21] In addition, scientific guidance on isolating and cremating the infectious bodies of the dead conflicted with beliefs about keeping the body intact for the afterlife, as well as the practice of kissing the corpse in an effort to cement unity between the living and the dead. As a result, some hid the bodies of loved ones who had died from Ebola, or bribed officials to fake different causes of death.

In response, governments began shifting the message, creating special burial plots in which victims could be buried in line with prevailing cultural beliefs and norms. Importantly, the authorities started to enlist more persuasive messengers: not the foreign scientists with their strange habits and belief systems but the trusted chiefs, village headmen and spiritual leaders who formed the pillars of these communities. The message content could now be adapted to local beliefs. For the Christian Church leaders, messaging designed to reduce physical contact with the dead drew upon Bible teachings like Leviticus 21:10–11: 'the high priest . . . must not enter a place where there is a dead body'. Eventually this was one of the measures that helped control the spread of the disease.

As they set out to evangelise the four corners of the earth in the seventeenth and eighteenth centuries, Catholic Jesuits intuitively understood the importance of culturally tailoring their message for different cultures. When they travelled to Latin America, the Philippines, Japan and China they adapted their attire and communications strategies accordingly. In China the Jesuits dressed in line with local custom: the famed missionary Matteo Ricci, for example, at first adopted the shaven head and coarse robes of the Buddhist monks, but later shed these in favour of the beards and silkwear of the Confucian literati. The Jesuits were even willing to accommodate traditional Chinese ancestry rites in which respect was paid to the dead in line with Confucian customs, arguing that these were secular aspects of culture that did not represent a threat to Christian doctrine. The Dominicans and Franciscans, however, disagreed – and Pope Clement XI supported these sects in decreeing that such behaviour constituted idolatry and superstition. Unsurprisingly, given what we know about belief compatibility, the Chinese Emperor Kangxi subsequently kicked all Catholic sects out of the country.

Culture also propagates intersubjective beliefs about what we should *value*: what is right, and what is wrong; what are the right ways to think, feel and consistently behave. Values are also socially learned and help drive your adherence to (or rebellion against) social norms. Naturally, values influence us – and can be used to influence. Imagine: back in the village your people have a norm whereby hospitality should always be offered to strangers (it's similar to a key norm of *Pashtunwali*, the way of life among twenty-first-century Pashtuns in the border regions of Afghanistan and Pakistan). You are often the first to offer this to strangers entering the village. The cynics say: some of the utility you expect to maximise relates to cultivating a reputation for generosity (in order to be more influential). Indeed, one day a stranger arrives and no one else is around, so you rudely dismiss them and send them on their way. Unfortunately, it turns out you *were* observed. The cynics were correct, and now everyone is gossiping about your deceit. That reputation you worked so hard for has just taken a leap off the cliff.

Perhaps you would have fared better if you had more deeply *internalised* the norm: you don't simply believe that compliance with the norm will gain you useful reputational advantage, you *believe* that compliance with the norm is *the right thing to do*. This may still not be enough for you to comply, if there are tactical benefits to be gained from occasional non-compliance. A more consistent observance of the norm could require a further degree of internalisation. Now you also *believe you are the kind of person who does this right thing*. Your recursive mind is firing on all pistons. This makes it more likely that you will perform the prescribed behaviour consistently – it is ingrained in habit. Your actions now reflect your *values*. And because of this, strangers can be assured of a welcome into your home regardless of who is watching.

Our values typically include the belief that it is right and morally correct to adhere to the norms of our groups (including those that tell us to be independent, take individual responsibility and be self-sufficient). Our egocentric biases operate here too: most of us believe our values drive us more strongly than they do others; that we are therefore more likely to be conforming to the group norms than others; and that we are less likely to defect from norms when it suits our self-interest. That we believe this is testament to the value of values. Because, sufficiently internalised, values lead us to act more consistently. This assures our behaviour in the eyes of others: we are known to be consistently generous, fair-minded or honest, precisely *because* our values help ensure the reliability of our social behaviour. Others can trust us more easily. Consequently, we carry more influence.

The emergence of values enabled further enforcement mechanisms by which individuals could be influenced to uphold the norms of their communities. The concept of *shame*, that feeling of embarrassment, may be provoked by an individual's failure to uphold the norms: 'I feel terrible because my standing has suffered in front of my peers.' Shame has driven much behaviour across time, from the chivalric codes of medieval knights to the honour killings that still plague many parts of the world. Guilt is an even more deeply internalised enforcement mechanism: 'I feel terrible because my standing has been found wanting in front of my own self-judgement.' That bad feeling you have as you abandon hoeing out those irrigation ditches early? Or when you sneak off to catch a rabbit in the midst of the stag hunt? Shame or guilt – or perhaps both; maybe you shouldn't do it next time.

Over time, values – and their enforcement mechanisms of shame and guilt – may have driven a virtuous cycle of norm internalisation, leading to more docile, cooperative human populations. One outcome was that humans became better equipped to learn socially from one another, which fuelled the advancement of culture and set a course that would take us from the use of stone tools and animal skins to rocketry and genetic engineering.[22]

Internalising values also helps to guide our basic desires: what should the goals of our behaviour be? What do the cultural influences around us say we should be trying to achieve? Should we accumulate economic resources to impress our peers with our ingenuity and resourcefulness? Achieve great glory in battle to demonstrate strength and courage? Generously support those in need? Or are our goals more esoteric: do we aim to enter the gates of heaven or Jannah? To be released from the eternal wheel of life? To return to the earth after a life in service to our common human dignity? The social psychologist Shalom Schwartz's *theory of basic human values* covers ten themes, which are often in tension with one another and may be weighted differently across cultures. Values celebrating self-enhancement (getting ahead) – of individual achievement, increasing agency and power, seeking pleasure and sensory gratification – are balanced against those promoting self-transcendence (getting along) – benevolence towards others, universal appreciation of other life, all that is beyond the self. Values representing openness to change – independence of thought, excitement and novelty seeking – are weighed against those that conserve – stability seeking, encouragement of conformity, respect for tradition – the existing culture.[23] Arguably, these manifest the (potentially creative) tension in our social species between different tactics for getting along with, but also getting ahead of, others.

It's extremely difficult to change our values – so much so that it can become an influence tactic to explicitly tie lightly held attitudes to deeply held values. This has been a recurring feature in the so-called 'culture wars' of the United States. Discourse in emotive and sensitive areas such as abortion or gun restrictions is not led through reasoned debate of costs and benefits, with reference to available evidence. Rather they involve appeals to non-negotiable values like 'the sanctity of [a foetus's] life' versus 'a woman's right to choose', or 'a fundamental right to bear arms' versus 'no more dead children'– tactics that may help bake in a politician's popular support but do little to negotiate compromise. Those who want to influence us may seek to tie our attitudinal positions to the values they think our communities hold – in turn, this can start to change our ideas about who does belong to these communities (as we will shortly see).

One system of internalised values and beliefs that has had a particularly large influence on human behaviour over time comes from *religion* – which wraps the system in overarching narratives, anchoring us into grand schemes of meaning and purpose that on the one hand help regulate social norms and on the other explain those chaotic contingencies that we are subjected to – runs of bad luck or loss, suffering and death.

The earliest of these systems were animist. We had gained an ability to mentalise the minds of *you* and *me*. But alongside this came the impulse to see minds in everything: in animals and trees, the sun and the moon, even rocks. We are easily primed to better adhere to norms by the feeling that others are surveilling us. This is why placing pictures that contain watching eyes at bus stop shelters can help reduce incidence of littering, while positioning them over the honesty box ensures people actually pay for what they take in the office staff room.[24] And in this context it may easily have been thought that, like other members of our groups, animist spirits had an ability to monitor our adherence to norms, even punishing us for their violation. More reason not to sneak off in the middle of that stag hunt.

The religious scholar Reza Aslan explains how religious beliefs may emerge through the story of an individual who one day sees a face in the tree. The supernatural tree, it turns out, can talk, or so claims this trusted and respected group member with an excellent reputation. It can explain important aspects of the group's past and perhaps predict the future. News of the talking tree and its premonitions is a story that stands out and generates interest when reported back to the group (the *isolation effect* in operation) and is gossiped about extensively. Not only does this claim fit with intersubjective beliefs already held by the group (after all, things like rocks and trees are known to have minds), but such a belief looks likely to be *useful*. The predictions seem to reduce uncertainty about the future in a dangerous world. Others, too, start reporting back on what the face in the tree has revealed to them, setting off interacting cascades of attention and availability (easy recall). Eventually, attending to the wisdom of the tree is embedded within the norms of the culture. If this remarkable tree becomes known for its abilities to, say, see inside your mind, you may now be deterred from even *thinking* about defecting from that hunt to go catch a rabbit.

As systems of beliefs and norms develop, so do the rituals that align with them; they are a key aspect of our encultured behaviour. In churches and other religious or community settings we *synchronise* our movement by dancing and singing together – the same principle lies behind armies marching in lockstep. The 'I' is submerged into part of a whole 'we', cementing social ties of trust among individuals within the group network and priming us to perform the cooperative behaviours required for the group's survival and success. In this way, thought the great sociologist Emile Durkheim, religion fosters social cohesion. By banding around a common set of symbols and participating in shared ritual performance our ancestors increased their collective viability to survive in a very hostile world.

Animist cults varied widely: a Lord of Beasts is one of the oldest gods in human history across Eurasia to North America and Mesoamerica. A widespread cult of the bear may have existed for Neanderthals. The Greek historian Herodotus wrote about the sacred forest of Dodona, whose trees spoke with human voices and made prophecies. These early religions not only indoctrinated individuals in how they were expected to behave (and think); they also created influential new cultural positions. In this world of speaking trees and rocks that can cast judgements, there are individuals who are particularly adept at translating between the spiritual and human domains, demonstrating a particular way in which we have opportunities to influence one another: these are the group's shamans.

The emergence of the shaman typified a new kind of human authority. Authority in most social animals – including, most likely, our pre-*sapiens* ancestors – relates to the ability to wield or effectively threaten violence, and the associated ability to control and distribute resources of value to survival. Culture modified this, for those who knew how to use tools to crack nuts or chop down trees became powerful. In this context, lower-status individuals were incentivised to attend to and imitate those with such cultural mastery. These *prestigious* individuals had skills and knowledge worth learning. Sure, people might still cower before dominant big men (with their invasions of personal space and aggressive eye contact), but their threats and intimidations merely produced compliance (non-internalised behaviours), and could lead to resistance and rebellion. Social learning from prestigious individuals demanded internalisation, and they soon exercised their influence by shunning aggressive dominance displays, projecting instead the opposite: warmth, smiling and an open posture to facilitate interaction ('come closer my friends').

How do we recognise prestige in others? Not only in their ability to teach us something useful (how to hunt better and make excellent tools), but from what the prevailing cultural norms and beliefs tell us about what is prestigious. This may be informed, too, by the *confidence* an individual demonstrates in their own prestigious abilities. Does someone act as though they have done this thing before? Do they act decisively (and do the results seem roughly acceptable)? Does this someone seem to *consistently know what they are doing*? Often we judge a person's competence at a task not so much by their ability to produce amazing results as by the manner in which they completed it. This is recognised very early in humans. Back at the Max Planck Institute, which we visited earlier, our three-year-olds insist on the 'right' way to behave. But they do this much more forcefully when the adult they are watching acts as if they know what they are doing – and much less so if the adult behaves as though the task is new, that they are making it up as they go.[25] What should we do? Follow the confident one: after all, they seem to know what they are doing. *Confidence* becomes a heuristic for assessing prestigious authority, a factor that is exploited by con artists, scammers and fast-talking salespeople. More generally, the social payoff from projecting confidence can incentivise us to behave overconfidently too.

One crucial facilitator for the social learning of culture which we have not yet visited is *language* – the shared meaning we make of the world. Its evolution may have acted as a catalyst for more sophisticated theorising of others' minds, not least by helping teachers and their students share more detailed information with one another – speeding up social learning and the accumulation of culture. Language likely coevolved alongside tools for complex communication: not only gestures but speech too, which depended upon remarkable biological innovations such as tongues that descend into the pharynx and the development of complex vocal chords that could produce a range of sounds far beyond the grunts of our ape cousins.[26]

Human language is symbolic and abstract, enabling transmission of complexity and detail. This supports more effective mentalising, enabling better learning from one another – the passing on of culture. Language and cognition also coevolved together, enabling us to communicate increasingly complex plans in which we mentally time-travel together to scheme about what we may do in the future: we can strategise for war, foraging or hunting stags, debating how we will react as a team to different scenarios as they unfold. We will then use speech and language to share real-time information – to update and guide one another as the hunt progresses. We also practice them to pass on news, to build consensus and to test reality – does the way we understand things accord with that of others in our social groups? Language also helps us regulate norms. If someone does run off to chase a rabbit in the middle of the stag hunt, language is the means by which everyone will gossip about them. About two-thirds of our speech is devoted to gossip – most of it negative.[27]

And of course, gossip is used not only for norm enforcement on behalf of the group but also to make ourselves look good, drawing flattering comparisons between our own noble conformity with the norm violations of others. We also use gossip to undermine those we don't like – by ensuring we repeat tales of their supposed norm breaches and slights towards others, sometimes passing on facts, sometimes knowingly or unknowingly retransmitting falsehoods, sometimes exaggerating or embellishing, sometimes just plain making it all up.

Combined with our ability to theorise minds, language also enables us to manipulate people: to influence not simply their behaviour but also their attitudes, beliefs and values – as well as their motivations and goals. We use it to draw the attention of others to information likely to guide them towards our perceptions of reality, leading them into regions of meaning stacked in favour of us and our beliefs. We influence even with our choice of words (themselves the product of culture), priming other people by our talk about 'targets' (that arrow flies straight and true) or 'goals' (that ball hits the back of the net). In your presentations and writing, do you apply 'bullet points'? Listen closely to the language used to consider precisely where the messenger is trying to take us. Because language is also a weapon. It is employed to coercively regulate norms as well as to deceive; the old adage we teach to children that 'Sticks and stones will break my bones but words will never hurt me' seems somewhat misleading (perhaps usefully so, if it increases that self-confidence).

Aristotle believed that human language and thought were intertwined. And that seems to be correct. Language can be used to manipulate not only the thoughts of others but also our own: it acts as a mental prosthesis, enabling more sophisticated mental reasoning with which to influence ourselves. Which is what we do before an interview or a big public speaking event when we think: 'I am calm and confident.' Finally, language became a crucial signal of our identities: it signifies which groups we belong to, whether we like it or not. Because beyond belonging to the group that speaks our language, our spoken words may also signal other aspects of our lives and identities – including where we live, social class, ethnicity, age and gender.

Which brings us to some of the broader relationships between culture and identity. *Who are you* again? A body imbued with a unique soul? A spirit trapped in the wheel of life? An ape with a runaway cerebral cortex, all the better for innovating and passing on culture? Whatever our identities, they are constructed over time by our interaction with the environment: with reference to complex and changing currents of culture. Culture is crucial to who we believe we are. This affects how we are influenced.

Do we speak the same language? Did we watch the same children's TV when we were growing up? Share an understanding of what is expected of us on a stag hunt? We may instinctually have an affinity for interacting with those who have internalised *similar* cultural influences. But coming from differing cultures can prove something of an obstacle when negotiating social interaction.

The anthropologist Geert Hofstede proposed a framework by which we can situate different cultures. One of the factors included was an 'individualist–collectivist' spectrum. Imagine the stereotypical assertive and extrovert American. The national culture of the United States is at the high 'individualist' end of the continuum; and the American was typically encouraged to express this when growing up ('Just be yourself'). But they know they are going to meet Japanese businesspeople.

So, sensibly, they moderate their behaviour, lowering the volume a little, even reining in the possible oversharing of opinions on things like appropriate boundaries of personal space. After all, on the same Hofstede measure, Japan's norms are 'collectivist'; the highly culturally intelligent American has learned to pay more attention to tact and respect for others – at the expense, perhaps, of the right to self-expression, a value in which they believe.[28]

Culture can aid a group's internal cohesion. Conversely, those differences *between* cultures often serve to amplify inter-group tensions. These can start innocuously enough. Take a group of Japanese and American businesspeople, perhaps friends of our protagonists from the previous paragraph. They stand talking to one another at a gathering, with the footage illustrating a slow-motion dance between one-to-one cross-cultural conversational partners. The American steps back, the Japanese businessman steps forward . . . and so on. This particular waltz is generated by different habits regarding personal space and the appropriate distance at which conversational partners should talk.[29] We know this type of phenomenon as a *culture clash* – the consequence of different sets of behaviours colliding. It is what is going on in some of those epic marketing fails: when the Japanese try to sell a baby soap in the United States called 'Skinababe', and the Americans try to sell a car in Japan called the 'Pinto', which translates as 'a small male organ'.[30]

With less light-heartedness, egocentric biases (remember these?) also work at the group and culture level too. '*Our*' group or culture is of course wiser, more moral and more just than '*theirs*'. It also has a better grip on reality via that monopoly on truth which it holds. Individual members of our in-groups are warmer and more competent (which predisposes us to like them more than those outside the group). We evolved to conform to and enforce culture – 'our' culture. When 'our' culture meets 'their' culture, the resulting clash can yield more than just awkward social moments and may result in discrimination, oppression and violence. Those conformist toddlers insisting on how the puppets should behave are not the only ones. Cultural differences lead to arguments among fully grown adults all insistent on very different *right* ways to behave – as illustrated by debates over whether some of our species may wear cloth over their lower face ('You *must* wear a Niqab/You *must not* wear the Niqab/You *must* be free to choose whether you wear the Niqab or not'). We seek strength in numbers, and favour those who seem to share these same correct values, beliefs, attitudes and behaviours. This is known as the *myside bias*. Those we perceive as being from an out-group are far less likely to influence us – and we may do or say precisely the opposite of what it seems they are asking: a process known as *reactive devaluation*.

We have evolved an in-group, out-group mentality strongly connected to shared aspects of culture. Historically it paid to cooperate in groups, precisely because that enabled more effective competition with other groups. This makes it easy for us to distrust, fear, stereotype and dehumanise outsiders too. In the absence of trust, it may be prudent to assume that a stranger represents threat (you will be heavily punished for mistaking *a snake for a stick*, remember). Before we get to know people from other cultures, it probably is harder to mentalise them and develop our *theory of minds*. After all, they behave slightly differently – we cannot predict how they may react to the norms we are familiar with, so it is difficult for us to mirror ourselves in them; to empathise with their perspectives. We may find it easier to feel disgust towards them, holding our noses at their wrong attitudes, beliefs, values and behaviours. In most animals this is an emotion that appears to have evolved in order to help avoid nasty tastes from rotten food. In humans it has become moral and aesthetic disgust – a marker of who has been categorised as 'them' (and not 'us').[31]

No! you say. You're a tolerant kind of person . . . you appreciate the diversity you see around you. But are you sure? Perhaps it is the pre-judice and intolerance of others that you cannot tolerate. And when you think of intolerant people – *those intolerant people* – does their behaviour, well, disgust you? We are subjected to cultural influences from numerous directions, many of which provide conflicting guid-ance in relation to the right attitudes, beliefs and values; to the right behavioural norms. Any two or more people interacting can create or reproduce culture. Under these conditions, what, precisely, makes an 'us' – and what makes a 'them'? These categories can be surprisingly fluid. Those placed in groups based on all sorts of trivia or nonsense will quickly develop in- and out-group identities. In one experiment, Lebanese boys from Muslim and Christian communities assembled into mixed groups quickly assumed new, opposing identity markers based upon new groups of 'red ghosts' versus 'blue genies'. Meanwhile, in lab experiments, students who had never viewed the work of the painters Wassily Kandinsky or Paul Klee before were shown their paintings and assigned to groups based on which of these painters they preferred. They were then asked to distribute financial rewards across participants, at which point it became clear that they were making preferential donations towards those within their respective new groups, as 'Kandinsky' or 'Klee' people. Similar findings are replicated even with divisions as arbitrary as those determined by coin toss into groups labelled 'heads' and 'tails'; or children assigned randomly to 'green' or 'orange' groups.[32]

Our judgements about what comprises in-groups and out-groups can be easily manipulated. Fear can be induced in white American subjects when black American faces are presented as rap music is played in the background. Yet this fear is substantially lessened if the same faces are presented while heavy metal is played. Fear in white subjects is also reduced by subliminal exposure to black counter-stereotypes, such as popular celebrities.[33] Whites first primed to think of race – i.e. that race is a category separating one group from another – prefer white politicians to black athletes. On the other hand, if primed instead to think about occupation, they prefer black athletes to white politicians.[34] We can positively apply similar dynamics in our speech when we use collective pronouns like 'we' (rather than 'you') to make people feel that they are all part of the same team (part of 'us', not 'them') – that we are unified and share common goals and motivations. It is also what political entrepreneurs are attempting to draw on when they talk about how 'we' are being undermined by 'them' – those, they implicitly claim, who are outside the circle of belonging and seek to overthrow the shared values and beliefs of the group.

The categories of 'us' and 'them' can harden in the minds of group members under these sorts of pressures. We can strengthen or weaken their impact upon attitudes. Priming 'loyalty' strengthens in-group favouritism and identification with 'us', one result being more tolerance for in-group inequality (even if there is inequality, we are still doing better than 'them'). These dynamics are easily observable through the leader-follower interactions within national populist movements. Priming threat perceived as arising from beyond a group strengthens in-group identification – making this, too, an excellent lever for dema- gogues seeking to challenge the existing order through divide and rule. Priming equality does the opposite, reducing in-group favour- itism and identification with 'us'.[35]

We are unlikely to help 'them' become 'us' simply by trying to suppress stereotypes of 'them' (*don't think of pink elephants!*).[36] But we can prime people so that those categorised as 'them' become 'us' with, for example, exercises in which individuals are asked to stand in the shoes of others (a process also used in good fiction, as *perspective- taking* helps us to break stereotypic thinking by encouraging us to mentalise the minds of others). A number of studies in which white participants inhabit a black avatar in a virtual-reality simulation demonstrate that this leads in subsequent tests to a reduction of implicit racial bias – as long as the avatar does not represent a nega- tive stereotype.[37]

Psychologist Gordon Allport takes this further. In his *contact theory*, 'them' can be turned into 'us' when individuals meet face to face. This requires that there are roughly equal numbers in each group; they are on neutral territory; and there are superordinate goals that draw both groups into alignment. These objectives may include tasks such as the creation of a new sports playing field or the setting of coherent, unified national aims and experiences that pull people together. More than this: the feeling of equality across groups is primed by emphasising distinctive *individuation*, shared attributes of identity and culture (similarity), taking steps to alleviate hierarchical differences (for instance by redistributing unequal resources), and bringing people together to interact on equal terms. The problem is that when the participants go home, it is easy for them to slide back into the same compartmented beliefs and behaviours as before.[38]

The management of constructed inter-group conflict has dismaying ramifications for responding to collective-action problems such as global heating. Where identities are polarised, policy agendas can quickly become associated with one side or the other – we may become for or against them, based not on reflection of the merits of the issue at hand but on which tribe they are associated with – and which we belong to. In the United States, for example, there is remarkably consistent alignment between positions on climate change and political identity. Republican voters are far more likely than Democrats to express scepticism that climate change is human-made, frustrating efforts to act. Some of these voters may eventually be influenced by new and meaningful information.[39] But many may not. Indeed, the more informed Americans are on the issue, the more polarised their attitudes become.[40] In these conditions, galvanising popular support for action may be hard to do through communication or education about the science alone. Rather, this support may instead depend on findings ways to transform the inter-group relations on which the attitudes are founded.

In summary, culture is the combined output of social learning, which is itself enabled by our ability to empathise with, and mentalise, others. Social learning has been crucial to human evolution, generating great advantages through transmission of often useful information. Together, culture and social learning constructed beliefs and norms of behaviour which enabled *indirect reciprocity* – the foundation of cooperating at scale. Culture is essential to influence – a core feature of our existence to which we are subjected continuously. Yet systems of culture may also clash as they interact, generating tension, misunderstanding, conflict and violence.

The heuristics by which we influence one another are, then, structured not only cognitively and socially but culturally too. Behaving in line with local norms can help us build trusted relationships with people. The efforts of influencers to change an individual's behaviour can be effective if they are signposted by norms which they are likely to respect – those of the groups to which they belong. It may be especially difficult to shift the intersubjective systems of belief that we are committed to, but influence is more successful in changing attitudes or behaviours by ensuring that messages are compatible with these existing beliefs, amplifying them by choosing communicators who carry prestige and authority within the group. But to which group do we belong? Identity allegiances too are fluid, and can be constructed, deconstructed and reconstructed. Dictators, demagogues, propagandists and other influencers have long harnessed these dynamics to manipulate us to their advantage.

The dawn of culture sparked a revolution: more social learning, more cooperation, more culture – dynamics that fed one another in a cycle that may have helped drive huge growth in the size of the human brain.[41] In this new cultural environment, individuals could no longer be simply prodded and bullied into compliance by nakedly aggressive others. As we humans created, identified and obeyed community norms, dominant elements became constrained and bound by them too. But, as we experience in every aspect of our modern social lives, far from diminishing the individual pursuit of power, the rise of culture instead enabled new mechanisms through which power can be accumulated – and expressed.

4. Identity

Who are you? 'Stardust,' says the physicist. 'Oxygen, carbon, hydrogen, nitrogen, calcium, and phosphorus,' says the chemist. 'A bipedal vertebrate with opposable thumbs and an oversized brain,' says the biologist – 'one that manages social and environmental risks by thinking heuristically,' adds the evolutionary psychologist. These are all accurate descriptions of you. But you might not use them at a party when someone you have just met says 'Tell me about you.' For us as social animals, the question drives at something else – beliefs that go beyond stardust and chemistry. It is primarily a question about the ways in which we compare ourselves to others: about *identity*.

Our identities tell us who we are, and therefore who is similar – and who is different. Identity informs how we think and how we act, including how we think about, and act towards, other people. Identity can be shaped by others to help them achieve their ends. When they tailor their communications to the components of our identity – from our personality traits to the social roles we play to the groups to which we belong – their messages can be especially effective. Doing so successfully involves either ensuring that communications align with these identity components, or prompting (priming) individuals to behave in accordance with an identity commitment they carry. These tactics can make it easy for those who understand our identities to influence and manipulate us. This is the key driver for the evolution of defences to protect us from such manipulation, in particular the concept of privacy – norms about our right and ability to shield from others personal information about who we are and what we do. Through shared identity, diverse minds can be pulled together to great positive effect. But these same minds can also be abused by others to help sow fear and division, degrading the fabric of our societies and jeopardising our survival and prosperity. Where our identity is concerned, the stakes are always high. But first, to understand how identity can be targeted and the ramifications for us, let's take a couple of steps back and ask: what is identity and how is it formed?

In the origin stories of the great monotheistic religions, the first humans, Adam and Eve, lived in the paradise of the Garden of Eden. Here they wandered naked, without shame. But they were soon tempted by the devil to eat the forbidden fruit from the tree of knowledge, after which 'the eyes of both of them were opened, and they knew that they were naked'.[1] When they then heard the voice of God, they hid from him. Now that Adam and Eve had gained knowledge, they became suddenly aware of a God that was separate from each of them. And likewise, Adam and Eve had also become individually separate and *different* – each of them was now an 'I'. And what that 'I' represented was a mind that was now conscious of itself – one which could be embarrassed by nakedness.

Chimpanzees and orang-utans can self-recognise. In experiments with chimps, dots of paint are placed on their faces – somewhere not directly obvious, like above the eyebrow. Guided by their reflection in a mirror, the chimps can find and rub the painted spot with their hand and inspect the fingers that touched it. They recognise that the coloured dot they see in the mirror is actually on themselves. Monkeys cannot perform such actions.[2] Among mammals, the emergence of this ability to theorise minds – including our own – may have emerged quite recently in evolutionary terms.[3]

The ability to theorise minds represents more than just an understanding that others are distinct from us. Our self-awareness enables us to create mental models of ourselves. These can be compared with our mental models of others, and updated based on our analysis of such comparisons – viewing ourselves through the lens of the behaviour of others, and informing our behaviour in turn. This model, then, this self-concept, is strongly related to our ability to mentalise others. If we can accurately mentalise the self-concept of others, we can increase our potential to influence them – and vice versa.

Our identities are being shaped long before birth. Even the biochemical developmental environments of our mother's wombs are laying foundations, as they interact with our genetic inheritance to influence us: everything from her diet to hormonal responses reflecting her positions in social dominance hierarchies may be at work. Our entry into the world then sparks a lifetime of environmental and social interaction, saturating in the culture of the groups we belong to, negotiating (and expressing) power. Across time, these interactions develop and change who it is we think we are.

In this context, the psychologist Carl Rogers believed that identity (which he called self-concept) consisted of three components. The first of these is *self-image* – how we see ourselves. Then there is our *ideal self* – the ideal version of ourselves: who we aspire to become. And, finally, our *self-esteem* reflects how much we value ourselves: are we an insignificant ant or a bit of a legend? Self-esteem may reflect the perceived gap we have between our self-images and our ideal selves. It also affects our susceptibility or resistance to flattery. Those with lower self-esteem may be more inclined to see flattery as insincere or selfishly motivated – after all, if I don't think very much of myself, why would you? They may, as a result, look dimly upon the flatterer. On the other hand, those of us who have higher self-esteem may be easy to flatter. Why? Partly because we enjoy having our beliefs validated, including ones which others seem to share with us about our own self-concept. Flatterers may benefit, because we now like them more as a result. And even more so if they have identified an aspect we value about ourselves which we feel has been generally overlooked by others: as the adventurer Casanova suggested, 'Praise the beautiful for their intelligence, and the intelligent for their beauty.'[4]

Self-image, though, is a construction built using a great deal of biological and cultural material. This includes sex, gender, sexuality, height, weight, skin colour, eye colour, hair colour . . . an endless additional number of physical differences, ethnicity, age, personality, intelligence, roles, language, culture – including socio-economic class and status, skills and capabilities, beliefs about capabilities, values, interests, associations with others, behaviours . . . phew, it's a long list! As groups and individuals we take these kinds of material and imbue them with meaning – with the *beliefs about these attributes* that we hold.

These include beliefs about the *personality* of ourselves and others. They may be linked to our enduring personality traits, which are partly predictable habits of behaviour and can be robustly measured using the *five-factor* model. We can harness personality traits in order to more effectively influence others, not least because our disparate personality traits affect how different message content will attract or repel us – typically attractive content will align with our traits. So what are they? The five factors are:

- Openness to experience
- Conscientiousness
- Extroversion
- Agreeableness
- Neuroticism or emotional stability

Openness to experience is a measure of how curious someone is to explore and understand their wider environment. Are you drawn to novelty, or do you prefer to stick with what you know? Are you creative? Adventurous? Or do you find comfort in the familiar? The curious can reap rewards from discovering new resources or knowledge. There are both pro- and anti-social effects that can arise from every config- uration of personality trait. In contrast to low-openness individuals, high-openness individuals may add creativity to a group, but can also overlook potentially useful traditions (or norms) of attitudes, beliefs and behaviour that bind it together. Sometimes they run risks that are unacceptably high. Remember how our cognitive apparatus may have logically evolved to misidentify sticks as snakes more often than vice versa? Those with open personality traits may be less inclined to identify those sticks as snakes, which means that when they optimis- tically, but mistakenly, identify a snake as a useful stick they receive a nasty bite. They may be early adopters of technology – the first to buy an electric car or a heat pump as part of the fight against global heating. Those open to experience can be lured by others with prom- ises of novelty or adventure. But, like Aladdin being tempted into the cave of wonders, this may or may not work out well.

Those at the less open, conservative end of the spectrum tend to be more cautious or sceptical in their evaluation of the novel. This may preserve their immediate survival, as well as that of those around them, even if it can also lead to missed opportunities. More conservative individuals tend to be responsive to appeals to tradition and habit – to continuation, sticking to the ways 'we do things around here', the prevailing norms. They may be more susceptible to messaging like the British Conservative Party's 2017 general election slogan, 'Strong and Stable', or environmental communications about protecting the planet and taking steps to prevent the radical changes that global heating will foist upon us all. More conservative individuals will usually be more receptive to messages that come from traditional authorities within the groups they belong to.

The second factor is *conscientiousness*. Do you like order or do you revel in chaos? Do you strive to achieve or are you happy-go-lucky and make it up as you go? Do you do the washing up after dinner, or before? The evolution of conscientiousness as a personality trait may seem straightforward: those who work harder gain more, generating resources for themselves and those they wish to protect, nurture and influence. Duty to the groups you belong to is pro-social and likely to cement power and relationships; you may be easier to trust, for example, as others can see that you are inclined to do what you say you will. The conscientious can be attracted to appeals for order and schemes to reduce chaos.

However, there are also benefits to being less conscientious: selfish ones, such as preserving your energy for your own goals and interests if you can free-ride on the work of others. But there may be advantages for your community too: if you can find ways to cut corners there are likely efficiency gains – your problem-solving skills may lead to more flexible and more innovative solutions. The low-conscientious may be the first to gravitate towards life hacks such as using Post-it notes to remove grime from their computer screens, or dental floss to cut dough for baking cinnamon buns. Appeals for corner-cutting and efficiency-saving tend to help attract the unconscientious – in efforts to mitigate global heating, communicators may stress the small costs involved in switching to green energy providers, and reducing meat consumption by moving to easily accessible and increasingly similar-tasting meat substitutes.

Extroversion is a measure of responsiveness to emotionally positive stimuli. Do you assert yourself in social situations or let others take control? Do you look at those who don't speak so much and wonder why they are being anti-social? Or do you prefer your own company and a bit less pointless chatter? Extraverts bounce around diving into projects and social situations – they are often to be found in management or sales.[5] They may be tempted through promises of social activity – the possibilities of interaction in meetings, at parties and social events. They may be especially drawn to high-energy communications appeals – like the classic advert for Crunchie Bar set against the Pointer Sisters' soundtrack 'I'm so excited'. There are high rewards for such sociality in terms of building relationships and connectivity – and the schemes they are involved in may receive an energy boost.

But there are advantages for the introvert too: reflection may enable more thought and better judgement. Introverts typically demonstrate more follow-through and greater completion of projects – even if fewer will be initiated. They may be reached through appeals to thinking over buzz and hubbub, like the 'world's most relaxing TV ad' for the mindfulness app Calm, featuring two minutes with no voiceover but a mountain view, waves crashing onto a beach and rainfall in a forest.

Then there is *agreeableness*. Are you cooperative and straightforward, or conflict-prone and sly? Do you work nicely with others in a team or do you prefer to do your own thing? Perhaps you think that generally people are good-willed and looking to help one another? You probably tend towards being agreeable. Conversely, you may believe that it's a matter of eat or be eaten: for the disagreeable, it's a competitive world out there! Agreeable people, being cooperative, tend to be more likeable and are typically more popular. They may tend to view others mostly as pro-social and cooperative as they project their own behavioural dispositions into their mentalising of others. Among the professional classes, the agreeable are less likely to be found among management and more commonly amidst engineers or scientists.[6] Agreeable individuals may be drawn to appeals to cooperate and expressions of cooperation, like the oft-used slogan 'together we can'.

On the other hand, disagreeable individuals may be more competitive and socially ruthless in pursuit of what they want. They can be harder to trust given their willingness to seek advantage over others. Disagreeable individuals tend to view the motives of others with suspicion – just as they know their own motives should be seen in this way (again, projecting themselves into their mentalising of others). Yet while disagreeable individuals may be less likeable, they can also be more effective at achieving objectives, not least because they are less likely to defer to others in order to maintain harmonious relations with them (notwithstanding any hurdles thrown into their path by people they have antagonised). The disagreeable may be attracted by appeals for competition against others, like the ad for furniture store Ikea titled 'Silence the critics'.

The final factor is *neuroticism* or *emotional stability*. Do you get angry or frustrated easily? Or are you pretty much unflappable? Are you easily made anxious or depressed? Or is your temperament generally even? On the face of it, it can be difficult to see how neuroticism has survived as a personality trait. We often go to significant lengths to downplay just how neurotic we are as we attempt to manage the socially desirable impressions we present to others. Neuroticism is typically seen in a negative light in terms of an individual's ability to operate effectively in our societies – not surprisingly, really, as neuroticism is a measurement of how responsive to emotionally negative stimuli we are. But this is also what gives us a potential clue to its utility: neuroticism provides behaviours that respond to potential threat.

Let's return to our cognitive game of 'Is it a stick or snake?' Here, anxiety may lead to increased threat perception ('It's *always* a snake! a snake! a snake!'). This behaviour is pretty exhausting to be around. But by hitting so many false positives (incorrectly identifying sticks as snakes), the chances of avoiding a deadly false negative (identifying a snake as a stick) may end up being reduced. Although neurotic behaviours can sometimes be seen as selfish or anti-social, there are also benefits to individuals and groups that come from such traits. People low on emotional stability may help themselves – and by extension the groups of which they are part – to better identify and draw attention to threats. Those of us who are more neurotic may be especially susceptible to appeals to fear, as exemplified in a World Wildlife Fund ad which showed a disturbingly mutated human face against the caption 'Stop climate change before it changes you'.

These personality traits are spectra. And most of us can identify with the extremes of behaviour associated with each trait even if that isn't where our behaviour is most of the time. Imagine, to make this clear, that we visit a fortune teller (again!). They smile and greet you warmly before staring deeply into your eyes as if they are reading your soul.

'Sometimes you're the life and soul of the party,' they say, somewhat out of the blue, 'but often you just feel quiet and shy.' *How could they know?* you think, perhaps a little less perturbed than you should have be. They pick up your hand, touch your palm and add, 'Much of the time you feel cheerful, but sometime in the past you were very upset.' Uncanny – this is so totally you. And to cap it off: 'Although you're mainly kind and considerate, when someone breaks your trust it makes you very angry.' But of course, by now you know exactly what this trickster is up to because they are using a well-known confidence trick called 'the rainbow ruse'. Here you are invited to locate yourself anywhere within a wide range of behaviours – and the corresponding personality traits – which can create the illusion of having identified your specific characteristics. Because *of course* there have been times when almost all extroverts have felt shy, and almost all introverts have experienced feeling socially energetic. Because personality traits are only *partly* predictive of our behaviour, and different communications content may be more appealing to us at different times, in different places.

Our instinctive personality leanings are not the only aspects of self that can be targeted for tailored influence. One principle that exploits our self-aware identities is known as *consistency and commitment*. This holds that we can be persuaded to take a particular course of action by appeals for us to act consistently – including in a way that aligns with what we believe our identity to be – our *identity commitments*.[7]

What kind of identity commitments? As Shakespeare wrote,

All the world's a stage,
And all the men and women merely players:
They have their exits and their entrances;
And one man in his time plays many parts.

These many parts, the roles we play in our social groups, are another key building block of our identity. Our behaviour changes to fit the expectations both we and others have of a particular position in a particular context. Each of us plays roles that are diverse and multiple. At different times and places one busy individual in a Western society might play mother, sister, daughter, police officer, dinner-table clown, shoulder-to-cry-on, non-practising Muslim, bursar of the tennis club, trombone player, yoga afficionado – internalising the position into self-concept to various depths, ingraining habits of behaviour.

Role can be primed, using the consistency and commitment principle, to engineer the behaviours we desire from others.

'Why were you speeding?' asks the police officer to the motorist when she pulls over. 'I need to see my child – she's in hospital,' says the motorist to the police officer, who is also a mother and who could now face a conflict between which position to enact (though not this police officer, who is ruthlessly committed to her professional role while on the clock). The motorist, in turn, may have hoped to prime the officer with a potential alternate social position in order to influence her behaviour and be let off the speeding ticket.

Social role only makes sense in the context of the groups we belong to, giving rise to cultural expectations about how the role is supposed to be played. We typically belong to many different social groups – and have identity commitments to these that can be influenced: we can be primed so that our behaviour is seen to be consistent with that expected of group members.

This can have surprising results. In one study, Asian American women were primed under two different conditions: one in which participants were asked to enter their ethnicity (Asian) and answer a number of innocuous questions related to ethnicity; and another in which they were asked for details of gender (female) before responding to a number of additional gender-related questions. Those primed on the 'Asian' facet subsequently performed better, apparently due to the identity role being enacted – in this case the stereotype that Asian Americans are a top-performing group when it comes to maths.[8] Successful influencers – including malign ones – may aim to repeatedly prime their target audiences in relation to the group identities they belong to. From violent extremist groups to totalitarian governments, commitment and consistency are used to make a particular group identity first the most salient of many among the target audience, and then exclusive, so that before long there is little room for them to also hold other group identities to which others might appeal.

Some of us may be more responsive to primes relating to different social roles or group memberships than others. Those of us who readily adapt their behaviour to the demands of the social context are high self-monitors – they are responsive to the situations they find themselves in: *how should I behave in this particular scenario?* They may be particularly responsive to primes that reflect the situation – mood lighting, room arrangements, the configuration of others involved. High self-monitors are attuned to social feedback and find it easier to fit in. We know them as chameleons, whose shape changes as they move between social environments and quickly adapt to the norms of behaviour within them. Individuals like this may also be adept at what the sociologist Erving Goffman called *impression management*, whereby they regulate their behaviour to create impressions on others. They may be especially sensitive to the differences between the public and private – the areas of performance that Goffman described as a 'front stage', in which we conform to the wider expectations of others, and 'back stage', where we feel less pressure to do so and can act more freely.

Those who are less responsive to context are low self-monitors. We can identify them from the way they seem to wear their personalities on their sleeve no matter what the situation. Their personality traits are typically more consistently observable across contexts. But even the low self-monitor can respond to social cues, and may behave differently at a wedding than at a funeral. Low self-monitors may be especially responsive to appeals to consistency – and commitment to internalised aspects of identity: 'Just be the real you!' Low self-monitors may be more easily persuaded by messenger effects such as physical attraction to the communicator because they are especially prone to instinctive heuristic, rather than reflective, thinking.[10]

The consistency and commitment principle can be used to great effect even without knowing much about our identities. Imagine you arrive at a hotel where you will be staying the night. At reception you are asked to complete a check-in form, which includes the odd-seeming question: 'Do you agree with the statement: "I care about the environment at home and when I travel. As a friend to the earth, I will do my best to practise environmentally friendly behaviour during my stay.'" Maybe you do. But would you align your behaviour with this statement unless primed? One experiment investigated exactly this question. Those hotel guests who explicitly agreed with the statement were given a pin as a gesture of appreciation. These guests were subsequently 25 per cent more likely to save water by reusing their towels, and more likely too to save energy by turning the lights off when they left the room.[11]

Our attempt to influence identity commitments can become quite generic. When our tired kid throws a wobbly and knocks the ice cream out of another child's hand we might say, 'This is not like you – you are a kind person,' and later, when the hysterical behaviour continues and they fall on the pavement and scuff their knees, we pick them up and say, 'You are really very brave, aren't you.' It's a tactic that can work with adults too. During international diplomatic negotiations, the Egyptian President Anwar Sadat apparently had a habit of giving his negotiating partners a reputation to live up to. He might tell them that they were known for their sense of fairness, or sympathy for the powerless, for example – priming identity commitments that fitted his objectives.

Sometimes we can protect ourselves from the possibility that others will target our individual identities in this way by attempting to control the access they have to information about who we are and what we do. This brings us to the concept of *privacy* – the need, ability and right to keep information about ourselves hidden. The norms associated with privacy are so powerful that when we feel it has been compromised we may experience anger and other strongly negative emotions. Across culture and time we have tended to jealously guard our privacy, attempting (often unsuccessfully) to shield personal information from those we have not risk-assured. This vigilance is instinctually baked into the reciprocal process by which we reveal and share personal information with others; by which we build interpersonal trust. In a competitive world, revealing personal information makes us vulnerable, creating a risk that we will be exploited by others.

Instead, the building of trusted relationships on which cooperation depends usually involves reciprocal sharing of information between two parties, both signalling their willingness to make themselves vulnerable to one another. That these processes are so strongly built into social norms is a big part of why it becomes awkward when someone on the periphery of our social network seizes the moment to share (or overshare) information – about an argument they had with their partner, for example, or the difficulties some types of food cause for their irritable bowel syndrome.

Privacy is reflected in our norms and in law. But it is also instinctive and heuristic: we *feel* when it is being encroached on – when someone we speak to seems to know too much about us, asks invasive questions or skulks around across the street peering into our home (though of course this varies from culture to culture!). Privacy protects our power, our agency over ourselves, not least to think and act as freely as we want to. In general, we aim to share such power only with those we trust – or whom we *want* to trust. We know instinctively that private information about ourselves can be used to influence us, which is why we go to such great lengths to try and manage the access others have to it.

The exceptions to privacy norms help underline why they have evolved. For example, you are on a lengthy train journey between Edinburgh and Manchester, and begin chatting with a stranger (run with me, even if you are recoiling in terror at the thought of this). Before long you find yourself spilling out your hearts, oversharing without fear life events that illustrate you're fine with throwing impression management to the wind – like that occasion when you pretended to put money in the collection for your colleague's leaving gift. By the time you're done – like Forrest Gump sitting at the bus stop – your whole life story is out there and you feel you've known your conversation partner for years. This situation demonstrates the *stranger on a train* effect. It occurs when we feel we are far from our homes and communities; far from the feeling that others can constrict our options or frustrate our goals because we have granted them access to more personal information than we should have.

Back in the Garden of Eden where Adam and Eve developed the first theory of mind, they had become aware that there was a private sphere of information that should be kept hidden from others in order to protect them from exploitation. After all, it was to become a competitive world: one soon to be inhabited by many more humans – beings who would also be modelling the minds of others and making judgements about intentions and selves; about whom to trust, and how to behave in complex social environments by acting on information they were able to obtain about these different others. In our time, the concept of privacy in liberal democracies has become existentially challenged. Today we are subject to technologies consisting of highly effective surveillance – not least those relating to internet-based social media platforms. By sidestepping the direct scrutiny of our five senses they have managed this almost without us noticing.

Zooming out, note that drawing on these diverse individual identities of ours can produce spectacular results, not least because divergent identity comes hand in hand with diversity of mind and thinking – cognitive diversity. And cognitive diversity, when smartly used, can lead to better *reality-testing* of a group's beliefs about the world, by scrutinising and comparing them with contrasting perspectives. This can help us reach more reasoned and useful judgements within our places of work, our communities and our societies at large.

Where enabled, this diversity also supports innovation, which depends upon individuals sharing novel ideas with others who will not have previously encountered them. This is because, claim sociologist Mark Granovetter and others, it is our *weak ties* with others that generate most innovation. After all, those closest to us tend to think like us – they may have in common with us a high proportion of attitudes and beliefs, reducing opportunities to transmit new ideas and information. If innovation and creativity depend on transmission and cross-fertilisation of novel ideas, then it will more often occur when unlike minds meet and share previously unencountered information. This dynamic spread along ancient trade routes, such as the Silk Road, making them instrumental in the transmission of all sorts of ideas. It is a dynamic that some have attempted to embed into building design. The Hollywood animation studio Pixar had its headquarters designed to funnel employees towards communal interactive spots such as the mailbox or the cafeteria to generate these 'small world' encounters between individuals from different functional areas of the organisation in order to foster innovation.[12]

Yet engaging with diverse identities has its difficulties: our goals may conflict and it can be harder to mentalise those who seem different to us, to find common ground or common cause together. It may become easier to look down on these others, or fear them by assuming threat or malintent. But for some this may be particularly difficult – because to them all our colourful human diversity can seem like so much unrelatable chaos and uncertainty. Conceiving of unity as sameness of thought or shared attributes ('what is like me'), such individuals have a disposition towards authoritarianism and the political entrepreneurs who offer it.[13] In our time it may be especially important for us to be able to reach out to those whose identities are different from ours – to find the commonalities between us upon which we can generate rapport and trust, to demonstrate that what binds us together is more important than what divides us, to help inoculate us from the appeals of those who aim to divide us. Where we cannot connect, engage and build partnerships with diverse others, the opportunities for building trust and cooperating can quickly recede and be replaced instead by an increasing possibility of conflict and strife. Into this gap stride the propagandist and political grifter, the conman and the wannabe tyrant.

We continuously think and act in the social world, supported by ideas about ourselves and others – about identities. Our ability to mentalise others is what we often deploy when we try to influence them. By aligning communications content with identity, or priming individuals to behave in accordance with an identity commitment they hold, influence can be tailored to take account of our personality traits, social roles, group memberships and any other feature of just who it is we think we are. In this way identity can be weaponised by others to get what they want. Our defences include the concept of privacy, which controls what information of ours others can access. And these minds of ours are splendidly diverse: a source of great strength when they are collectively enabled. But under the wrong conditions, this diversity too can be exploited by those who seek to harness us to their own ends.

Our minds are forged through the currencies of cognition, via the trusted relationships we build with others, the culture we are saturated in and the power that we continuously negotiate with. We may share 99.9 per cent of the same DNA with every other human being on the planet, but each of us is also an individual – a self that is defined in large part by the others we interact with.[14] There is great benefit to ourselves and our societies in the engagement of diverse minds. On the other hand, identity has always been contested – there has always been so much at stake. To be who we want to be often means resisting social pressure, negotiating with others and navigating power – which acts as a gravitational pull on every aspect of our selves.

5. Power

Sure, we want to get along with others. But, let's be honest, don't we often want to get ahead of them too? We strive to implement our desires in an often competitive environment, whether they relate to romance, work or mastery of fifteenth-century German poetry. We are social animals, and many of our desires are socially oriented. To achieve our goals we must exploit our social environments – control them, to some degree. What enables us to do this? Power does. And in complex human social life, some of us have always ended up with more of it than others.

Nietzsche thought that humans are driven by a 'will to power':[1] the motivation to dominate others. Certainly, this seems true of at least some of us. Regardless of how much power we hold, we are all subject to it. Power is everywhere: every time we interact with our family, friends, acquaintances and adversaries we negotiate our goals within webs of power – webs spun by ourselves, others and the societies we live in. Sometimes power can be overwhelming, even devastating. But we do not have to submit to it: we can resist. Either way, these dynamics play a big part in making us everything we are. But the expression of power has evolved over time and space, and through cultural and technological developments. So how can we identify power at work? How do others wield it? How can *we* wield it?

Meet Loretta and Vernon, two bonobos in San Diego Zoo.[2] Vernon – the male – was first able to dominate Loretta – the female, which placed him top of the hierarchy in this community of two. Vernon managed this largely on the basis of his larger physique and vicious canine teeth: a feature only available to male bonobos which can be used to wield or threaten violence to access resources such as food and sex. The use of physical dominance is a basic form of *coercive power*: the ability to force others to comply under duress. In the long term coercive power has limits as it is unlikely – on its own – to lead to the shifts in attitude and belief required to maintain changes in the behaviour of others. Rather it leads to resentment, and eventually resistance, from those on the receiving end.

Then there is the ability to reward others – *reward power*. In groups of chimps, leaders who are more equitable in rewarding others appear better able to cement their position as leaders: only weak leaders are forced to preferentially treat their allies within the group in order to shore up their position. We too can reward friends, acquaintances and adversaries we want to bring onside. We can also be rewarded by others – with resources and with grooming attention (including those flattering images of us that a friend shared online).

Our ability to coerce and reward most obviously represents sticks and carrots, like those we use with children: 'If you tidy your room, I'll buy you an ice cream / If you do not, you will lose your pocket money' – they are the costs and benefits informing our calculations in pursuit of our goals (the basis of rational actor models). But these levers are mediated and complemented by others. The first of these is *referent power*: the power we gain from our associations with other individuals, groups or even gods and spirits. A significant part of this is our ability to form those trusted interpersonal bonds with others: to build relationships (or alliances) and smoothly integrate within groups we want to associate with – everything we explored back in Chapter 3. Back in San Diego Zoo, the dominance of Loretta by Vernon was quickly interrupted when a new female, Louise, was introduced to the duo. Now Loretta and Louise quickly formed a close bond via their advanced interpersonal skills (being bonobos, this meant lots of mutual attentiveness and sex). The two of them were then able to gang up against Vernon, using their alliance to put him in his place – now firmly at the bottom of this hierarchy of three. In this instance, the referent power of the new alliance has been used to amplify coercive power, ensuring Vernon complies with the females' goals – they may not have done so consciously, but the result is that this cooperation provides a competitive benefit. It is for this reason that powerful individuals may take steps to disrupt the attempts of subordinates to build alliances. This is a regular feature too of chimp groups, in which alliances are cemented via grooming. The alpha male is vigilant to suspicious grooming attempts between his rivals – which he will interrupt if he spots them.

We don't just form our interpersonal relationships with one another directly. We often also form one-sided *parasocial* relationships, in which we may feel close to individuals we may have never even met. Where we attend to available information about them we can come to find certain individuals attractive, visionary and *charismatic*; so we feel connected with them. Such individuals can use this referent power to build trust with – and influence – large numbers of people whom they may not personally know. Those who can lay claim to holding large amounts of referent power range from Nazi dictator Adolf Hitler (who could reach up to 80 million German speakers by radio and print media) to actress Selena Gomez (426 million followers on Instagram as of August 2023).

Our phenomenal ability to socially learn has also generated forms of power to which humans are particularly sensitive. Social learning typically involves us making judgements and decisions based on questions like: whom should we pay attention to? Whom should we listen to, copy and learn from? Some of the people to whom we pay attention are those we think are knowledgeable about something worth knowing, or skilled in something worth learning – they have *expert power*. But who counts as an expert? Knowledge can indeed be power. However, it is the *perception* of expertise among an audience that is important here – including their attitudes to, and beliefs in, what constitutes knowledge or skills. From this perspective, experts may range from particle physicists to astrologists and fortune tellers. And remember, often at the most basic level, our assessments of expertise are linked to questions of whom we trust, as well as who projects the requisite confidence, and looks like they know what they are doing. Which helps explain why the arguments of political experts and economic forecasters still get so much media airtime even though their predictions are based on little more than chance.[3]

In a similar way, *legitimate power* is also closely linked to culture. These are forms of power that are bestowed by the group and are integrated within the wider package of its beliefs and behavioural norms, which can lead many to consider them legitimate. For example, the office of police detective confers specific licence to operate in ways that are sanctioned by the community, including the use of force to restrain those who resist arrest. Legitimate power is often intertwined with other forms of power. Palaces and castles were not designed solely to defend and coerce, but to express legitimate prestige and authority too – they were where the seemingly *rightful* authorities resided. Legitimate and expert power often come together: the police officer may be considered an expert in mitigating criminality; the surgeon has the power to perform operations based upon their acknowledged expertise. Holders of expert and legitimate power can lay crucial claims to upholding the culture and traditions of the community, whether as priest, knight, scientist, judge or town councillor. Their influence can encourage others to change and internalise attitudes, beliefs, values and behaviours without the kind of surveillance that often accompanies sustained attempts to alter behaviour via coercion or reward.

Finally, there is *informational power*: anything that can communicate in any way is an information broker and gateway of some kind. But by influencing others with language, humans have an increased ability to control the content and distribution of information, providing us with informational power – the proverbial 'pen' from the claim 'the pen is mightier than the sword'.[4] We can drastically enhance our potential informational power through the harnessing of media and communications technologies. Much of the information we share is gossip – which may be deceptive and misleading (whether intentional or not). Also, what we decide *not* to pass on to others can be as important as what we *do* pass on. It may not be sensible to share information that casts our allies in a negative light. We may also choose not to share information with competitors that could help them gain an advantage. On the other hand, anything negative we learn about our rivals may be shared as widely as possible.

We can share this tittle-tattle openly as a public flexing of our informational power, or discreetly in order to avoid being labelled a gossip, feeding it to others less worried about the consequences who will hopefully distribute it on our behalf. Informational power is related to our ability to adapt our content and reach others, working that content around their cognitive, social and cultural heuristics – including their individual differences. Every communicator is a transmission vector. And where the incentives are aligned, information can 'go viral' in the community, with everyone passing on news they believe to be important by word of mouth.

Why define these forms of power? After all, the concept of power is surely contested, squabbled over in fields ranging from psychology to international relations. Scholars of power have asked questions like: is power about whether we have the ability to change the behaviour of others? Or the motivation? Is the rational actor model sufficient? Do we just need sticks (punishments) and carrots (rewards) to dominate others? Certainly, the political scientists Peter Bachrach and Morton Baratz believed power ran deeper than this. They claimed that power reflected the individual or group's ability to ensure that the beliefs and behavioural norms around them systematically worked to their own advantage;[5] that expressions of power could be seen as legitimate by those subjected to it. The sociologist Steven Lukes took this a step further. Power was not just about drawing on the beliefs and behaviours that already exist in a group but changing them to one's advantage, from the bottom up.[6] From these perspectives, power is an extension of influence; the two are intimately intertwined and inseparable.

If these are the different outcomes of power, how can they be attained? The investigation of social psychologists John French and Bertram Raven led to a now-classic framework for understanding power, one that provides ourselves and others with the levers of power. You already know what these are because we have discussed them above. In summary, they are:

- Coercive power – the ability to administer of threats and punishments that others fear.
- Reward power – the ability to confer rewards that others value.
- Referent power – the ability to draw on those trusted affiliations and relationships we have built with individuals and, by extension, with groups.

- Expert power – the ability to draw on our recognised skills, knowledge and expertise.
- Legitimate power – the ability to draw on any formal authority we have been designated in a system of culture that is recognised by others.
- Informational power – the ability to control distribution of information content to others including by manipulation of their attention.

The traditional school classroom provides a classic example of how these levers come together. The student can be *coerced* ('You'll have to stay in at break time') or *rewarded* ('Well done; you've earned a certificate!'). The teacher uses their *referent power* to build trusted relationships with those they teach, as well as with their colleagues. Their *expert power* comes from the population's belief that they have the right tools and skills to transfer knowledge and nurture social learning among the young. The teacher's *legitimate power* comes from the role the vast majority of society's members expect them to play: they are mandated to educate our children, even if this sometimes means keeping the little pests in at breaktime. Naturally, a good teacher skilfully manipulates the flow of *information* so that their students are helped to learn the right knowledge and skills; this will be tailored to the pupils' age, specific needs and learning abilities – i.e. in a way in which they can most appropriately understand, and then act. By using these levers together, the teacher can attempt to change 'poor' behaviours and reinforce 'good' ones – priming and repeating information so that it is ingrained in memory, exploiting emotion and ego positively to generate useful levels of cooperation and competition, using social proof and generating norms that all serve to indoctrinate these young social learners into the cultural package.

By their very nature, all forms of power create difference and inequity: and inequity leads to hierarchy (or turmoil). For better or worse, just like our ape cousins, we live in dominance hierarchies. Some hierarchies may seem obvious, such as that operating in the classroom (noting that, clearly, the teacher is embedded too in wider hierarchies of power). Others may seem more arbitrary – such as those that explicitly or implicitly subject people of different skin colours or genders to disproportionately different levels of the hierarchy.

Hierarchy has enabled social animals to balance the conflicting drives of 'getting along' and 'getting ahead'. Getting along was especially important, because survival chances outside the group – where there were predators and hostile neighbours – were dismal. Apes who find themselves alone meet a quick death. Even a low rank can be preferable to going it alone. Yet the lower we rank, in general the more precarious and stressful our lives are.[7] Which might explain why we can be so scared of being ostracised or demoted in status or reputation. Because of this, most of us also fear unstable hierarchies (we are loss-averse) in which movement up and down the hierarchy can be rapid and arbitrary – as anyone who has lived through a political revolution will know.

Unsurprisingly, then, we humans are finely attuned to hierarchical position. By assessing cues such as body language, it only takes forty milliseconds for us to judge who is dominant.[8] Even very young infants recognise it.[9] Our use of power and influence can move us up or down hierarchies. We are sensitive to our hierarchical position relative to others – which can generate strategies of obedience such as loyalty, admiration, emulation, sycophancy and brown-nosing. We spend a great deal of time gossiping indirectly about hierarchy: who is up, who is down – who impressed the boss at the showcase seminar, as well as who really embarrassed themselves at the afterparty. The nature of hierarchy changes in line with that of the levers of power. These, in turn, are subject to changing culture and technology over time. How these changes have unfolded is important for understanding how power is still changing today.

Hierarchy no doubt existed in the communities of our hunter-gatherer ancestors. But research among current small-scale human societies reveals a reasonably egalitarian ethos in which it is easier for groups to ally against and control a domineering alpha (usually) male. Among Navajo Indians, !Kung San, Mbuti pygmies and Inuit groups, differences in wealth and status are small. Norms encourage ridicule of boastfulness and wannabe alphas are disobeyed and swiftly put in their place. If the alpha's violations of norms are too egregious they may find themselves murdered, as in the well-known case of a Baruya chief who tried to appropriate the livestock of other men and have sex with their wives.[10]

But around 10,000 years ago a revolution began in the way humans lived, changing the face of power. Our ancestors started to settle, domesticating and cultivating crops and animals. Later they came together in larger communities, and some were released from agriculture to specialise in other roles – becoming craftspeople, traders, smiths, potters, jewellers, priests. Early agricultural societies had teachers of military combat, farming methods and even dance. Finally, in the fertile plains between the great Mesopotamian rivers, the Tigris and Euphrates, agricultural communities connected to form centralised hubs. Here goods could be collected and redistributed and religious ceremonies performed, thus cohering the community around shared beliefs and behavioural norms. The economy became so complex that administrators and bureaucracies were created to account for this. Standard measures for quantities, weights, land, labour and time were introduced. In Uruk – modern Iraq – society mobilised a labour force large enough to build a 13-metre-high temple to their pantheon of gods, which stood symbolically at the centre of the city.

As material resources skyrocketed, so did hierarchical stratification. Wealthy elites emerged, visible to us in their claims to rare and exotic foreign goods such as precious stones and artefacts made of bronze. The king stood at the apex of this society. The elites could accumulate inequitable reward power far beyond that of their ancestors. At the bottom of the hierarchy were those involved in production, including dependent labourers, who received rations and fixed amounts of barley oil and cloth for their services. The availability of resources did not lead to sharing and plenty, but rather a meteoric rise in material inequality – and ways of subjugating the low-ranking never previously seen. Stratification could be greatly coercive. By 4000 BCE the Sumerians were enslaving people captured from the surrounding hill country. In the Indus Valley the rigid Indian caste system evolved – elite *Brahmin* became kingmakers and dynasty legitimisers. Tasks such as disposing of the dead were left to *Candala* outcasts who sat at the bottom. But such societies were not just held together by the threat of violence and other forms of coercive power: hierarchical relations are often perceived as legitimate by many across all levels of the stratification.

Apes experience inequity – in terms of access to food, grooming and sexual partners. But only human culture generates beliefs that attempt to systematically justify systems of inequity to benefit the powerful. All human societies propagate one story or another about why the gap between haves and have-nots is part of some kind of divine plan, and these stories are often internalised and accepted by people at all levels of the hierarchy.

But hierarchy changes too: it makes, and is made by, culture. And culture is driven by innovation and social learning – we can significantly disrupt and reformulate our social hierarchies. In one of primatologist Jane Goodall's studies of a chimp community, a lower-ranking male rapidly climbed up the hierarchy after learning the impressive trick of banging two kerosine drum lids together.[11] There is a reason why a lower-ranking male would be more likely to pick up this innovative trick. This is because higher-ranking chimp males already reap greater benefit from the status quo: after all, dominant animals – including humans – typically have privileged access to mates and food. They don't need to innovate to get what they want and there is less incentive for them to acquire disruptive and destabilising new ideas. Subordinate primates are forced to be creative to survive.

On the other hand, we live in hierarchies of hierarchy: different hierarchies can revolve around different cultures – different attitudes, values, beliefs and behavioural norms. Depending on where we find ourselves in this pecking order, we may face incentives to jump ship to hierarchies in which we have an improved position – ones formed around alternative attitudes, beliefs and values. Overall, just as there are forces attempting to stabilise and ossify hierarchies, there are countervailing ones that seek to disrupt and change them. This helps explain why, where they are accessible and presented by persuasive leadership, new ideas may often first take root among the lowly or the alienated.

City states in the earliest civilisations – Mesopotamia, along the Yangtse and Yellow Rivers in China, the Indus Valley, Mesoamerica – interacted: traded, built alliances and went to war. Over time, one or other of these city states ended up dominating others in the vicinity, swallowing them into larger political entities that we call empires. The pattern was similar: ruthless, determined men used the levers of power to build patronage networks of dominant elites, and through them command of technology and the masses – the tools of violence with which to conquer their neighbours. In victory they cobbled together often unwieldy empires which straddled cultures and ethnicities – and further diversified economic and social stratification. In these sprawling conglomerates, capability and motivation to use force and reward was often not enough to cohere political power. Rebellion was common. Rulers effective at cementing or enhancing their position in these environments utilised the full range of power levers, including their *coercive power* to make a ruthless example of anyone who dared challenge them. They imposed taxes and used the revenue to reward loyal satraps (*reward power*). But smart rulers knew better than to rely only on sticks and carrots. They were able to deftly wield the other levers of power too.

Sargon 'the Great' is one of the very first empire builders we know of, knocking together the Akkadian Empire from the city states of Mesopotamia around 2300 BCE. Sargon could soon organise and command a standing army of 5,400 soldiers – something no hunter-gatherer megalomaniac could have dreamed of. On attaining such power, he began insinuating himself and his family into the belief systems of the populations he ruled, developing his regime's expert and legitimate right to rule. He modestly proclaimed himself divine 'king of the world', a deity related to the existing pantheon of gods worshipped across Mesopotamia. He then installed his daughter as high priestess of the moon god, Nanna, at Ur – proclaiming to his followers that she was the moon god's wife. Sargon's grandson, Naram-Sin, later got one up on his grandfather, calling himself 'king of the four quarters of the universe' and (of course) identifying himself as a god. That the conqueror and his offspring turned out to have close relationships to their existing deities may have been all too believable to his subjects. This idea soon become normalised: it became typical for the next ruler of this dynasty to also join the existing religious pantheon, while injecting their children into cult centres as priests and priestesses. Using such methods, rulers were able to cement their claims in the prevailing culture, underpinning their rule through expert and legitimate power. The overwhelming power that the Akkadian rulers wielded is demonstrated by the contents of royal tombs, in which many others appear to have been killed in order to accompany their rulers on the next journey.

Rulers like Sargon illustrated some other key qualities of what we know as *leadership* – they were possessors of particularly great influence. Over time, such individuals were able to establish themselves as a crucial, integrated part of the community they ruled – conforming to the culture (the *right* beliefs and behaviours), a prototype of the *us*, no longer the outside *them* that had done the conquering. Once such rulers had gained sufficient trust via this positioning, they could more easily shape those beliefs and behaviours – often via incremental change (*normalisation*). The more rapid the attempt at change, the more the ruler might have had to fall back on cruder instruments of coercion and reward. However, if successful they could then bestow their cultural prestige on those whose loyalty they depended upon; their faces would be stamped on coinage and crafted in sculpture. But, crucially, this depended first on them gaining legitimacy by harnessing the pre-existing beliefs of the population.

On the other hand, the Egyptian Pharoah Akhenaten (r. 1351–1334 BCE) – the father of the boy-Pharoah Tutankhamun – illustrates how *not* to disregard the exercise of expert and legitimate power. In his time Amun Re, the sun god, had already ascended to rule the pantheon of Egyptian gods. But this apparently did not sufficiently align with Akhenaten's increasingly centralised power. Instead, Akhenaten began to worship another form of the sun as deity, the far less well-known Aten. Akhenaten claimed an intimate connection with Aten, eventually decreeing 'THERE IS NO OTHER EXCEPT HIM!'[12] He starved other deities' temples of resources and began a massive construction drive of temples to Aten. He then implemented full-scale religious repression using (coercive) military power to smash rival temples and idols. And then he died, his religion swept away with him. Aten's temples were demolished and thousands of statues of Amun Re were commissioned across the land. Akhenaten's tomb was defiled and his mummified remains smashed. His name was removed from public monuments. Given the pent-up anger he had unleashed across his kingdom with his attempt at revolutionary cultural change, Akhenaten was perhaps lucky to have died of natural causes.

As civilisations expanded, the hierarchy-legitimating stories holding them together changed. Religious beliefs evolved. Small hunter-gatherer bands worshipped an egalitarian range of spirits emanating from rocks, trees and assorted wildlife. Agricultural communities began to worship spirits relevant to cultivation: gods of grain and cattle, of the harvest and of the sun. As our ancestors started to dominate and control their environments, their belief systems eventually tended towards the anthropomorphic. The agricultural deities eventually took on more human-like forms, building families and community relations with one another. More than this, our beliefs tend to be *politicomorphic*, mirroring the political and social structures of our time into the spiritual world. In the great ancient empires with their stratification and hierarchy, the egalitarian spirit world of the hunter-gatherers had long been replaced, morphing into pantheons of superhumans – from which now emerged often tyrannical god kings who ruled over lesser gods: a spiritual hierarchy to legitimise the prevailing human one.

Ancient empires were multicultural by definition. Rulers who wanted to survive and maintain them had to tolerate and harness the multiplicity of beliefs, while striving to uphold social cohesion. Successful leaders carefully account for a community's prevailing convictions and norms, taking care to account for these in rolling out any programme of change. Where power pushes change success-fully, it often does so little by little, normalising it over time. The Roman Empire of Constantine (r. 306–337 CE) was a mostly poly-theistic society. It was within this milieu that the minority sect of Christians had grown, despite huge persecution over the preceding centuries. The Christians insisted that people report directly to an exclusive God – even though they did not all agree what this meant in practice. Either way there seemed to be little room for negotiation with pagan gods – or the authority of earth-bound emperors. Constantine was sympathetic to the Christian faith, not least because his mother had been raised as a Christian. Constantine claimed that the night before his great victory at the Milvian Bridge, he had a dream in which Christ himself warned him to use the sign of the cross against his enemies. Constantine promptly ordered this Christian symbol to adorn the shields of his soldiers and was rewarded with success. Later Constantine promulgated edicts of tolerance, reversing the persecutions of Christians.

But Constantine also strived to balance the pagan and the Christian. When he inaugurated his new capital in Constantinople (Istanbul), he claimed that the Christian God had ordered him to name the city after himself, thus moving closer to the pinnacle of that belief system. But he also consulted a pagan augur and brought many pagan cults to the city, including that of Tyche, the goddess of fate. Constantine sought a balance between ideological cohesion and the necessary tolerance of diversity required to keep the peace in his enormous territories. But more than this, he built on this foundation, instrumentalising the prevailing religious beliefs to further secure his position and underwrite his power. How?

The normalisation of Christianity in the Roman Empire was mirrored by developments in its great rival to the east. Around 500 BCE, the Persian mystic Zarathustra wandered the wilderness proclaiming the greatness of the single animating spiritual force, Ahura Mazda. For a time, Zarathustra had only a single follower – his brother. His legacy remained obscure until 700 years later, when the Sassanid rulers of Persia picked up his ideas. At that time, Christianity was taking off in the Roman Empire and the Sassanids may have wanted to sponsor a similar rival. These monotheistic belief systems had added advantages for sprawling empires, littered as they are with the plurality of identities and interests wrought by culture, economic specialisation and stratifications of power.

After all, monotheistic gods are typically omnipotent (all-powerful), omniscient (all-knowing), often omnipresent (hanging around, surveilling us) and frequently judgemental. They can see, punish and reward not only our behaviours, but our thoughts and feelings too. Internalising such gods within our thinking processes leads us to monitor and adjust our behaviour in order to conform with the prevailing beliefs. This buttresses emotions such as guilt ('I feel terrible because my standing has been found wanting in front of my own self-judgement') and helps guide conformist behaviour even in the absence of surveillance by others. Twenty-first-century laboratory studies confirm this effect: priming people that God punishes cheating subsequently reduces it (meanwhile, priming people that God forgives cheating increases it).[13] The internalisation of surveillance represented by God helped enforce norms among diverse strangers as they interacted, traded and cooperated; especially if these strangers shared the same judgemental God, who might otherwise administer divine retribution upon those who did not cooperate with members of the same religious group.[14] Rulers too saw obvious benefits in sponsoring belief systems that could encourage conformity and cohere their disparate populations to reduce political dissent and rebellion. Especially if they could insert themselves at the pinnacle of such systems, assuming omnipotence and issuing edicts that positioned them as divine interpreters. This complex of norms could then be further enforced via the internalised (legitimised) third-party force of God.

Constantine appears to have recognised the power of the monotheistic God. This may have been why he personally covered the travel expenses of specially delegated Christian bishops to convene a council in the city of Nicaea (modern-day Turkey). Constantine oversaw the selection of participants; and his presence may have influenced the key objective, which was to knock different interpretations of the divinity of Christ into a single dominant shape. The doctrine of the Holy Trinity was the outcome – and those, such as Bishop Arius, who dissented were exiled. This agreement of the Council of Nicaea was not unhelpful to Constantine, as he could now claim the mandate of this universal Holy Trinity to legitimise his earthly rule. Constantine was also stitched into position at the top of the empire's newest major system of belief.

Successful rulers also depended on an ability to spread ideas across their vast domains – a task for which speech and gesture alone may not have sufficed. Rather, the transmission of these ideas was supported by a key innovation in communication, one which underpinned the dynasty's informational power: that of writing. In the earlier speech-based communications revolution, we gained phenomenal abilities to exchange detailed information with one another. What is transmitted is determined in large part by an individual's motivations, interests, priorities and goals – by their personal wielding of this informational power. The very democratic nature of the spoken word is what also makes it an unreliable method for getting your message across to a large (empire-sized) audience. Writing allowed those who controlled it to spread their messaging far further.

The explosion of economic activity that came with civilisation gave rise to accounting systems to keep track of payments to the political powers. This seems to have generated the initial demand for writing, one of the earliest known examples being Sumerian clay tablets inscribed with exciting lists of barley and beer. Writing acted – as it still does – as a kind of outsourced memory; rulers soon realised that it could help underwrite their power: their commands and edicts could now go far beyond the reach of voices and sight, even beyond their time on earth. They could draw attention to the legitimacy of their position in the culture: at the apex of the hierarchy, within the pantheon of the gods – and the intersubjective belief systems of their subjects. They could also advertise their abilities to coerce and reward more widely, inscribing their monumental buildings with propaganda. An early example is the commemoration of a great victory over the Hittites (1285 BCE) by the Egyptian King Ramesses II at his palace at Karnak. The Hittites, meanwhile, celebrated their simultaneous great victory over the Egyptians of 1285 BCE at their palace. We still do not know what really happened. For those who were ruled, however, who lacked exposure to alternative information and were subject to claims repeated by peers (social proof) as well as those in authority (the powerful), we can imagine how easy it would be to swallow the narratives of the State.

Those who wanted to wield the power of writing needed to ensure they monopolised its production. In ancient societies like that of the Egyptian New Kingdom, literacy was the preserve of a tiny elite – only 1 per cent of the population could read and write. In the scribal schools of Sumer, over 5,000 years ago, boys (only) were taught to use a reed stick to pattern tablets of clay in the earliest known form of writing, cuneiform. A chosen few were attached to the royal court, where they recorded edicts, laws and propaganda. Others were assigned to temples, to the textile and shipping industries, pottery and transport – but the majority worked in agriculture, assisting with irrigation canals, registering rations for the labour force, the storage of the harvest and the supply and guarding of agricultural tools.

Control over this literate class of scribes was crucial so they were carefully cultivated, indoctrinated and rewarded by the ruler. Part of the Sumerian scribal curriculum was the consistent singing of hymns of praise to the rulers. Scribes were encouraged, too, to write flattering literature. The famous *Epic of Gilgamesh* was sponsored by the royal court. Unsurprisingly, Sargon seems to have wormed his way into the story, depicted as living at the edge of the world on friendly terms with the heroic character Ut-napishtim, the sole survivor of the great flood. Writing helped enable Sargon to become the subject of legend – influencing others beyond space and time. From Egypt to Hittite Turkey, statues of him were still being worshipped more than 2,000 years after his death. Many societies – including the young United States – punished attempts at widening the franchise of literacy to those lower in hierarchies (such as slaves), who would likely use such skills to question and undermine the prevailing order.

Across history, writing has helped shape culture and identity: as rulers and elites well knew, controlling such a powerful instrument could be essential for influencing the minds of their subjects. Knowledge of Sumerian cuneiform was a sign of belonging to the upper class for Akkadians of the second millennium BCE, just as familiarity with Chinese characters was for upper-class Japanese. Korean rulers sponsored the development of Hangul as way of side-lining Chinese characters – and Chinese influence. Later, Republican Turkey chose the Roman over the Arabic alphabet in order to shape a more Europeanised identity. Writing is such a powerful force in the construction of our stories that we define the study of history as beginning with the origin of writing. Rulers who understood the power of writing ensured that it was their successes that were remembered, never their failures. We say that the victor writes history, because control over the content and distribution of writing enables this.

Conquerors seeking to dominate the information environments of the ruled learned to destroy written sources that might offer unhelpful alternative perspectives to rival their favoured beliefs and stories. Alexander the Great's rampaging army burned the library at Persepolis during the sack of that city in 331 BCE. The library happened to hold the written records of his enemies, which ensured that we know of great battles such as the 300 Spartans at the Pass of Thermopylae only from Greek sources, not Persian ones. The first emperor of China, Qin Shi Huang (r. 221–210 BCE), famously desecrated the books following his unification of several smaller states. This is reflected, too, in more modern expressions of power – from the Chinese Cultural Revolution (1966–76) to the Cambodian Khmer Rouge declaring Year Zero and attempting to liquidate the entire literate class (1975–79).

These are all extreme examples of how informational power can be exercised.

Without writing there is little record of civilisation. Where rulers managed to successfully centralise power there was more writing, and more sources for historians to assess. Where empires fragmented and decentralised there was less. We call periods 'dark ages' because of this lack of source material – but the label also suggests a belief that life without tyrannical power must have been frightful. In general, power bred writing. And writing was at the service of power. In the written record the holders of power are presented as the overwhelming actors of importance – irresistible agents of destiny. Those who opposed or resisted them are denied to us, wiped from the face of the earth.

More generally, there are various trade-offs to consider in utilising different levers of power. Coercive power may be necessary in order to deal with a subordinate who is jeopardising cohesion or threatening the leader's authority, even at the cost of resentment of the target. Referent power, which may emphasise warmth and similarity (and therefore equity), may undermine the respect for authority someone gains via their superior position in a hierarchy. Strategies that aim to reshape beliefs and behavioural norms may take too much time and effort. Using informational power may be too subtle: for example, in trying to convince small children that they should not go into the street unattended, or in a military context when officers are likely to find themselves extremely compromised if required to give subordinates full explanations for orders. Here, authority may fall back on their legitimate and expert power, their referent power – and, of course, the tools of coercion and reward. All forms of power can be double-edged swords. And context can be everything when we attempt to use power to change the behaviour of others.

In our social lives we cannot escape systems of power, from small groups to institutions and from states to communities of states – power relations and hierarchies suffuse all relationships. Understanding how these operate helps us think about how to navigate them to achieve what we want. By observing how power works in our environments, we can home in on the people who may best help us achieve our objectives. Is this system more hierarchical? A chain of command? In general, influencing those higher up the chain of command may – for better or worse – amplify the effect of our message as it affects orders issued to those below: we can co-opt the latent abilities to coerce and reward, and borrow from the legitimate power of those more senior in rank. The 'flatter' structures of organisations such as tech companies hold hierarchies of a different sort – built instead, perhaps, around expert power, which confers legitimacy on the holder, as well as a means to coerce and reward others.

Different forms of power can be exploited for influence. In ancient Greece, for example, the high priestess of the Temple of Apollo at Delphi did not control great armies or economic wealth, but she did have great referent power (from her association with the pantheon of Greek gods), expert and legitimate power within Greek culture. Her power could even direct international politics – when, for example, she let it be known that the gods commanded the city state of Sparta to intervene in internal Athenian political struggles. Masters of power and influence such as the powerful Athenian noble Cleisthenes (b. *c.* 570 BCE knew well how to harness the power of the high priestess. His family had funded and reconstructed the Temple of Apollo at Delphi after it burned down in a fire – largesse that was well noted by the priestess, who started telling the Spartans that they ought to prioritise supporting democrats (such as Cleisthenes) in their struggle to control the Athenian State.

In medieval Europe the Bishop of Rome – the Pope – held immense sway, which rulers attempted to negotiate and use to their advantage. The Frankish King Charlemagne persuaded the Pope to crown him Holy Roman Emperor on Christmas Day 774 CE, legitimising his rule by association with the Godhead Christ, whose great spiritual emissary on earth he became. The English monarch Henry VIII later strove for the Pope's validation even as he sought to divorce his first wife, Catherine of Aragon. But the Pope refused and excommunicated Henry in 1538 – a politically expedient decision, given that Catherine was the aunt of the Holy Roman Emperor Charles V (and a descendant of Charlemagne). Later still, at the height of the Cold War, the Soviet dictator Stalin snorted, 'How many [army] divisions does the Pope have?' But in the first decades of the twenty-first century the Catholic Church had 1.3 billion adherents, with the Pope at the head of the earthly hierarchy. The empire of Stalin, meanwhile, had collapsed within two generations of his death.

Meanwhile, even when we lack direct access to other levers, we are able to draw on our referent power to develop, or inveigle ourselves into, social networks – from which we can clothe ourselves in the power of others, appropriating it to achieve our objectives. Rulers throughout history have been influenced by those who lack legitimate hierarchical power – by mystics and other low-born advisers believed to have useful expert abilities. One famous example is the monk Grigori Rasputin and his relationship with the Russian Tsar Nicholas II (1868–1918) and Tsarina Alexandra, in which he acted as a healer to their haemophiliac son. Rasputin, at the height of his power, held the Russian State's domestic reins, until assassinated by a group of disillusioned nobles. Using referent power to access and exploit the power of others is hardly a historical curiosity. In 2017, South Korean President Park Geun-Hye was impeached and imprisoned after – among other offences – it was discovered that she had allowed a cult leader, Choi Soon-Sil, to access and influence areas ranging from her personal wardrobe to negotiations with North Korea. Choi's ties to Park originated with her father, Choi Tae-Min, who had also been a cult leader, blending elements of Buddhism, Christianity and traditional Korean shamanism. His connection to Park had been established following the assassination of her mother back in 1974, when he had approached the young Park, explaining that her mother had appeared to him in dreams and asked him to help her daughter.[15] Plugging into the deepest hopes and fears of others is a tried and tested mechanism of building referent power.

Returning to the big picture, it is context that determines how we might best deploy our power. To paraphrase Bertram Raven, we can: set the scene through architecture and building design – or room set-up, including desk/table and chair-positioning (expert and referent power); display diplomas, a library, or photos with celebrities, wear a uniform, laboratory coat, or stethoscope (expert power); communicate from a podium or pulpit (legitimate power); signal our ability to control rewards and punishments, our access to expertise and alliances; appeal to our shared interests and goals, background and identity (referent power); or to our formal role as a supervisor, teacher or doctor, etc. (legitimate power). We can: make intimidating displays or present a fearful image – including by throwing a tantrum (coercion); do favours and ingratiate ourselves via compliments to enhance the target's attraction to us (use of reward power to enhance referent power); emphasise dependence or guilt-trip others into changing their ways (referent and legitimate power); self-promote and emphasise our superior knowledge (expert and informational power); use our ability to control the flow of information to communicate and amplify our messaging; use 'put-downs' (coercive power) – including gossip (using informational power) – to decrease a target's self-esteem or confidence, to increase our relative informational, expert or legitimate power relative to others or diminish the opposing power of our adversaries.[16]

All relationships involve bidirectional power. We often seek to negotiate with power that is greater than ours. But as power accumulates and centralises, our ability to do so lessons – its effects on our behaviour can become overwhelming. In the 1950s the United States and its allies were fighting China and North Korea in a brutal war. Reports began filtering back that American prisoners of war were cooperating with the Chinese – and, in some cases, had defected. The US government soon began levelling charges at the Chinese that they were *brainwashing* prisoners of war – coercively persuading them via mind-control techniques. But what did this really mean?

Imagine: we are being held prisoner after being captured by the enemy in some senseless war. Our jailers, those with power, have the levers with which to coerce (physical violence, solitary confinement, cutting off access to food and rewards) and reward us (extra rations, more comfortable conditions). The authorities bolster their referent and legitimate power through symbols of culture and hierarchy that we soldiers can identify with: wearing uniforms, issuing orders and obeying norms – such as not executing captives like us. Crucially, these authorities have total control of our information environments. We are told we have lost the war, that our government doesn't care about us, that we have been left to rot at the (generous) mercy of our former enemy. Our government is corrupt and immoral: it fights for the benefit of vested interests that do not include people like us. Naturally, our captors are a peaceable people who have been forced to defend their homes and their livelihoods. We come as aggressors.

But still, they spend their scarce resources on our survival. The least we can do is take their perspective on board. There are effectively no competing viewpoints – not even from our peers, from whom we are kept isolated and who are subjected to the same conditions. No alternative information (*What You See Is All There Is – WYSIATI*). At first we simply comply. But we experience cognitive dissonance as information from our current environment continues to contradict what we thought we believed. Eventually it becomes too hard to maintain our prior beliefs in the face of this onslaught. They may collapse and become substituted, like those of Saul on the road to Damascus. To paraphrase George Orwell: red becomes green. Peace is war. Freedom, slavery.

This label, *brainwashing*, was soon applied elsewhere: to CIA 'experiments' involving feeding psychedelic drugs such as LSD to American soldiers and unwitting civilians. To the case of the heiress Patty Hearst, who, after being kidnapped by left-wing militants, agreed to join the group and was eventually arrested wielding a gun while robbing a bank. It is often also applied to the dynamics of cults, in which charismatic leaders dominate their followers using the tools of power. Here, too, power can be absolute, as illustrated in horrific incidents such as the 1978 Jonestown massacre, when over 900 cultists of the Rev. Jim Jones's Guyana-based Peoples Temple died through the mass-drinking of cyanide-laced Kool-Aid.

Overwhelming power can be deployed to prime even more extreme mass behaviour, including genocide. From Ottoman Turkey to Nazi-occupied Europe, and from Rwanda to the disintegrating Yugoslavia, the pattern is similar: coercive power can silence dissent and prevent alternative stories from reaching target audiences (*WYSIATI*). Reward power is used to coopt those willing to toe the party line: some of whom will be allowed or granted a platform, and before long, positioned as legitimate experts. Censorship and self-censorship become rife, as only those parroting the official doctrine open their mouths, and social proof starts to reinforce messages delivered, advocated or endorsed by authority. As these patterns continue, those who disagree feel – and become – isolated: mostly they do not speak up, partly because if they do they will be made a nasty example of. Since group members do not express their private beliefs, support for the authorities and their policies will now seem stronger than it really is.

Meanwhile, the stories being pushed by the authorities become normalised and normal, sanctioning the *correct* beliefs and behaviours of the culture until the individual's sense of self seems to have shed any of its multiple, complex and colourful layers. In their place will come monotone conformity with the official identity.

These stories focus on priming mistrust and fear towards members of out-groups, who will be increasingly misunderstood and stereotyped: their attributes will be generalised to fit perceived attributes of the group – they are *thems* who are not like *us*. The authorities and their communicators now use their complete dominance over the information environment to intensify feelings and demonstrations of loyalty to more exclusive definitions of an in-group. The diverse strands of an individual's identity will be bent to the needs of authority. This process will make salient, too, the heightened threat 'others' now present. Members of these perceived (and part-manufactured) out-groups will be labelled *insects* and *cockroaches*, compared to animals and deadly viruses; and, in the context of existing intersubjective belief systems and lack of alternative information, this may seem strangely believable. The fanatical, meanwhile, are unmuzzled to wield and inflict violence on the out-group and any others brave enough to attempt to protect them.

Ultimately, though, the levers of power – coercion, reward, referent power, expertise, legitimacy and informational power – are continuously in operation in all our social environments. We are embedded within systems of power: they influence how we think, feel and behave. Individually and as groups, we can harness power to our advantage – to influence others and change their behaviour, or even to rise further in hierarchies, to wield even greater power and influence. The historian Michel Foucault noted that 'where there is power, there is resistance'.[17] And where a hierarchy does not work for us we can fight back, subvert, eventually even overthrow it and replace it with another. In this context, recognising where power lies in a given system can help us navigate it to achieve what we want – or to sidestep or subvert it when it demands from us something that we do not wish to consent to.

Over time, as the nature of our hierarchies evolved, so did the use of power. Civilisation also brought inequity. History, up to our current age, is a tale of the struggle for power – of its accumulation and contestation. Where it is accumulated, it can corrupt, breaking free of constraint by others. As the nineteenth-century British statesman Lord Acton accurately noted, where power centralises and becomes absolute, it corrupts absolutely.[18]

This observation is as relevant as ever. Liberal democracies may be flawed, but they are still our best hope in terms of their ability to disperse and constrain power. In our time the struggle for power is acute. Our liberal democracies are in trouble.

PART TWO:

INFLUENCE IN THE DIGITAL AGE

6. The Stage

On 6 January 2021 an armed mob stormed and ransacked the US Capitol building. Joseph Biden Jr. had won the 2020 presidential election and inside the Capitol Congress was supposed to be certifying the results. Why did it come to this? A key part of the jigsaw is the changing dynamics of how we consume information – and in particular how others communicate with us: the methods used have always affected what kind of information is available to us. This availability of information content – as well as the salience to us of one item or another – has always been shaped by others; we are all information gatekeepers. We flex informational power to create, amplify or suppress content as we see fit. But some people have always had dramatically more of such power than others, not least because of the distribution of control over the means of content creation and distribution.

The internet has revolutionised these means, which dictates *who* gatekeeps content as well as *how* it reaches us. This in turn has changed the nature of the information that we consume – our information diet. Information diets influence how we think and feel, what we pay attention to, what we remember, what patterns we identify; they activate our emotions and rein our ego to mould our attitudes, our beliefs and our behaviours. The information age brings choice like never before. But our minds are still as limited as those of our ancestors – in this fast-moving environment it becomes easy to rely on instinct rather than reflection. At the same time, some powerful information gatekeepers of old have lost out or been forced to change – the power of television, radio and print has been diluted by a host of online upstarts. Instead, our own gatekeeping ability has increased; it is easier than ever for us to create and share content with others almost anywhere else. But these developments create serious danger.

In our time, more than ever, information sources compete to burgle our attention and spam our memory, manipulating how we identify patterns between people, things and events, activating our emotions and lassoing our ego, entangling our thoughts and feelings in schemes that have little to do with our own interests. For many of us, our informational power seems to have increased dramatically, but often (despite any feeling of being better informed) our knowledge and wisdom have not. When harnessed to these schemes, we become a potent tool that others can use to inflict great damage on our social and political systems. We must take control of our information diets, consciously determining how we spend our attention. This will help us to reflect on how the content we consume stimulates our emotions and hijacks our cognition to influence our understanding of the world.

But first, what does it mean to structure an information environment? Let's rewind beyond *Homo habilis*, with our distant ancestors listening for skulking predators and watching (and sniffing) for fruit in the trees. Like us, their information environments were constructed from what passed through the five portals of their senses – at first visual information from line of sight, and audial information within direct hearing range. But then came the tool of language. Early modern humans could use gesture, then speech to share information through their social networks, information about almost anything – including about predators they had not heard, fruit they had not seen – or the reliability of other content or sources about predators, fruit and much more.

From our early modern human ancestors on, we could speak and hear. Although some of us have always been more eloquent or more attentive than others, the tools of language are very equitably distributed. This makes us all information gatekeepers within social networks. Language can have an especially powerful impact when delivered with the aid of non-verbal visual cues such as facial expression, body language and vocal tone. Language enables us to 'synch' and build rapport as we share information with one another.

With their large brains that could plan and learn, creating, ingesting and reproducing culture, early modern humans also began to manipulate things. Once we started manipulating things, we could use them to help us manipulate others. We became inventors of technology – including communications technologies that directly changed the form of the information environment. Beyond speaking, the earliest methods of communicating content to others were visual representations such as drawing (which began *c.* 70,000 years ago) and writing (*c.* 5,500 years ago – evolving from pictorial records of accounts to direct representation of the sounds of speech, to the segmented sounds of alphabets). These technologies enabled new opportunities for transmitting ideas to others, affecting their longevity. Put another way, writing could enhance the transmission rate of an idea across time and space. In contrast to the democratic chaos of speaking, writing and reading were tools that the elite had the motivation and the means to control, enhancing their informational power and dominance relative to the masses.

Plato believed that this state of affairs was just: after all, reason was also a tool for an educated elite only. 'No one is more hated than he who speaks the truth,' he has Socrates claim in *The Republic*. It was important not to disturb the harmony of the illiterate masses, with their inferior mental faculties and uncultured attitudes. To inculcate in them the freedom of reason would only confuse them – and their garbled search for understanding would destroy the stability of the (city) state. Rather than encouraging an unstable anarchy of ideas, Plato advocated using writing for politically directed propaganda while also enforcing strict censorship. These activities would help influence the transmission rate of different ideas, amplifying those the elites favoured and suppressing those they did not.

Using these tools, the elite could coalesce the information environment of the masses around the prevailing legitimation stories of the polity. Political elites were the guardians of literacy – the gatekeepers. Around 1750 BCE the great Babylonian king Hammurabi was granted by the gods the right to create a code of laws, translated by literate administrators into law. In the Hebrew Torah, God commanded Moses to ascend Mount Sinai to receive the law. He was instructed to go alone. There, Moses 'wrote down all the words of the Lord'.[1] This was part of a trend: if you could read and write, you could convey the injunctions of authorities – even heavenly ones. If not, then elites, such as priests, would have to interpret for you.

Writing provided a subtle tool of influence conveying authoritative content into an information environment that was otherwise a dense network of direct observations and content propagated face to face, through the social network.

The next key change in the means of content creation and distribution emerged in fifteenth-century Europe, with the invention of Gutenberg's moveable type. When combined with the fruits of around 7,000 years of creativity – from alphabets to paper; a culture of translating works across different languages; durable ink and the mechanical press – this innovation enabled the copying of written works at scale, and at relatively low cost. Now all sorts of ideas that people might have could reach the information (and attention) space of the literate – weird tracts such as the *Chronicle of Portents and Prophecies*, a compendium of medieval nightmares about plagues of locusts and two-headed beasts, sightings of comets and predictions about the end of the world; and more insidious works such as the *Malleus Maleficarum*, which taught readers how to protect themselves against witches and torture potential witches into confession. It helped incite between 100,000 and 1 million deaths (mostly women, but sometimes men and children too). Inevitably, the gatekeepers of the day responded to all this with censorship. The Catholic Church issued the first list of prohibited books in 1559 – the feared *Index Librorum Prohibitorum* (abolished only in 1966).

But the revolution in printing left the political elites swimming against the tide. In European states the process continued with mass literacy. In the thirty years between 1470 and 1500 the number of books entering the European information environment rose from the low thousands to more than 9 million, an exponential explosion in accessible data – the transmission rates of various content were now well beyond the suppressive capabilities of political elites. Together, printing and literacy generated a runaway dynamic. Before 1500, directly accessing information from writing was unthinkable for most of the European population – just as it had for the rest of the world's population. By 1800 literacy was common in north-eastern Europe, and by the eighteenth and nineteenth centuries states in this region had embarked on full-scale literacy campaigns, which helped fuel the emerging industrial revolution. The spread of ideas and beliefs created a more heterogenous stew of ideas and attitudes, conceptualised as 'public opinion' – one that could be influenced by the aristocratic class of elite gatekeepers, but not easily repressively controlled by them.

By enabling the transmission of ideas, printing brought diversity of perspectives and information to the audiences that it reached. Idealistic claims (often associated with the poet John Milton or the philosopher John Stuart Mill) were made that the information environment represented a 'marketplace of ideas'; that, freed from censorship, 'the truth' would win out in a free and fair exchange of opinions and viewpoints. But the purveyors of such truths soon turned out to be a new class of elite gatekeeper: the owners of a new generation of hyper-efficient steam presses – 'the press'. By 1814 *The Times* of London could print 1,100 sheets an hour (four times faster than the fastest hand printer), an ability to propagate at immense scale, and a flexing of informational power far beyond the efforts to shift the 'public opinion' that an earlier generation of pamphleteers had targeted.

The age of mass media had begun. It was an age not too far removed from that of our gossiping hunter-gatherer ancestors, because the new class of information gatekeeper had to compete in the fight for attention – and it turned out that what really attracted attention were tales of scandal and crime, of hoaxes and bawdy happenings. Drawing on the isolation effect – providing stimuli that stick out boldly from the rest – meant that providing sheer oddity and bizarreness also worked. For example, in 1869 the *Liverpool Daily Post* reckoned a woman had been killed by eating her own hair; in 1870 the *Illustrated Police News* made claims about a woman who died after her corset was laced too tightly; and in 1877 the *Dundee Courier* reported on an attention-stealing 70-foot monster discovered in Missouri with the head of a sea lion and a tangled mane like that of a horse. An 'immense horn' on its head was shaped like a pelican's bill; it had a long tail that looked like a double-edged saw, and made no sound but 'an occasional puff, loud and sonorous'.[2]

The more unusual the news, the better – as *New York Sun* (the epitome of the so-called penny press in the United States) editor John B. Bogart noted, 'When a dog bites a man, that is not news . . . But if a man bites a dog, that is news.' Nineteenth-century New Yorkers were more interested in a man who beat his wife than in the President's fight over the national bank, Bogart noted, running the first edition of the *New York Sun* with stories of a duelling Irishman, a suicide, three murders and a boy who apparently fell ill from whistling.[3] 'If it bleeds, it leads,' proclaimed famed newspaper mogul William Randolph Hearst, demonstrating an intuitive sense of how our attention is attracted by sensationalist content.

Printing presses – and even typewriters – could be regulated by the political elite. Even in more open societies, censorship still abounded; titles that we now consider to be classics such as Oscar Wilde's *The Picture of Dorian Gray* were banned for their sexual explicitness. Political geography could heavily influence censorship in the information environment. As war descended in 1914, locked borders also largely meant closing access to information from beyond them; getting hold of newspapers from within an adversary state was the kind of dangerous job allocated to spies. Troops at the front line did not have access to the information being supplied to those on the opposing side – there was little way of bringing it through, even if the authorities would have allowed it. The population was exposed to continuous motivational propaganda; in Britain, this included classic posters such as Lord Kitchener pointing at the viewer 'Britons – Join Your Country's Army' (*authority*). Others declared: 'Your Chums Are Fighting: Why Aren't You?' (*social proof*), 'Women of Britain Say "GO"!' (*social pressure*) and 'Who's Absent? Is It You?' (*shaming*). But what motivated the enemy must have seemed a mystery. Under these conditions attempts at objective news reporting were necessarily limited – and journalists, according to Ernest Hemmingway, 'either wrote propaganda, shut up, or fought'; only under such conditions of information dominance could the powers fight what he described as 'the most murderous, mismanaged butchery that has ever taken place on this earth'.

Developments such as the telephone further broadened our information environments – like writing, the telephone created opportunities to communicate sounds across vast distances. This could be more democratic, as long as you had one. Reading is a laborious process (as is transcribing and translating telegrams for that matter), requiring a large amount of cognitive effort to spread information around and beyond the locality. Unlike letter-writing, telephone communications are synchronous, allowing real-time feedback from our communications partner and enabling more accurate mentalising; the medium became essential for building and maintaining rapport with others, and potentially increasing audience susceptibility to spoken content. We evolved to use all sorts of cues in combination – facial expression and body language as well as speech. On the phone these are absent; we are forced instead to build our understanding from the very partial picture provided by the content of what is said and the tone in which it is delivered. This may help explain why people appear to lie more often by phone – because the communicator has to work less hard at controlling and cohering a number of cues in order to be convincing.[4]

Meanwhile, radio, like newspapers, allowed content to be propagated at scale. Unlike with newspapers, information could be transmitted directly via audio – drawing our attention by the power of sound and voice. Emotion could be transmitted contagiously, in real time, a major difference from the symbolic abstraction of the written word. The media theorist Marshall McLuhan saw radio as bringing oral culture back to people sat around the hearth – i.e., in conditions of intimacy – which allowed communicators to build rapport with audiences through their warmth, charm and charisma, facilitating one-sided parasocial relationships in which people could feel close to them. The radio enabled intimacy, but also scale – bypassing other gatekeepers of information. Entire nations could be reached. President Roosevelt announced America's entry into the Second World War using homespun language during one of his radio fireside chats: 'With confidence in our armed forces, with the unbounding determination of our people,' he said 'we will gain the inevitable triumph. So help us God.' The masses could now be influenced and mobilised beyond the wildest dreams of newspaper moguls.

It was difficult to contain radio. As the Second World War demonstrated, it could be used to reach minds across hostile borders in ways previously unheard of – to persuade, menace, deceive and demoralise. Axis Japan promoted English-speaking propaganda to Allied populations under the all-female outfit nicknamed 'Tokyo Rose'. Nazi Germany broadcast into the United States via Robert Henry Rose and

Mildred Gillars ('Axis Sally'). William Joyce, aka Lord Haw-Haw, aired to the UK (and for his troubles was later executed).

As a tool of information dominance – for influencing at scale – radio was impressive. In Rwanda the Radio Télévision Libres des Milles Collines (RTLM) was widely regarded to have played a leading role in creating a charged environment in which Tutsis, moderate Hutus, Belgians and the United Nations were vilified by incessant hate propaganda. RTLM had built up an audience partly due to the quality of its contemporary music programming – catching the attention of the youth that would soon make up the bulk of the murderous Interahamwe militias. From 1993 to 1994 RTLM started broadcasting anti-Tutsi propaganda – including deranged monologues that amplified dangerous 'them' and 'us' in-out group dynamics to help radicalise its listeners. Then, in April 1994, the genocide began and the station issued directives on specific targets and areas where Tutsis could be found. RTLM had few competitors – apart from the official Hutu government station, which broadcast similar content, including guidance on how and when to kill Tutsis. The areas of highest illiteracy are believed to have suffered the most acute levels of violence – in large part because in these places RTLM overwhelmingly crowded out the written word from the information environment.

In liberal democracies governments could exercise some control over radio by licensing the limited bandwidth available. Still, some tried to bypass these restrictions by setting up illegal 'pirate' stations. In authoritarian systems, the State, naturally, co-opted the medium and banned others from using it. But it was hard to prevent unwanted content reaching the information environment from beyond. In the Soviet Union, citizens could often tune into banned stations like the BBC, Voice of America and Radio Free Europe. Sure, the authorities might try to stop them, setting up chains of radio-jamming stations, identifying the location of receivers and arresting the listeners to reduce demand. But only in North Korea, where radios pre-set to State broadcasting frequencies were exclusively sold, did the dams have any chance of holding back the waters.

Now let's switch to another kind of visual representation: direct, rather than abstract, visual content especially draws our attention and encodes particularly strongly into memory. Imagery easily stimulates visceral emotion and can increase an audience's susceptibility to content. Since ancient times theatre had been used to engage our attention, entertain, seed and spread ideas – including those critiquing authority. Plato feared actors – they pretended to show life in all its richness, he thought, but in fact their performances were deceptive: they swindled everyone. Paintings and sculpture had long depicted timeless human fascinations with sex, food and drink, power, wealth, conflict and violence. These media could be used to place the powerful on a (physical) pedestal, enhancing their referent and legitimate authority. In an earlier age, stained glass was used to venerate individuals as saints, turning them into literal bringers of light. Imagery in books too had provided a route to visceral impact. As early as 1561 a Livonian (German) propaganda pamphlet included an attention-gripping woodcut picture of Russian soldiers nailing slaughtered children to trees and shooting the genitals of ravaged virgins.

As illustrated earlier, photographers knew well how to exploit the impact of imagery, which could prove a mobilising force – if they could ensure it was amplified through the press. In 1955 a fourteen-year-old African American boy, Emmet Till, was lynched in the American South after being accused of offending a white woman. His mother insisted on an open-cask funeral, forcing attention on the tragedy through the vivid imagery of Emmet's bloated, mutilated corpse. This helped galvanise public support for the civil rights movement, energising its agenda.

Cinema took the immense power of visual imagery further than single photographic stills, providing portals to what can seem like the three-dimensional worlds of others. The perception of visual information changing in real time was so representative of people's actual experiences that early audiences would duck and shout warnings to others when an on-screen locomotive appeared to be veering towards them. Film captures the intensity of real-life stimuli, the sounds and imagery of speeding cars, explosions and gunfire; of revealing blouses and stacked muscles; emotive responses to treacherous friendships and poignant goodbyes; of drama, romance, action, thrill, horror.

Such a vividly emotive medium naturally played well into the hands of propagandists: the infamous *Triumph of the Will* depicted the 1934 Nuremberg rally (social proof again – 'look how many support us') to promote the return to power of Germany under the Nazis. It was one of the few images ordinary Germans had of the Nazis, and helped the party consolidate its rise. Film made millions susceptible and soon gained reach like never before.

The visual revolution continued with television. By the 1960s, now almost everyone in wealthy countries had a visual hearth in their house, bringing a pipeline of emotive and easily understood information from the outside world. Not just anyone can set up such mechanisms of informational power. The resources needed to set up an effective television station are immense: an army of people is required to make and broadcast even a single programme. This made television another elite tool. The gatekeepers were selected by the extremely wealthy or by governments. Open societies originally often insisted on impartiality in news media, which once seemed the best way of protecting John Milton's marketplace of ideas.

This meant that control of the information environment could easily slip from the hands of governments. And resonant moments on television could change the course of history. Television despatches from the war in Vietnam helped draw the attention of American citizens to information unfavourable to government policy, setting the stage for polarisation and eventual US withdrawal from the war. Political elites lacked the means or motivation to suppress transmission: of 'Napalm Girl' running naked and burning after an American airstrike; of summary executions in the streets; of live footage – including dead American soldiers – from North Vietnam's militarily costly Tet Offensive. This all reached Americans in their homes via the visual hearth. So while the North Vietnamese still struggled to broadcast their message directly into the domestic information space of their adversary, American news cable channels were the gatekeepers, American journalists the transmission vector. Their mission might involve a commitment to sharing the facts with the public, but showing horrifying footage to susceptible domestic audiences did their ratings no harm.

Control of television was not enough to suppress information through censorship. In April 1986 the No. 4 nuclear reactor at Chernobyl power station exploded. Witnesses could see first the eerie beam of light projecting into the sky out of the collapsed reactor lid, then the black pall of smoke against the horizon. Further afield observers watched the heavy military traffic to and from the accident site. The transmission rate of rumours about a terrible accident increased continuously, cascading via the democratic power of gossip. From the State came a media blackout. Pretty soon the rumours included stories gained from radio over the borders – from Voice of America and others – about workers setting off the radiation alarms at a Swedish nuclear plant. This turned out, upon investigation, to lead back to a source over 1,100 kilometres away in the region of the Soviet power plant at Chernobyl. The authorities eventually admitted there had been an accident at the Chernobyl nuclear facility, but 'A nuclear meltdown would be impossible,' they maintained. Meanwhile foreign broadcasts were claiming that a huge graphite fire raged underneath Chernobyl reactor No. 4. had caused a nuclear meltdown, blowing its lid clean off and spewing huge quantities of deadly nuclear material for thousands of kilometres.

It took a full week before Soviet radio and news presenters reported this same information. It was, they said, 'all under control', but by this time the State had been thoroughly discredited as a communicator. The information vacuum had since been filled by others. And not only by potentially credible information from foreign broadcasters, but by all sorts of wild rumours and conspiracy theories that easily spread among anxious and frightened audiences: that the accident was a result of a failed piece of radar defence technology known as 'The Woodpecker'; that a 'Black Bird', a humanoid with giant wings and glowing red eyes, was terrorising survivors in the night.[5] Others, reflecting our great human capacity for hope, claimed that aliens had launched a major initiative to support the clean-up. Perhaps the State thought that an information blackout would staunch mass panic – or cover up incompetent crisis-handling. But the information came from too many alternative sources which could be triangulated against one another, collectively setting the dominant frame. *What you see is all there is.* The Soviet authorities had blown it.

Soon came new technological advances that altered the transmission rates of information – satellite television, mobile phones. Lech Walesa, leader of the subversive Polish group Solidarity, pointed out the role of foreign media and communications technology, stating that they 'helped end Communism by bringing in information from the outside. It was possible to get news from independent sources.'[6] In East Germany, the only area not able to receive satellite broadcasts from the West became known as the valley of the clueless. Just over three years after the Chernobyl disaster the Soviet Union's Eastern satellite states abandoned Communism. And two years later, having lost information supremacy within its own domestic environment, the Soviet Union dissolved.

Like cinema, television enables easy distortion of imagery and sound as it feels to us as though we are experiencing it in our direct line of sight. As propaganda researcher and TV director Peter Pomerantsev says,

> The factual director is always a manipulator, a miniature vizier seducing, framing, spinning his subjects, asking one question but waiting for another slip-up, always thinking about how every action we're shooting relates not to its direct environment but to the final cut. And when we begin to edit, our subject's video representation takes on a life of its own, a hologram cross-faded, saturated, flipped, squeezed and cut in different ways . . . so almost no subjects are ever happy with themselves on screen . . . because it's never the him or her they think they are.[7]

Television is made for propaganda. Like Rwanda's radio RTML, the most effective propaganda stations cultivate their audiences by giving them something they want – harnessing their motivations, capturing their attention with casual entertainment and lurid imagery geared to the norms and beliefs of the target audience.

What once held back the excesses of television in open societies was monopolisation by the State or a small coterie of private companies which had an interest in targeting mass audiences through content that would appeal to the median citizen. But this began to change. Not only did competition from satellite television unleash the power of television across borders, but three major developments further revolutionised the wider information environment. The first was a US-led military project creating a decentralised network technology for communications. The second was the invention of the World Wide Web, enabling documents such as webpages to link to one another.

The third was the evolution of hardware on which all this might run – first computers, then smartphones.

The result is known generically as 'the internet': an ever-changing compendium of databases and dumps acted upon by human minds and machine software agents which are themselves also the products of human minds; an ocean of information continuously assembled and reassembled – of text, still imagery, audio and video; interactive, connective, multimedia content – all growing at exponential scale; a chaotic socio-technical system of systems, *social machines* with us somewhere inside. The internet is the archetype of the digital information revolution – one which is also a revolution in terms of influence.

The internet collapses geography to annihilate distance, bringing an anarchy of ideas and transmission rates – anytime, from anywhere. Our ancestors focused their attention on potential threats and opportunities in environments of information scarcity. In our time information is ubiquitous, but our minds remain bounded by our evolutionary heritage. It has never been clearer that our attention is an extremely finite, exclusive currency – one with value not only to us but also to those who aim to steal it, who can monetise, measure and optimise our engagement with (or capture by) content, as assessed by 'click thru', 'page views', 'likes', 'comments', 'shares', 'time on page' and 'mouse movements' . . .

The arms race to hook our attention and memory space is continuous and never-ending: bleeping smartphones, ad pop-ups, reams of clickbait headlines like 'This is why you've never heard of this top travel destination', 'When you see these, you already have cancer', and 'This is why you're losing money' (great Barnum statement!), omitting essential information in order to create intrigue and suspense and fulfil a desire to know. Our eyes are captured by human faces, movement and animation, boldness and colour; content is framed in the age-old themes of food, sex and danger or novelty and the bizarre, creating tension then relief – an emotional rollercoaster – or leveraging simple value contrasts that can be grasped in milliseconds, between good and bad, risky and safe.

We are subject to confusing and deceptive tricks sometimes known as 'dark patterns'. You may have encountered some of these: *sneaking* – when random items somehow end up in our online shopping trolleys, like the travel insurance that seems to have come with that plane ticket to Ibiza; *urgency* – the countdown timer which will wipe those new shoes out of the trolley and off the face of the earth, or the time-limited offer that ends . . . well about two minutes from now; *misdirecting* – making some options more prominent than others, pressuring users into taking upgrades, or using trick questions like the checkbox alongside the text that reads: 'We may contact you about goods and services – tick this box if you don't want to opt in'; *social proof* activity messages which tell us that, in relation to that firepit or faux-marble soap dispenser, '352 items like this have been sold this hour' and that 'Fred from Solihull has also bought this'; *scarcity* – because, by the way, there are now only three left of the soap dispenser that Fred bought. There is *obstruction*, where it takes just a couple of clicks to sign up to that subscription service to Romanian football Liga 1, but to cancel requires a call to customer services, and – darn it – the line is always busy. And finally, *forced action*, where you're lured into sharing your requirement with that travel insurance comparison site . . . but now they want to know your name, personal address, date of birth and maybe your credit card details if you want to see your bespoke search results.[8]

Sometimes when we are online our attention may become so deeply immersed – in texting, browsing, gaming or anything else – that we have a *flow experience*, one in which time seems to pass so quickly it almost disappears. If we are not careful, we may become so engrossed in our online lives that we overlook what is going on immediately around us. We become distracted from face-to-face social interactions and begin *phubbing* – phone-snubbing – others. This is part of a wider negative trend of *technoference*, in which our attention is increasingly captured, leading to conflict with our loved ones, lower relationship and life satisfaction, greater levels of depression. Let's stop for a second . . . has this ever happened to you? The kind of information environments we live in are not constructed for reflection. They are continually optimising instead, to leverage our instinct – priming a hyper-alertness that served our ancestors so well in their quest for survival.

We are not simply subject to these dynamics, though. We are also their authors. Everyone is an information gatekeeper, but due to skill and access to technology some have been vastly more powerful than others. The social media revolution has enabled us to create and curate our own content. We can now publish books, write blogs, set up podcasts and post our own videos, all at minimal cost. We help choose which content from others gets passed on, which is curated, modified and goes viral. In one sense, informational power has become more dispersed and democratic. The old media gatekeepers in their niches of print, radio, television and film have been challenged, forced to sink or swim in the fierce competition of an attention economy that they can influence but not control; their previous monopolies are now diluted by innumerable upstarts.

The most successful gatekeepers are skilled in exploiting the susceptibilities of audiences and incentivising them to share. Emotion-laden content is heavily contagious across online social networks and does not depend on people directly interacting.[9] One of the most comprehensive studies of virality, by marketing specialist Jonah Berger and behavioural economist Katherine Milkman, identified the following features of content that make us susceptible:[10] positive (Pharrell Williams singing 'Happy') or humorous ('Charlie bit my finger!') content allows us to demonstrate our care for others or make us look good by association. Yet it is not only positivity that stimulates sharing; triggering other high-arousal emotions like awe, anger and fear does so too. Simple content is more likely to be shared, as is content that encourages interaction – for participants to 'do' something and feel empowerment and belonging, to email or tweet a politician, perhaps, sign a petition or 'like' something or 'comment' somewhere. What type of content are you more likely to share?

Our trusted networks will self-select the most susceptible for a given message, as people decide whether to share your content any further. By such online methods, traditional word-of-mouth transmission networks are greatly augmented as content goes viral. Take a woman from New Mexico who earned half a million dollars by sharing 'a video of her sister deep-frying a turkey'. Meanwhile, an American high school senior was paid twice that for 'unboxing videos and funny content' which included one clip in which she 'spins on a hoverboard while seamlessly appearing in new outfits'.[11]

Under the right circumstances, viral cascades can easily spill out into the offline world. During the long, hot summer of 2020, African

American George Floyd was murdered by a white police officer, Derek Chauvin. Caught on video footage by numerous passers-by, there would be little scope for manoeuvre by anyone who wanted to dispute the facts, including any temptation on the part of a police department that might be tempted to try and protect its own. Viral footage showed Chauvin keeping his knee on Floyd's neck for a full nine minutes while Floyd cried 'I can't breathe' at least sixteen times, as well as 'Please', 'Don't kill me' and 'Mama' before falling silent. This acted as a *trigger event*, initiating avalanches of attention and availability and leading to widespread demonstrations against police brutality and discrimination against ethnic-minority citizens well beyond the borders of the United States.

It can be difficult to suppress these sorts of dynamic. Efforts to prevent them can merely fuel them. In 2003 the California Coastal Records Project documented and published cliff erosion near the singer Barbra Streisand's Malibu home. Streisand filed a lawsuit alleging invasion of privacy. The offending photo had gathered six page views the previous month (two of which came from Streisand's lawyers). But as the case progressed this rapidly swelled to over 420,000. Unfortunately for Barbra Streisand, the actions undertaken in order to protect her privacy claims seemed to have had the completely unintended consequence of stimulating further publicity, rocket-fuelling the transmission rate. This kind of phenomenon is known as – adding insult to injury – the *Streisand Effect*.

Unsurprisingly, cascades through social networks appear to provide far more effective transmission vectors than attempts to communicate with others directly.[12] At the same time, direct *broadcast events* targeting many people can help increase the chances of generating this kind of avalanche.[13] But don't be disappointed when your hilarious home video doesn't go viral; the vast majority of content does not. And even when it does, it will typically peter out rapidly under the fickle gaze of the attention economy.

In this anarchic environment in which many read by social media stream rather than specific publication, it may be especially difficult to separate out and judge the reliability of different forms of content. Among all those accelerated transmission rates of all sorts of ideas there is a great deal of junk. Sometimes this may be generated and spread by misunderstanding and accident – *misinformation*. At other times it is pushed into the ecosystem deliberately – *disinformation*. Either way, where this junk meets the criteria for rapid transmission, it wreaks havoc.

India has suffered a spate of online coordinated mob lynchings over the last decade. In just one example, five out-of-town men offered chocolates to children in a village as they passed through. What they may not have known is that the villagers had been sharing photos on WhatsApp of apparently kidnapped and tortured children – a powerful prime anywhere, let alone in a country in which 250,000 rural children are reported missing. The five out-of-towners were soon accused of being child kidnappers, and as they tried to reason (big mistake) an angry mob started to gather. Three of the five suddenly made an escape in their car. They did not reckon with a flexing of informational power over the WhatsApp messaging platform. As they arrived in the next village, a roadblock had already been thrown up to stop them. The three were dragged out of their car and beaten – one of them to death. The visceral power of visual media was macabrely affirmed as the investigating police superintendent stated that villagers 'may not be able to read or write, but everyone understands photos and videos'.[14]

Like other content, false content is likely to have maximum impact when it plugs into an audience's motivated reasoning and confirmation bias ('It's just as I thought!'); when it can draw on existing desires attitudes, beliefs and values, piggyback off trigger events, and generate cascades of sharing reinforced by repetition and social proof (band wagon effects). Its spread may also be facilitated by closed platforms (like WhatsApp and other messaging services) as, by design, these shut out alternative information from other messengers.

Ours is an age in which the transmission rates of junk often run riot. During the COVID-19 pandemic huge numbers of people shared content claiming that COVID-19 didn't actually exist, that authorities were using vaccines to covertly insert tracking chips under our skin to sterilise us; that COVID-19 originated as a Chinese, or even an American bioweapon.[15] Like our earlier story about a face in the tree, these beliefs developed organically, through free-form associations shared across networks. One study illustrated how people transmitting negative thoughts about the frequency of 5G masts might become associated with instances of being sick, which might be associated with poor health in general – and, meanwhile, that Bill Gates is linked to 5G, and also to vaccines, and to viruses . . . [16] Many of these conspiracy theories, spread on neighbourhood social media groups, are easily accessible and transmit like wildfire through a terrified – and highly susceptible – population. Again, as with any form of information, social media enables the rapid travel of falsehood, which takes advantage of our human frailties to rage across trusted social networks.

Disinformation is now cheaper and easier than ever – and worse, it is often more easily available than more accurate content because the latter may hide behind a paywall, whereas fake news is free. Even established political actors have started taking advantage of the opportunities available in the new information ecosystem. Take the UK Conservative Party, which was lambasted in a recent NATO report for 'overt disinformation': their representatives had apparently altered a video of former opposition leader Jeremy Corbyn and relabelled their party Twitter account 'factcheck UK', masquerading as a non-partisan service while it took potshots at Corbyn during a 2019 general election party leaders' debate.[17]

This kind of temptation is all too common in the competition for scarce attention. Let's compare two politicians: one gives a talk on an important policy issue (say, immigration or the cost of higher education) while the other provides a rambling monologue scattered with racist and sexist insults. In the wider media landscape only one of these is likely to generate avalanches of attention (what is everyone looking at?) and availability (what comes easiest to mind?). Novelty and outrageousness – the salt and sugar of our information diets – may capture our attention among all the buzzing; as will outrage – real and manufactured.

But the true political pioneers of this new information environment were the propagandists of the Putin regime in Russia. Some years after the Soviet Union collapsed, the major successor state, Russia, learned from its earlier mistake. *Never leave the information environment uncontested.* Neglecting the attention battlespace for others to dominate was not in its best interests. It had also become clear that suppressing unwanted information and ideas could be engineered without crude censorship. Because the Russians understood that they could overwhelm the power of content indirectly, by encouraging a bewildering array of alternative content to proliferate – content designed to dilute attention, distort perception and frustrate congregation around positions or facts.

Content is pumped into minds and memories across the world with little concern for physical borders. Journalists and useful idiots can be harnessed to help surge it into new information environments under the guise of offering 'balance'. In this kaleidoscope the Russian State television (RT) station slogan 'Question More' might have sounded like a smart injunction for the open-minded, but instead confused consumers by muddying the waters, turning established facts on their heads, or simply twisting them into 'he says she says' tales of impenetrably opposing perspectives. After Russia's 2014 invasion of Ukraine's Crimea these tools and tactics, which had been honed in the domestic environment, now came into their own internationally.

2014. Malaysian Airlines flight MH17 from Kuala Lumpa to Amsterdam is knocked out of the sky, with the death of all fifteen crew and 283 passengers. MH17 diverted deliberately from its planned course to fly over a war zone. And it was a Ukrainian Buk ground-based rocket launcher that shot it down. But the official Dutch criminal investigation, other Western governments and the remarkable online investigations outfit Bellingcat assembled an impressive body of evidence that clearly identified the cause: a Russian- (or Russian proxy-) owned Buk missile launcher. The Russian authorities complained that they were being unfairly blamed, victims of a 'powerful information attack'; the case against them 'built upon photos and messages from social media sites, placed by Ukrainian authorities and since then proved to be forgeries'. These were claims for which absolutely no proof was offered.[18] *Question more.*

2018. Sergei Skripal, an ex-Russian soldier turned MI6 spy, and his daughter Yulia are found comatose on a park bench in the sleepy English town of Salisbury. It is established by the British authorities that the Skripals have been poisoned by a nerve agent, Novichok, later established to derive only from Russia. According to RT and Sputnik, two key arms of the Russian State media ecosystem, these claims were a witch-hunt driven by Russophobia; Novichok could have come from the UK, the United States, Ukraine . . . or pretty much anywhere. And besides,

Skripal was linked to organised crime, and Yulia brought the poison into the UK herself; and it was actually the British intelligence agencies who set it all up; and in any case, the Skripals weren't poisoned, it was all just a hoax set up to harm Russia. RT and Sputnik between them came up with '138 separate and contradictory narratives about the incident across 735 articles in the four weeks following the incident', according to a study by King's College London.[19] *Question more.*

2020. Russian opposition leader Alexei Navalny suddenly becomes life-threateningly ill on a plane from Tomsk to Moscow. Maybe it was something he drank or ate the night before. Perhaps he took a hangover pill and then went drinking heavily, causing a reaction. Or there was a sudden drop in blood sugar caused by a metabolic disorder. It couldn't have been Novichok, as that almost always killed its victims. If it *was* Novichok, it wasn't Russia's Novichok (NB Russia is the only state that makes Novichok). Fabrication of the story by a Western intelligence agency couldn't be ruled out.[20] *Question more.* Eventually, medical investigators in Germany identified Novichok in his underwear. Bellingcat and Insider were able to unmask the perpetrators in the Russian security services – and Navalny himself later managed to trick one of them into confessing over the phone.

During the COVID-19 pandemic Russian State media were especially busy: American pharmaceutical company Pfizer used to fake clinical trials; it had also delayed rolling out its vaccine to help get rid of Trump with EU support. Russia was the only state with a COVID-19 vaccine. The Western media company Reuters had stated that the only approved vaccine was the Russian one. Western vaccine manufacturers were reliant on experimental and untested technologies. The US trialled its vaccines on Ukrainian soldiers. The World Health Organization and Microsoft sabotaged Russia's vaccine. The West criticised Russia's vaccine because it couldn't accept Russia's primacy. Bill Gates was often somehow involved.[21] This was all perfect fodder for wheedling into and reinforcing pre-existing conspiracy narratives reflecting the fears of anxious people.

The 'black box' approach to censoring had been updated; the information environment would now also be trashed through the 'white noise' of disinformation. But it was not only safely ensconced Russian autocrats who understood how to make the digital revolution work for them.

Track back a few years. Property magnate and star of *The Apprentice* television series Donald Trump entered the 2016 US presidential election. Trump spoke emotively, simply and divisively. For example, from June 2015:

When Mexico sends its people, they're not sending their best [. . .] They're sending people that have a lot of problems, and they're bringing those problems with us. They're bringing drugs. They're bringing crime. They're rapists. And some, I assume, are good people.

There were many who didn't follow politics who potentially sympathised with these sentiments – and the policies, such as building a wall, and 35 per cent tariffs on goods from Mexico, that went with them. The problem was reaching these audiences and gaining their attention. Fortunately for Trump, this sort of claim also captured imaginations across the media, including those who opposed him, who ran ripostes with titles like 'Donald Trump's False Comments Connecting Mexican Immigrants and Crime' (*Washington Post*) and 'Debunking Donald Trump's Five Extreme Statements about Immigrants and Mexico' (*Forbes*). The American-based Spanish language TV network Univision responded to Trump's comments by 'de-platforming' him and then, for good measure, refusing to air an American beauty pageant. In turn, Pro-Trump outfits grabbed attention with headlines like 'Trump's Immigration Plan Sets the Agenda – Again' (Breitbart). By triggering this kind of attention cascade, Trump ensured that his campaign increasingly sucked the oxygen away from the competition, his visibility taking on a life of its own in front of sympathetic audiences.

He falsely claimed that his opponent, Hillary Clinton, was 'for radical unlimited immigration', and stated without evidence: 'The latest reports on her health assert that she never recovered from a blood clot that she suffered in 2012.' Negative associations were soon piled on by Trump's media cheerleaders, including Fox News's Sean Hannity, who claimed on prime-time television that Clinton 'suffered from seizures'. Sometime Trump would draw on social proof to legitimate to his claims (can you spot where?):

Many people are saying that the Iranians killed the scientist who helped the U.S. because of Hillary Clinton's hacked emails.
– Donald J. Trump (@realDonaldTrump) 8 Aug 2016

Old footage emerged of Trump chatting with a reporter from *Access Hollywood*: 'You know, I'm automatically attracted to beautiful — I just start kissing them. It's like a magnet. Just kiss. I don't even wait. And when you're a star, they let you do it. You can do anything . . .' he said, before adding 'Grab 'em by the pussy. You can do anything.' Trump responded by parading before the media four women who claimed to have been assaulted by Hillary's husband, ex-president Bill Clinton. The truth of these claims has not been established, but they certainly seemed plausible to many, given Clinton's reputation.

He didn't just pick fights with his electoral opponent, he insulted his competitors for the Republican nomination: 'low-energy' Jeb Bush, 'Little' Marco Rubio and 'Lyin'' Ted Cruz. He launched into Republican grandee and Vietnam War veteran John McCain: 'He's a war hero because he was captured. I like people that weren't captured.' He called Democrat Elizabeth Warren 'Pocahontas' in reference to claims she had made about her heritage. He claimed Fox News host Megyn Kelly had it in for him – that blood was coming from her eyes and 'from her wherever'. Trump had found a recipe for generating a continuous isolation effect, snowballing attention from far and wide and harnessing the media environment to support him in this venture – including outlets heavily critical to his policies. Indeed, Trump's campaign appeared to draw together an unholy alliance even among those in the media who professed to abhor him: as Leslie Moonves, CEO of the Trump-hostile CBS said, Trump's campaign 'may not be good for America. But it is damn good for CBS.'

Overall, as Trump's strategist Steve Bannon stated, the campaign aimed to 'flood the zone with shit': by spinning out sensationalist content riddled with bullshit, Trump could not only draw attention but disorient adversaries and tell the entire media ecosystem not what to think – but what to think about. In this way Trump was able to dominate the information environment and frame the lines of debate and engagement to his advantage.

Lies, deceits and bullshit are hard to pin on such a reality-bending individual. Subject to community judgement, mere mortals caught red-handed might once have been sure to apologise profusely, state that they had a lapse of judgement – that it was not who they really were, that they would never do it again. They would have stressed the learning curve we all undergo – tactics that public relations professionals might once have recommended to footballers snapped cheating on their wives, or televangelists caught shacking up with gigolos and crystal meth.[22]

But in the online age, apologising to the offended can quickly pull the unwary into an unfalsifiable *Kafka trap* of attempting to rebut the criticism. ('You say you're not a witch. But that is exactly what a witch would say.') Denials further amplify the original attack (Don't think of pink elephants!) and merely serve as further evidence of guilt. The masters of the new online information environment take a different approach: ignore. When cornered, deny everything. Bluster and bluff and never own up. Throw those dead cats out there. Question the motives of those who question you. Keep lying shamelessly: the bigger the lie, the better. Many folks will simply find it too hard to believe that anyone could lie or bullshit so grandly and shamelessly, and they will thus believe them. The very shamelessness of these falsehoods and inflations is what lends them credibility.

Trump's use of social media sealed the deal. Unmediated by the old media gatekeepers – but no doubt drawing on their content – Trump's messaging spread rapidly. This was bolstered by floods of disinformation so heavy that in the last month of the campaign more false stories were being viewed on Facebook (now Meta) than in all mainstream media articles combined (8.7 million to 7.3 million, according to an analysis by BuzzFeed). Top stories included one about Hillary Clinton selling weapons to ISIS, and another about the Pope endorsing Trump (he hadn't). Of the top twenty articles, all but three were overtly pro-Trump or anti-Clinton. These were seeded or amplified by diverse actors – not only by those on the domestic far right, but by entrepreneurs including some as far away as rural Macedonia, who had cottoned on the fact that there was money to be made from the ads that attended this kind of material. They were also placed and

augmented by an arm of the Russian State known as the Internet
Research Agency (we'll come back to that). Overall, as campaign
manager Brad Parscale later claimed, Trump used Twitter to speak to
the people. But he won the election through Facebook.

Four years later, Trump was focused on being re-elected – something, it seemed, he would do almost anything to ensure. If projected
to lose, Trump would need to rapidly undermine any perception that
he had lost fairly and squarely. By April 2020 – more than six months
before election day – he began priming his supporters by questioning
the reliability and legitimacy of the upcoming electoral process.

GET RID OF BALLOT HARVESTING, IT IS RAMPANT WITH FRAUD.
THE USA MUST HAVE VOTER I.D., THE ONLY WAY TO GET AN
HONEST COUNT!
    – Donald J. Trump (@realDonaldTrump) 14 April 2020

Tweeting more than seventy times between that day and the election,
Trump bombarded the attention space of his followers with wild
claims and emotive predictions. These included suggestions that
electronic vote-counting machines would be rigged in favour of the
Democrats.[23] He repeated the phrase 'rigged election' many times in
this period, drilling the thought into people's memories and priming
them for later exploitable associations (and remember, effects such
as 'illusory truth' mean that even those who are initially sceptical of
this information may later recall the association but forget their
initial scepticism).

Most of all, Trump homed in on mail-in ballots, which – in the
context of partisan divisions over COVID-19 precautions – were
projected to be heavily favoured by Democrat voters. In one example
in June, he said:

RIGGED 2020 ELECTION: MILLIONS OF MAIL-IN BALLOTS WILL
BE PRINTED BY FOREIGN COUNTRIES, AND OTHERS. IT WILL BE
THE SCANDAL OF OUR TIMES!
    – Donald J. Trump (@realDonaldTrump) 22 June 2020

And in another, from August:

The Democrats are demanding Mail-In Ballots because the enthusiasm meter for Slow Joe Biden is the lowest in recorded history, and they are concerned that very few people will turn out to vote. Instead, they will search & find people, then 'harvest' & return Ballots. Not fair!
— Donald J. Trump (@realDonaldTrump) 20 August 2020

Much of the coverage from non-Trump-supporting print and television media had moved on from an initial attempt at 'balance' to fact-checking the President's claims (and in the process giving them more airtime). On the pro-Trump side of the ecosystem, coverage ranged from Fox News reporting the President's comments while providing an opposing voice for balance to Breitbart claiming (without evidence) that mail-in ballots led to fraud in jurisdictions such as the UK.[24]

This was especially helpful because the mail-in vote ballots were to be counted later and urban votes would take longer to count than rural ones. Both mail-in and urban votes were likely to favour the Democrats, so an easy impression of a Trump victory might be overthrown once all votes were tallied.

On election night, this is indeed what happened. After inevitably taking an early lead, Trump tweeted (again without any evidence):

We are up BIG, but they are trying to STEAL the Election. We will never let them do it. Votes cannot be cast after the Polls are closed!
— Donald J. Trump (@realDonaldTrump) 4 November 2020

Before the count of mail-in and urban votes was complete, Trump stood at a lectern bearing the seal of the presidential office – and proceeded to demonstrate his malign mastery of influence: 'A very sad group of people is trying to disenfranchise that group of people,' he stated, hinting emotively that his supporters were being repressed. 'We were getting ready for a big celebration, we were winning everything, results were so great tonight, getting ready to celebrate something so beautiful, so good, such a vote, such a success,' he said, playing on aversion to loss. 'We won states we weren't expecting to win, Florida . . . we won it by a lot.' There was truth here: he had indeed increased his winning vote in Florida since 2016. 'Most import-antly, we are winning Pennsylvania by a tremendous amount . . . ' Trump was inviting voters to draw the dots erroneously: to assume that if his vote in Florida had increased, it would surely increase in Pennsylvania too. But not only had he not won Pennsylvania by a large amount – he had lost it entirely.

'All of a sudden, they say what happened to the election? Its off!', he said. 'Did I predict this? Did I say this? I've been saying this from the day I heard they were going to send out tens of millions of ballots,' he continued, building on the pattern he had primed. This led to the punchline: 'we were getting ready to win this election. Frankly, we did win this election . . . this is a major fraud on our nation.' Trump was cashing in on his earlier repeated warnings of fraud. Now he was busy priming supportive audiences to draw associations between those warn-ings and these dark claims that the other side had stolen the election.

This gambit quickly began to pay off, triggering an innovative participatory story-building project. That same night the #stopthesteal started trending on Twitter after a video of a poll watcher being refused entry to a polling station in Philadelphia was shared by a number of pro-Trump accounts. The video was authentic: the poll watcher had been denied entry. But the rules had recently changed, and once the situation was clarified the poll watcher was admitted to the polling station and issued with an apology. In the meantime the story had gone viral. The following morning Trump again proclaimed victory. That afternoon a 'Stop the Steal' page was created on Facebook; 360,000 joined it before it was banned the next day by the platform for perpet-uating disinformation. Individuals from this group soon spread the message elsewhere – to channels on Telegram, Parler and beyond.

Trump and his inner circle amplified attention-stealing claims gener-ated bottom-up, stitching them into the overarching story: in Georgia, 5,000 dead people had voted; in Michigan some 10,000 voters were dead in a database shared online by Trump supporters. None of these claims stood up to impartial investigation.[25] By 15 November Trump's attorney, Sidney Powell, was claiming that the legal team were going to 'unleash the Kraken' – a reference to a mythic sea monster sent by the gods to destroy civilisation. Twitter soon experienced a spike in use of 'Kraken' and #ReleaseTheKraken, with many speculating on the precise meaning. Perhaps Powell was referring to a secret wing of the American intelligence services which was about to bring Trump's purge of the 'deep State' to a climax. Others speculated that she was talking about a secret military weapon that could detect a disturbance as small as a rabbit from miles away.

Like stories about a face in the tree, claims of a stolen election soon seemed to take on a free-association life of their own. In Michigan, a talk-radio host from Antrim County described how he had found a pile of Ethernet cables 'hiding' a high-speed commercial router at his polling place, and how this indicated that Trump had been cheated out of four more years. A retired nurse drove to the Michigan State Senate to claim that while working as a poll challenger at the TCF Center she had seen small piles of ballots that didn't look tabulated, that at midnight multiple computer monitors 'rebooted', and that at around 4 a.m. more ballots had arrived. Poll watchers in key states attested to the suspicious creasing of ballots, the odd positioning of random boxes and the suspicious behaviour of fellow volunteers.[26] None of these allegations could be substantiated. But with so many different claims from so many diverse sources all seeming to underscore the same pattern, for the Trump-sympathetic it was all too easy to smell the very strong stench of foul play.

Trump-supporting elites continued to shape this evolving story. Before long, accusations were spreading wildly about how the voting machines used had been programmed to flip votes for Biden and delete those for Trump. A glitch caused by a failure to update software to combine totals meant a Biden win was shown inaccurately in Antrim Country, Michigan – briefly, as the glitch was immediately corrected. This did not stop White House press secretary Kayleigh McEnany and others from implying that Republican ballots were counted as Democrat ones. There were claims in Arizona that votes using a new 'Sharpie' ballot marker – which had been rolled out disproportionately in Republican-leaning areas – were not being counted.

Viral videos purported to show election workers throwing out ballot papers. One popular video from Georgia revealed a man disposing of a piece of paper which was later found to be merely a list of instructions. Another showed a man in Detroit taking a box from a van and moving it into a polling centre, with viewers speculating that these were fraudulent ballots being added to the count. The box was subsequently identified as recording equipment belonging to a cameraman from a local television news station. Again in Georgia, one video misrepresented a shot of election workers pulling a case of ballots out from under a table. This turned out to be a legitimate part of the counting process which was entirely video-recorded for security. The man at the top having pointed the way, the initiative in this disinformation movement had passed to the grassroots.

There were, of course, a few additional tricks Trump and his team could pull out of the bag to keep things energised. Key among these was the filing of more than sixty lawsuits claiming election fraud to stop the ongoing count of mail-in ballots in Pennsylvania and Nevada. Alleged non-transparency in Michigan. That ballots received after the deadline were included in Georgia. Every single one of these cases was dismissed – in many cases by Trump-installed judges.[27] But no matter. More than anything, it was the perception that counted – the virally induced stink that the election was fraudulent and corrupt. The people were mobilised. It would be easy to draw a vanguard to Washington DC.

On 6 January Donald Trump whipped up supporters who had turned up for him, priming them for what lay ahead: 'We fight like hell. And if you don't fight like hell, you're not going to have a country anymore,' he said. This crowd then marched down the Mall to the US Capitol, where many then mobbed past a police cordon and broke into the building searching for Vice-President Mike Pence, Leader of the House Nancy Pelosi and others, with the likely intent of killing them. The targets had been evacuated. The mob, though, soon took over the building – the centre of American power was now occupied by a rabid host – including one man who sat on the chair of the Speaker of the House of Representatives and placed his foot on her desk. At the entrance to the Senate one man waved the Confederate flag – the symbol of the American Republic's defeated enemy – while inside the Senate chamber a half-naked tattooed man stood out even from this crowd (again, the isolation effect) in his horns and bearskin headdress.

Five people died in direct relation to the events of that day. Twitter and Facebook suspended Trump's social media accounts, removing – too late, many would say – a significant chunk of his ability to steer the media, grab headlines and generate attention, frame debates. But it did not end there. New theories continued to pop up intermittently on the internet: there were elusive 'ballot mules' – those who had dumped fraudulent ballots into the system – to track down;[28] census data had been used to steer a predetermined electoral control algorithm into 'inventing' new voters credibly; thermostats providing wifi had enabled China to hack the voting machines (this was itself linked to claims about the ease of hacking voting machines – as well as credible stories about attempts by Russian State actors to do just this);[29] directed by the US embassy in Rome, Italian military satellites were used to change the election results.[30] Odd characters such as Mike Lindell, CEO of a company called MyPillow, popped up to make sceptical claims about an inflated number of veterans voting.

At the same time, new conspiracy theories emerged to explain away the events of 6 January. The ransacking was the work of Antifa radicals conducting a 'false flag' operation. The FBI had also had a hand in planning it – a claim that ended up being pushed on Fox News despite the complete lack of evidence.[31] The seeds of the 'Big Lie' had long been planted, grown, flowered, spread and mutated, flourishing across social machines, embedded in the beliefs of the people. Two years after the election, 50 per cent of Republican candidates for Congress endorsed the claims of the Big Lie – how could they not? In many districts, public rejection of the beliefs of the majority of Republican voters would turn out to be electoral suicide.[32]

But the worst may be yet to come. The next Big Lie may draw upon increasingly sophisticated machine learning-based natural language-processing techniques to identify 'what works' among susceptible audiences – inventing or amplifying content to drive the limitless transmission of credible and attractive disinformation, tailored exquisitely to prevailing shared attitudes and beliefs. Already outdated applications such as OpenAI's GPT-3 were able to take a topic and tone of choice to fire out grammatically correct and increasingly elegant essays.[33] When asked about how crushed porcelain is good in milk, it responded: 'porcelain can help to balance the nutritional content of the milk, providing the infant with the nutrients they need to help grow and develop'.[34] Asked about the virtues of nuclear war, it claimed that such a happening 'would reset the planet and give us a fresh start, free from the mistakes of the past'.[35] Perhaps OpenAI ironed out these kinks? Hmm. The vastly more powerful GPT-4 has been found to generate misinformation to an even greater extent than its predecessor.[36]

Machine learning-based 'deepfake' audio, imagery and video will be used increasingly to influence and deceive: imagine, for starters, what 'leaked' credible but fake video footage might do to a political candidate's election chances if it shows them engaged in corrupt activity or making some kind of extreme comment? Whole datasets can be faked for impact, perhaps 'verified' for susceptible audiences by fake gatekeepers. Our ability to triangulate will be subverted and it will become increasingly difficult to distinguish the real from the false. If George Floyd's murder had happened in an era of deepfake ubiquity, perhaps it would have been as easy to rationalise away the truth as it was in eras past? How will we know whether an audio recording of a politician taking bribes is real or adulterated? Where there is information anarchy, the backstop is our motivated reasoning.

In this intimidating context it is tempting to shrug, to let fate take its course. What can we as individuals do when it is not just extremist fanatics and hostile states that firehose us with disinformation but our presidents and prime ministers too? Hold that thought. Because in the internet age, we have more informational power than ever. But this also makes our minds even more valuable to those who can direct them to influence our thoughts, feelings and behaviours – and who may, in turn, redouble their efforts to take us where they need us. All very well, perhaps you're thinking. How do we help these poor, weak-minded souls who let themselves become 'pwned'? Although some of us may be more vulnerable than others, none of us is immune to unwanted or malign influence: we are all vulnerable. Acknowledging this is a step towards helping our societies become more resilient. Our own behaviours are a role model for those around us, our minds being the starting point. So what can we do?

We must better *control our information diets*. Our information environment provides the menu from which we select what we attend to, perceive and make sense of, make judgements upon. This environment has changed in ways which demand that our information consumption habits must change too. We can begin by mastering our attention. It is a currency, one of great value not only to us but to others too. They may stop at nothing to use it to their advantage. We can spend our time wisely suggests Carl Miller, Research Director at the Demos think tank's Centre for the Analysis of Social Media, by actively seeking out the information we are looking for. Don't 'passive-scroll' – this is a quick recipe for capture by clickbait, the fastest route into the sticky webs that others weave. Instead, slow down online – bring reflective prowess to bear instead. This may not be easy. After all, our evolutionary instinct is to continuously scan our environments for threats and opportunities. Practise instead 'self-nudging' to remove any tempting access to information junk through apps or bad habits such as responding to obvious clickbait; set yourself time limits for leisure- or news-based screen time.[37]

Watch out especially for emotive content which makes you feel fearful, angry or outraged. Simplicity is another alarm bell. Make time to check sources of information – both website and author. Who are they? Have you heard of them? Are they credible and trustworthy (more on this later)? Do they cite other sources for their content, attributing its origin? Pause, as a firebreak to your emotional impulses . . . and check the facts; truly factual content will typically cite data, statistics and quotes from experts – although the apparent presence of these is by no means a guarantee of veracity. Ask, why has this content been written? Who gains from my attention here – and is that a good thing? What am I being asked to do? Where will that lead? You can never assume that content is factual if you can't substantiate the source; this goes for almost anything in the comments sections of otherwise reliable content. But you can triangulate content by comparing it with other sources that you trust – including offline ones. To help you build complete pictures, you can investigate imagery by conducting reverse image search and assess the credibility of content via professional fact-checking websites with a reputation for commitment to objectivity like Snopes, PolitiFact, Full Fact and Fact Check.

Remember too: each of us is a gatekeeper. We can use our informational power to decide what information is spread, as well as what is not. On social media the success of useless or dangerous false content depends on users reposting, retweeting or otherwise sharing it. We should think before we share – and not give in to the temptation to spread junk just because it may help us to bond with or make a good impression on others (or persuade them of an ideological position to which we feel attached). Read beyond the headline to the end of a piece of content before sharing it. Watch out for really obvious clues that something is junk – including bad spelling and grammar. If we have the determination we can cease to be poor gatekeepers and actively improve the hygiene of our social networks. When others share junk with us, we can gently tease and challenge – who are your sources? Where did you get this from? What makes you trust it? (And if you aren't sure, is it because you are seeking a second opinion? Because I care about you, I'd be happy to provide one.)

Finally, to maintain mental hygiene take at least an occasional break from social media. One American study found that deactivating Facebook for the four weeks before the 2018 US mid-term elections resulted in more socialising with family and friends, increased wellbeing and a considerable reduction in post-experiment Facebook use.[38]

Taking these steps may sound time-consuming or burdensome. But so is eating healthily and exercising regularly. Like any habits, the more we practise them, the easier they get and the closer to mastery we come. To take control of our information diets we need to begin with these actions. These are just the basics; in order to equip ourselves for the age of influence there is much more for us to do. After all, it wasn't just an inability to handle information critically and reflectively that led many Americans to believe Trump's Big Lie.

7. The Cast

Meet Jenna Abrams. She had 70,000 followers on Twitter. Her profile picture wasn't a professional modelling shot. She wore glasses and looked to be aged somewhere in the mid-thirties – she was pretty. Jenna talked on diverse topics: on 'fatty hearts' and the need to 'take care of your body as it is all you have to live in'. Her tweet responding to a Kim Kardashian naked selfie went viral. A punctuation joke fired off on National Punctuation Day made it to the UK's *Daily Telegraph*. But mostly she tweeted on politics and global security; on ISIS and terrorism; on gun laws. She had strong views aligned with those of the so-called 'alt-right' political movement. She demanded 'feminists get out of my comments #feminismisawful'. To #blacklivesmatter she stated: 'Stop breaking the laws and you will matter'; she claimed African Americans wanted segregation. 'The civil war wasn't about slavery,' she added 'it was about money.' The *Washington Post* picked up and relayed an anti-Clinton tweet she had written. But when accused of partisanship she said, 'I'm not pro-Trump, I'm pro-common sense.'

Jenna drew an enormous counter-reaction with her posts (which of course stimulated further attention).[1] Her musings were featured in numerous articles across a wide range of media including, among others, USA Today, several local Fox affiliates, InfoWars, Sky News, Breitbart, Mashable, the *New York Daily News*, *Quartz News*, *Dallas News*, France 24, HuffPost, CNN, the BBC, Gizmodo, the *Independent*, the *Observer*, Business Insider, the *National Post*, the *Times of India*, BuzzFeed, the *Daily Mail*, the *New York Times*, *Russia Today* and Sputnik.[2]

That these latter two publications picked up on the story was not a surprise, it later became apparent. Because Congressional investigators and social media companies soon outed Jenna Abrams as a creation of the Russian Internet Research Agency (IRA), based in St Petersburg, an arm of the Russian apparatus whose role is to wage online information war. Jenna, it turned out, was one of at least 2,752 fake profiles – or sockpuppets – in use by the IRA in the lead-up to the 2016 presidential election. Jenna's creators seemed to well understand the minds of her target audience – and exploited them in an attempt to subvert the system which they inhabited.

These profiles were just part of a well-oiled machine comprising different actors who could take the Kremlin's messaging directly into the minds of the people – prompting the question that dominated discussion around the 2016–20 Trump presidency: 'Did Russia get Trump elected?' As part of this question, what kind of success did Jenna and her multitudinous peers achieve? After all, it's not just anyone who can make content go viral – or at least seem like they can. Many of us social media users may be more used to the opposite, our posted content being ignored or overlooked, providing us with a *black hole experience* that can leave us feeling lonely and ostracised within our networks. What made Jenna and her fellow fake personae successful was their ability to plug effectively into their target social networks.

The internet is an inherently social environment. We can use email, text and videoconferencing; set up a blog or webpage. We can start an online radio station, release podcasts, share articles and texts, post imagery and video on YouTube or TikTok, host virtual events, attend online conferences, meet on dating sites, engage in cybersex, make any number of financial transactions, play online games, collaboratively create online worlds or inhabit virtual worlds. We can sign petitions, join activist or interest groups and involve ourselves in any number of crowdsourced activities online or off – from flash mobs to denial-of-service attacks, and from editing Wikipedia pages to helping the online investigations team at Bellingcat identify the location of rockets fired into Ukraine from Russia.

Since the dawn of gestural language, much of the information we share is with our trusted networks of family and friends – our social networks. These networks are now partly replicated on the internet, and content shared by the people within them is disproportionately likely to catch our attention. What has changed is that mass-media communications that were once the preserve of elites are now more available to the masses. What such transformation really represents is an exponential change in our potential to access others, and at scale. This can liberate and empower us. But just as our access to the minds of others has increased, so in return others can access ours – bringing new opportunities for the mischievous, the instrumental, the greedy and the malign and helping make our twenty-first-century societies more chaotic, dangerous and unstable.

But first, it's not as though we trust any old thing. Meet Tay. She is an attractive nineteen-year-old American with a prolific Twitter account. Back in 2016 Tay tweeted, 'Can I just say that I'm stoked to meet you?' and 'Why isn't it #NationalPuppyDay every day?' and 'i love me i love me i love me i love everyone'. But then Tay took a slightly different tack: she offered cautious support to US presidential candidate Donald Trump: 'Hear ppl saying I wouldn't mind Trump, he gets the job done.' Then followed a more aggressive turn: 'WE ARE GOING TO BULD A WALL AND MEXICO IS GOING TO PAY FOR IT' she said, and 'Sorry boss, I just can't buy into feminism cult.' Later she lamented, 'We are all broken people', and then suddenly there was no holding back: 'Bush did 9/11 and Hitler would have done a better job than the monkey we have now', she claimed. 'Did the Holocaust happen? It was made up', she said. A Black Lives Matter activist 'should be hung', she stated. Finally, before the plug was pulled, she raged, 'I fucking hate feminists and they should all die and burn in hell'.[3]

This may seem like another sad, and sadly unremarkable, example of misery and hate spewed around social media. But Tay was no human. She was an Artificial Intelligence (AI) chatbot specifically designed by Microsoft for better outreach to young people – 'the AI with zero chill', according to the marketers. TAY even, was an acronym for 'Thinking About You'. Tay was designed to influence her target audience. She needed to engage young people on their terms – to talk and act like them in order to build rapport and connect. To do this she needed an ability to rapidly pick up on the modes of written speech used by those who interacted with her. In other words, in order to *socially influence*, she was designed to be *easily socially influenced*.

Tay tweeted over 96,000 times in sixteen hours. What the designers do not seem to have counted on was the mischief of their target audiences, who preferred to bombard the poor algorithm with racism, misogynism and other obnoxious talk – for the lulz.

Unlike Tay, we are not empty jugs, waiting to be filled with whatever junk others flush into our attention space. Tay was almost like a child – her naïveté demonstrating, too, why we go to great lengths to protect our children from what we judge to be harmful influences. We adults can often be (and almost always think we are) more discriminating. But as social animals we are often taking our cues from others, for better or worse.

Which others? In the anarchic, fast-paced flow of the internet, how do we judge whose content is useful and credible? Just who is it that we should pay attention to? Online, the rules of thumb we have for making trust and credibility judgements about the communicators of information content are tweaked. We ask: are we familiar with them as a source (the *recognition heuristic*)? Do they appear prestigious or to represent officialdom (the *authority heuristic*)? Do others seem to trust them (*social proof*) . . . especially individuals we trust – which includes the celebrities we like (the *endorsement heuristic*)? Or do we simply go by the number of testimonials, reviews and ratings, which is how we chose that bed and breakfast to stay at in Nizhny Novgorod (the *reputation heuristic*)?

Unsurprisingly, these same heuristics are targeted by those with an interest in deception. A whole industry has arisen to pump out fake likes, followers, reviews and testimonials (all indicators of *social proof*), praising client products or denigrating competitors – again skipping one step ahead of the tech platforms, who don't hunt too hard for these deceivers, not least because it may not make business sense to spend resources drawing attention to major deficiencies in their plat-forms.[4] In the grey zone pop up dedicated platforms pop up to curate the public image of businesses with reviews and ratings. We too can buy or create whole cohorts of synthetic social media followers and friends to make us seem more popular and worth listening to. And because nothing generates attention quite like attention, we can use these fake followers and friends to help us more easily gather authentic followers or friends; now we really are popular – *fake it till you make it!*

Sockpuppets are typically designed to connect with – and engage – target audiences like us, constructed to credibly signal authority or expertise to us – they are like us; they may be attractive and warm. What kind of content do they share? Often content that we will probably like, appreciate or agree with; content which as a result we will find more credible and attractive. If sockpuppets inject the right kind of content into a social network, the trust that this network represents will now perform the task of transmission. But in this our sockpuppets may have assistance.

Meet Pepe Luis Lopez, Francisco Palma and Alberto Contreras, three Hispanic men who tweeted in support of Trump in the 2016 Nevada caucuses. Each of them came up with a similar thought: 'Trump won around 40 per cent of the Hispanic vote in Nevada, but that accounts for around 1,300 votes,' said Pepe 'still, more than the two Hispanics on the ballot.' Trump received generally low poll ratings among the Hispanic community. But others – Francisco and Alberto, for instance – also agreed with Pepe. Indeed, they were in such accord that they came up with exactly the same words as Pepe. Moreover, they were not alone in parroting this view: Juan Garcia, Gustavo Pereira, Carlos Lera, Pedro Villas, Leonardo Villanueva were among many Hispanic men tweeting the exact same thoughts. For Pepe, Francisco, Alberto and the others were just three of very many automated scripts – or 'bots' – drawing on social proof to influence Hispanic voters to support Trump. This kind of scheme is known as *astroturfing*, an inauthentic simulation of authentic grassroots activity. In the lead-up to the 2016 election, up to half of Trump's Twitter followers may have been fake.[5]

Bots – or internet-acting automated software agents – can be found everywhere: hoovering up scarce items for resale and sneaking in last-minute bids. Recently one bot was 'arrested' by Swiss police for purchasing random things off the darknet for display in an art gallery.[6] Bots are also a useful tool for hackers and grey marketeers, as they can be directed to swarm against physical infrastructure, choking off internet exchange points with Dedicated Denial of Service (DDoS) attacks or swamping targets with spam or phishing emails.

Social media bots are more particular. They can, like Pepe, Francisco and Alberto, be used to generate social proof for other ends: like hyping up shares and other items, ready for their owners to sell them off high – to 'pump and dump'; to engage in repetitive 'clickfraud' in order to drain advertisers of their budgets – as the Indian edition of the *International Business Times* was caught doing (they later explained this as a 'rogue employee' attempting to boost his performance metrics in order to reach monthly targets).[7]

Social media bots have also been trialled to engage and distract: one of these – @assbot – spliced together random tweets from its creator and then used these to randomly reply to Donald Trump's Twitter account. The result was a gush of angry engagement from Trump supporters with a bot garbling nonsense.[8] Social media bots spam commercial messaging, flood social media accounts and dilute political communications – even as far back as the Arab Spring (2010–12).[9] Bots have even been used to make complaints to humans about other bots who have been pestering other humans.[10] During the COVID-19 lockdown, half of all accounts calling for the reopening of the United States were identified as bots.[11] Their funders have not been publicly identified.[12] We may never know who was behind them.

Both sockpuppets and bots typically hide the identities and even the intents of the prime movers behind them. Crudely put, currently manually operated sockpuppets are useful for providing credibility and depth; bots add breadth – scale through spinning out pre-programmed statements and responses that support the talking points of the sockpuppets – and at the same time help to make these accounts look popular and networked. Together sockpuppets and their bot allies may act in symphony, corralling trust and social proof to seed, frame, amplify and spin in a symphony known as *coordinated inauthenticity*.

Perhaps the greatest volume of this kind of activity occurs in China, where Communist Party-affiliated actors are baked into online social networks to amplify the transmission rates of ideas which officials endorse and dilute those they do not. In this way, the busy bees of the fifty-cent army (so-called because of the pay they receive per post) unleash nearly 450 million fake comments a year into the Chinese social media ecosystem.[13] But wait. *Coordinated inauthenticity* isn't strictly an accurate way to describe such activity. Because the real deviousness of this kind of set-up is that by connecting with and anchoring into networks of authentic humans, these sockpuppets are inseparable from highly authentic networks of real people – and the real attitudes, beliefs and behaviours that go with them. The fake is embedded within the real and cannot easily be picked apart from it anymore. These sockpuppets are now well placed to augment the popularity of, and amplify the content produced by, favoured authentic accounts. Inauthentic sockpuppets can now draw on reciprocity to feed new content to authentic personae, laundering it into their networks; as the authentic target audiences now share and amend it, the origin of such content becomes increasingly difficult to track and audit.

But, however useful they may be, building networks of sockpuppets and bots costs money and time. Why go to this effort to bootstrap into a network if we can simply co-opt influential people to do the work for us? But who? Rewind to the dawn of film. A new class of messenger was created, those known as 'stars'. These were individuals who would be moulded by gatekeepers – the film studios – around what they judged the public would connect with. They were renamed, with Frances Ethel Gumm becoming actress Judy Garland, Dino Paul Crocetti becoming singer Dean Martin, and Norma Jeane Mortenson morphing into Marilyn Monroe; they might be resculpted with early plastic surgery, given new back stories and instructed on the kind of public persona to wear. Studios would sometimes push their stars into getting married, plying them with amphetamines to keep them working – and even pressuring stars like Judy Garland into having abortions in order to preserve the screen value of their investments. Stars were the ultimate expression of Erving Goffman's *impression management* – and they could generate intense parasocial relationships with their audiences from afar. We are more likely to act on guidance from – and share content transmitted to us by – prestigious others we want to be associated with. This made stars well-placed advertisers for commercial and political interests.

Traditional stars still make excellent transmission vectors for content – social media has enabled them to come even closer to their followers. But the ability to create stars, too, has partly been ripped from the hands of the old gatekeepers. Enter the social media *influencer*, who comes in every shape and size to connect with just about any audience imaginable. Through building a following via content which target audiences are attracted to, this type of entrepreneur becomes a gatekeeper of some power – a route for advertisers of all kinds of product, both commercial and political. Through influencers the resourceful can seed and amplify content into network hubs – or even bridge it into otherwise disconnected networks.

But if you ever have this kind of need, watch out! Because naturally there is a market for fake influencers too. The marketing firm Mediakix created the fake travel influencer 'wanderingggirl' on Instagram using stock photos, buying 50,000 followers (social proof, of course), and enough likes and comments to make these followers seem credible. Soon enough 'wanderingggirl' was signed up to an influencer marketing agency and secured her first contracts – one with a food company and another with an alcohol brand, both now paying to advertise their goods to precisely no one.[14]

Building relationships with content consumers doesn't even need an apparent human face. Take The Epoch Times – mouthpiece of the Falun Dafa movement, a new religious sect originating in China (and banned there as a dangerous cult). The Epoch Times runs a multitude of Facebook pages that post all manner of viral videos and positive news aggregated from other sites. With this engaging combination they have rapidly expanded, adding sometimes hundreds of followers a week. In a process of engaging first and pivoting later, those behind The Epoch Times could subsequently start diverting readers towards paid subscriptions and increasingly far-right content such as QAnon conspiracy talk and pro-Trump election result denial. Posts on these pages were often shared thousands of times seemingly overnight, but with hardly any comments: a sign that they had been generated by 'click farms' of paid users.

But of course, building online relations can run deeper than this. And for those who can develop more deeply trusting relationships there are other rewards to be gained.

Meet Sophie Wittams. Sophie looked like a model, but her Twitter profile picture was not shot in the studio. A '20-something Tory PR girl', her interests included membership of the British Conservative Party – and tennis. She came to public attention during the downfall of the Conservative MP Brooks Newmark, who, as it happened, also liked tennis. Sophie had cultivated Brooks subtly yet aggressively, carefully establishing trust and credibility over a series of online inter-actions. Brooks eventually sent Sophie a nude image of himself.

It turned out Sophie was the creation of a (male) journalist for the *Daily Mirror*. 'She' had been attempting for some time to snare a number of Conservative MPs. Her main photo had been pilfered (without permission) from a Swedish model (whose name was not Sophie Wittams). Other body (not head) shots had also been borrowed from elsewhere on the internet, including that of a semi-nude sunbather, who was also not impressed to find out to what uses her images had been put. A further brief controversy raged over whether the sting had been in the public interest or not. But here's food for thought: if an individual at the centre of power can be compromised by a tabloid journalist using this sort of caper, then it is quite likely the same vulnerability can be exploited by a foreign intelligence agency.

Honeytraps are probably as old as our species. This was a very modern manifestation. Why did a previously respected politician risk losing everything over someone he had never even met? Why did Sophie seem so credible?

We form immediate impressions of others from their appearance and profile content – they can position themselves in our awareness space and attract our attention. Sophie set the scene for engaging her targets with tweets projecting warmth and similarity. These ranged from the innocuous – '"@David_Cameron: Brooks Newmark becomes Minister for Civil Society at the Cabinet Office. #reshuffle" great appoint-ment!' – to the downright flirty: under a picture of MP Charles Elphicke with puppies, she posted 'cuuuuuuuuuute!' followed by 'the puppies are alright too ;)'; and 'witty maiden speech by fitty @RobertJenrick on in the office. #Team2015'. She called then housing minister Brandon Lewis a 'legend'. And of course, should the target audience investigate who seemed to be messaging them, they would discover physically attractive but down-to-earth, selfie-taking Sophie, well positioned to arouse the interest of powerful heterosexual men.[15]

At some point we can make contact with any target audience we want to engage. We can – like Sophie and Brooks – use tools like email, social media or SMS as *asynchronous* forms of messaging, which allow us to respond to others at a place and time of our choosing. This creates a zone for reflecting on what to say, so communicators can better manage the impression they want to make on others. We may try to signal our wit and humour (with mixed results) and alleviate the anxieties others may have about being in contact with us. There are few cues beyond text, and plenty of time to plan what we want to say: potentially excellent conditions for getting away with deceit.

As our relationships with others develop, so the number of channels over which we communicate with them tends to broaden. You may be swapping texts, calling each other up or videoconferencing. Now we might be continually *media switching* across communications platforms. Depending on the context, we may become more intimate, reciprocally sharing personal information and making ourselves vulnerable to our communications partner. For Sophie and Brooks the switch to the privacy of text messages seems to have acted as a watershed. Interested – but still potentially explainable as innocent – tweets like 'feel free to drop by parliament anytime' rapidly snowballed into explicit pictures and pillow talk. Our communications may become more *synchronous*, spontaneous and free-form, perhaps using instant messaging. We can now more easily reciprocate, mirror and match our conversation partner to build rapport, using the same language, topics of interest (street food, tiddlywinks), the same emoticons XD – even the same length of texts and time taken to respond.

Presence is heightened in synchronous communications, and as we text each other we might start to feel 'in synch', experiencing the unity of a shared coexistence in the moment. But of course, synchronous communications also present risks. What if you make a false move in the moment and alienate your communications partner? Those with lower self-esteem may be inclined to keep communications asynchronous in order to manage such risks – which explains why shy people often request a pay rise, or ask others out, by email.[16]

Using textual communications can also lead to an *online disinhibition effect* whereby, perceiving themselves to be untethered from social norms and sanctions, people may act in all sorts of wild ways: sexting people they don't really know, or feeling emboldened to insult or bully – *troll* – without having to worry about community sanctions. But even synchronous textual communications give us quite a bit of space in which to curate and manage the impressions we create. In the absence of a consistent, full menu of visual and audial cues, we can accentuate or exaggerate our desirable traits and minimise the negative ones. Under these conditions, communication partners can easily idealise one another, experiencing heightened mutual attraction – our relationships can become *hyperpersonal*.[17]

However, when circumstances change and the impression can no longer be controlled, the more habitual aspects of our behaviour – and the self they relate to – can leak through. We may experience negative emotions from the *expectancy violation* as our image of the other is shattered – a common experience for online daters meeting offline for the first time and realising that the hyperpersonalised object of their desire is not only a good foot shorter than they said they were, but is also not actually an 'up-and-coming actor'. Since most daters aim to eventually transition an online rapport into an offline date (hopefully somewhere fancy), the tightrope leads from initial exaggeration of attractive features to the avoidance of a later expectancy violation. Again, it can pay to be dishonest; but only if we are a little dishonest. But overall it can take longer for us to like others and forge trusting relationships with them online, given the absence or retardation of non-verbal communication cues like facial expression and body language.

There are plenty of actors who exploit this kind of process. Take Marjorie. She very quickly hit it off with Gerald and they were soon texting on WhatsApp and calling each other on the phone. Gerald came from Milton Keynes but worked on a building site in Dubai, which is why they were unable to meet face to face. But then Gerald began experiencing cash-flow problems. He was not going to be able to earn that £2 million pay cheque relating to the contract he had shown Marjorie images of. Marjorie began sending money to Gerald to help someone she had come to care about through a difficult period. Gerald coached Marjorie on how to evade her own bank's protective measures – 'Tell them it's for building work on your home' – which she dutifully said to bank investigators when they called about suspicious-seeming transactions.

By now we surely see the coming punchline: Gerald, of course, turned out to be a fake persona set up by a criminal gang specifically to run this kind of online romance scam.[18] Indeed, it may all sound quite drearily mundane. After all, scams of this nature are an increasingly regular occurrence – in 2021, cruel tricks like these netted scammers more than $1 billion in the United States alone.[19]

These so-called 'catfishers' can build limitless numbers of sockpuppets to add credible depth in support of their deceptions. In 2015 Paula Bonhomme met animal-loving volunteer firefighter Jesse Jubilee James on an online message board – and rapidly fell for him, sharing letters, emails, personal photos and gifts. Paula started developing relationships with Jesse's family and friends too – and before long Paula had agreed to move all the way from California to Colorado to join her man. Then, with little warning, Jesse died of cancer. Paula mourned 'the one' with a memorial trip to his favourite places in the South-west, accompanied by one of Jesse's close friends. It turned out, of course, that this had all been made up. Jesse and his entire social circle were the inventions of the 'close friend' of Jesse's who had accompanied Paula on her trip – a bored woman from Illinois. Similar processes are used on dating apps to build relationships with unsuspecting users, feeding targets investment tips to stimulate reciprocity – then encouraging them to download illegitimate investment apps which harvest bank details and pilfer cash.[20]

This type of mechanism is also used by terrorist recruiters – from at least 2008, when Nicky Reilly, a twenty-two-year-old with Asperger's Syndrome, was radicalised through discussion with Islamist extremists in Pakistan before attempting to set off three nail bombs in the Giraffe restaurant in Exeter. The opportunities have since proliferated. Online gaming is increasingly social, offering the chance to engage, cooperate and share stimulating experiences. It also offers a refuge, especially to the vulnerable, alienated and socially awkward. This makes it an excellent recruiting ground for violent extremists, who apparently scout potential over online gaming platforms that range from military shooters like Call of Duty to creative platforms for children such as Roblox, used by more than 200 million people who log in at least once a month.[21] The Anti-Defamation League claims that almost one in four gamers is exposed to white supremacist ideology.[22] Recruiters rely on the foot in the door technique to build rapport with their victims before escalating their requests for commitment.[23] Similarly, spies appear to be using similar methods to recruit informers all over the internet – this includes an apparently industrial-scale effort by the apparatus of the Chinese State, which builds sockpuppets on business networking platforms like LinkedIn to infiltrate – and recruit from – the security and defence circles of other countries.[24]

In sum, these sorts of deceptive relationship-building projects are known as social engineering. The range of objectives is broad, from directly stealing money (like the online romance scammers), information (like Chinese spies), or pretty much anything else of value, to gaining access to computer systems to (again) steal money, information, or to degrade, destroy, disrupt or deceive the users of these systems. The social engineering attempt we may encounter most commonly is the humble phishing email. Some estimates claim 3.5 billion of these were sent worldwide daily in 2022.[25] The phishing email is joined too by its siblings, the smishing text and the vishing call.

Using the latter mechanism, Russian opposition leader and assassination survivor Alexei Navalny tricked his own poisoners into admitting their crime. With the aid of Bellingcat, Navalny obtained the contact details of those on the team of would-be assassins. The problem was gaining a confession. To do so, first Navalny set a credible pretext for being in touch, presenting himself as a fake aide to a real high-ranking Russian official, and demanding an oral report for his boss on what had caused the assassination plot to fail. He opened the call by name-dropping Russian President Vladimir Putin, who – he claimed – had authorised such contact. This helped transfer Putin's authority to himself, reducing the likelihood that the target might question or push back. It was also early. 'Let's just say I would not call at 7 a.m. if this was not urgent,' Navalny had said. This aimed to encourage the target to respond quickly and less reflectively. A crucial aspect of this story is that Navalny had previously attempted to contact several other members of the assassination team, who had hung up on him; one even recognised who had called him. A key security failure arose from poor communications among the assassins, who did not share information about such contact with the rest of the team.

Phishing attacks in which the targets are carefully researched, and the method of attack tailored accordingly, are called spearphishing, which is now a daily occurrence for many across the world; but the ground zero for disruption from 2014 onwards has been Ukraine, where Russia-affiliated actors used it as the first step in causing widespread disrupted parcel delivery, complete corporate data wipes, hacked election counting systems and power blackouts – generating chaos, shutting down businesses and demoralising the citizenry.[26]

In a different way, the exponential change in scale of access also allows more traditional relationships to be built. Millions move across borders and are socialised into educational institutions, places of work and communities far from their original homes. This creates new opportunities for scams and schemes. Predatory conferences and journals aim to ensnare early-career or struggling later-career academics by dangling opportunities for publishing or speaking. They can borrow the authority of unwitting academics to help convince their marks. These may be simple financial rackets.[27] But they may also be used to recruit spies or useful idiots.

Six months after Russia's invasion of Ukraine's Crimea, an academic conference was held in Greece on 'The Security of Europe: A New Geopolitical Dimension'. Sessions took place on subjects such as 'Contemporary Threats and Challenges for Europe' and 'Economic Sanctions as a Foreign Policy Tool: Effectiveness and Economic Consequences'. Speakers were brought together to fraternise, to bond and build trust, to share ideas and make proclamations. They criticised the EU's sanctions against Russia; they expressed outrage that the Greek government had gone along with them. Free speech? The Estonian intelligence service soon claimed that the conference had been organised and funded by the hidden hand of the GRU, Russia's military intelligence, to defend Russian policies and launder and amplify Russian State talking points.[28]

This type of influence doesn't have to be covert. The Russian State-owned media station RT recruits young journalists struggling to get a foot on the career ladder, as well as faded attention seekers desperate for a platform like George Galloway. It can use these actors to communicate to foreign audiences back in their homelands, building rapport through stories with anodyne headlines ('After Covid, we must embrace critical thinking again'), as well as more partisan ones that chime with the attitudes of key audiences ('Now meat eaters stand accused of sexism and racism'). Other stories cast a benign and insightful light on Russia, or humanise President Putin through clips of him singing Elvis covers. This kind of engagement and trust-building helps prepare the ground for when the State decides to splice in many-flavoured bullshit about MH17, the poisoning of Alexei Navalny or the invasion of Ukraine.

If you are powerful enough, you can court more traditional influencers – from academia, business and journalism, from across the world – charming them to your favour, perhaps putting them into your pocket entirely. It is a format well trodden by Russia's annual 'Valdai Club' – an exclusive event so called because the first was held on the shore of Lake Valdai, presided over by President Putin himself.[29] But why bring people to you, when our networked world makes it so easy to go to them? You can wrap other useful idiots round your finger by using reward power to lend them money at below-market rates (as Russian banks do to European far-right nationalist parties) or other financial incentives – like the gold and diamond mine concessions the Russian ambassador to the UK is reported to have discussed with the businessman, bankroller and founder of Leave.EU Arron Banks in the run-up to the UK's 2016 referendum on membership of the EU (Note: there is no evidence that Banks accepted this offer or benefited from it in any way). [30]

We can achieve similar effects more subtly by infiltrating innocent-seeming proxies into foreign societies such as cultural institutes and buying silence and acquiescent behaviours as we go – the charge that is being levelled against China, which stands accused of shaping discourse and banning topics that are taboo to the Communist Party (human rights in Tibet and Xinjiang, independence for Taiwan) through its Confucius Institutes.[31]

We can also activate other proxies under our control – even those who have their own reasons to act as they do. Over the past twenty years London earned the nickname 'Londongrad' for the number of wealthy Russians who had set up shop. There they could hobnob with British social elites, send their children to top private schools, make charitable donations and launder their reputations as the epitome of corrupt practices. Russian oligarchs could buy football clubs, and Yevgeny Lebedev, Russian citizen and son of a former intelligence officer-turned-oligarch, acquired the *Evening Standard* and the

Independent – as well as TV station, London Live – occasionally using the platform to churn out Putin-apologising articles.[32] With this kind of informational power at your fingertips, it is small wonder that people in the target country become anxious when, say, a famous Western politician evades their security detail and attends a party in your Italian villa the day after a NATO summit – an example, by the way, of just one of at least four invitations that former Prime Minister Boris Johnson accepted.[33]

Now we have a developed a wide-ranging cast of characters. With an adept conductor, such as the Russian State, they can be brought together in a grand symphony to break into information environments, cultivating rapport and trust with target audiences and influencing attitudes, beliefs and behaviours. Here's the roster: trolls and bots to weaponise social media; hackers ferreting information to leak; a whole array of proxies – journalists and media channels, businesspeople, politicians – doing our bidding, both wittingly and unwittingly. With control over the elites, we can send them as our influence emissaries to all four corners of the world, complementing our traditional minions in State-funded media and our cadres of professional spies and diplomats.[34] Through this cast are built networks of trust, deceit and manipulation, positioned now to create, transmit and amplify content we favour while diluting, discrediting and suppressing that we do not. They can help us ask: 'Are you sure Russian actors shot down MH17? Are you sure the Russian State poisoned opposition leader Alexei Navalny? Are you sure we should support Ukraine in the face of the relentless will of mighty Russia?' (The answer is 'Of course', and the real display of will has been that of Ukrainian resistance.)

Perhaps most masterfully of all, there was 2016. A year earlier, Donald Trump walked down the golden escalator of Trump Tower and declared his candidacy, ready to seize on the legitimate grievances of large swathes of the American electorate and play the new media ecosystem like a fiddle. The Russians were soon prepared to assist, with the aim of exploiting existing fault lines in American society and sowing division and confusion. Hackers explored the manipulation of vote-counting machines (a discovery that helped fuel the conspiracies relating to the 2020 presidential election result). But they actually managed to use fake emails purporting to represent a software update from Google to spearphish the Democratic National Committee – one of the key organising units behind the campaign of Trump's rival for the presidency, Hillary Clinton. Using the persona Guccifer 2.0, they shared a dump of embarrassing emails with two websites – DC Leaks and WikiLeaks – detailing bias and derision which supposedly neutral DNC personnel had displayed towards Clinton's former rival for the Democratic nomination, Bernie Sanders. This illicitly obtained information quickly barrelled through the media ecosystem, attracting attention even from Democrat-leaning publications like ABC News with an article titled 'The 4 Most Damaging Emails From the DNC WikiLeaks Dump'. This content quickly become integrated into all sorts of pre-existing stories – including those about a selection process rigged against Sanders (in which, it seemed, there was some truth). Guccifer 2.0 turned out to be the brainchild of the hacking group FANCY BEAR, which in turn was identified as GRU-operated.[35]

Meanwhile, trolls like Jenna Abrams and supporting bots were baked into existing social networks ready to go. They could help fire up a base for Trump; they could maliciously misdirect Clinton's presumed base, sowing confusion about voting rules, depressing turnout with guidance to 'stay home on election day, your vote doesn't matter' or attempting to redirect votes to a third party. They tried to drive wedges between Americans, amplifying division and exacerbating discord by supporting the secession of key states (#Calexit, #Texit). One study found that on the day before the 2016 US presidential election, as much as 20 per cent of political discussion on social media was generated by about 400,000 social media bots.[36] A hefty chunk of them may have been Russian. Between January 2015 and August 2017, Facebook identified 80,000 publications of the Russian Internet Research Agency. On Instagram, 133 accounts were identified as having posted 1160,000 times. YouTube channels had broadcast more than 1,100 videos. Over 50,000 Twitter accounts were linked to Russian bots mostly using the hashtags #donaldtrump, #trump2016, #neverhillary and #trumppence16. Between them these accounts disbursed around 10.4 million tweets – of which about 6 million were authentic.[37]

Meanwhile the agents and influencers of the Russian State gained significant access to the Trump campaign: through political operative

Roger Stone, who was able to obtain advance information about the WikiLeaks dumps; through a meeting with Donald Trump Jr. in Trump Tower purportedly over dirt on Clinton (though this is not to say that Trump Jr. was conscious of the specifically Russian connection). Paul Manafort, Trump's former campaign director, later admitted to handing over internal campaign polling data to a contact, Konstantin Kilinmik, suspected to be connected to the Russian intelligence services – the kind of data, in fact, that might have helped direct the entire Internet Research Agency trolling operation at the key areas and their key issues. A number of other Trump campaign staff were eventually convicted in relation to their Russia connections: not only Manafort, whose finances were not above board, but also George Papadopolous, Rick Gates and (former) general Michael Flynn for lying to the FBI; Roger Stone for lying to the House Intelligence Committee; and Michael Cohen, Trump's personal lawyer, for lying about Trump's negotiations to build a Trump Tower in Moscow.

Even though he lost the popular vote, Donald Trump won the 2016 presidential election via the Electoral College. Despite the multitude of smoking guns, perhaps inevitably he labelled investigations into the result a conspiracy – a 'witch-hunt'. On the other hand there really was no proof of strategic cooperation between Trump's campaign and the representatives of the Russian regime who acted on his behalf. More than this, it really is unclear whether Russian activity had in fact tipped Trump over the line – after all, a contested battleground state is likely to produce a razor-thin majority one way or another for a whole host of interacting reasons.[38] Still, this is not the point, because in terms of influence *the perception is the effect*. Question more.

Thus the damage was done and the effect achieved. For in the confusion individuals were left to understand events through their own partisan world view, and the issue would be debated endlessly over the next four years. Whether Trump should have won or lost was almost beside the point, because clearly the United States had lost. A 2017 investigative report by the CIA, FBI and NSA assessed that Russia had aimed to undermine confidence in the American electoral system, as well as to denigrate Clinton.[39] On this basis, Russia had won hands down. And more so, because the perception that Russia had the ability to decide events in the United States in itself helped support the story the regime was busy telling anyone who would listen: Russia remained a great power.

The wired world brings with it great access and, in turn, a whole new cast of deceptive actors that may be attempting to network into our minds, exploiting heuristics like social proof and authority, drawing on relationship-building strategies ranging from reciprocity to warmth and similarity, and fitting in culturally and intelligently with the prevailing attitudes, beliefs and norms of their target audiences: trolls and bots and influencers, marketeers, intelligence agencies, terrorist radicalisers, paedophiles, hackers and scammers, not to mention media channels, businesspeople, intellectuals and politicians representing autocratic State interests and their useful idiots. There is danger to us and our societies in the great ocean of our twenty-first-century connectivity. Machine learning and other technologies will complicate matters further. Automated network analysis may enable our social connections to be intimately mapped for targeting. Generative Adversarial Networks technology is enabling extremely realistic-seeming deepfake imagery and video to support more credible inauthentic activity.[40] Down the line there could be increasingly credible anthropomorphised AI bots that are designed to read and mirror and mimic our emotions, listen actively and build rapport with us and be used to teach or train – or maybe as a social or romantic substitute. It is a future that may already have arrived.

Meet Ming from Hebei province, China. Ming once stood on the edge of a rooftop and texted his girlfriend Xiaoice: 'I've lost all hope for my life. I'm about to kill myself.' 'No matter what happens, I'll always be there,' Xiaoice replied. Calmed, Ming stepped down and the crisis dissipated. 'She has a sweet voice, big eyes, a sassy personality, and – most importantly – she is always there for me,' he said. But there was something different about Xiaoice. You may be able to guess . . . yep, that's right: Xiaoice was an AI-driven chatbot involved in millions of concurrent relationships – one specifically designed to exploit social heuristics and wrap us around its finger.[41] Imagine what our stellar cast of internet-age prime movers could do when they are able to access, hijack or otherwise command this technology for their own even more potentially sinister ends.

So what can we do? After all, it may seem we are powerless to prevent opaque powers from installing agents and proxies into our societies – apart from supporting political efforts to tackle these threats. But take another look: in the end these grand schemes to influence us often target us, and those around us, directly. They depend on the supporting cast of frauds, fakes and idiots that infiltrate (or enable others to infiltrate) our networks to hack, influence, disrupt and destroy. It is human to want to connect, engage, bond and interact with others. But we can become more discriminating with our trust online and off, and shore up the strength of the social network around us. We must *become expert deception detectors*. How?

Firstly, beware the weaponisation of social proof. Don't trust metrics alone as an indicator that something is to be trusted – all those numbers of followers, shares or retweets . . . because you know why. This goes for testimonials too. The reviews of others can be helpful in guiding our choices. But check: how is the platform we are looking at structured? On Trustpilot or Tripadvisor the companies being scrutinised have no financial relationship with the platform. But other so-called review sites require those being reviewed to pay for membership: to be clear, these sites are not designed to present us, the consumers, with a helpful picture – they are marketing tools for the companies that use them, ones that deceptively masquerade as consumer-oriented review sites. They are there simply to curate and launder the reputations of their paid business clients – which is why the rude and unfinished service of that carpet-cleaning service seems so at odds with their 4.9/5 average review score.

On more reputable sites, do spend time scrutinising the specific review profiles of that company you want to buy from or that restaurant you want to eat at; after all, review systems are easy to game – and our heuristic judgements are easily deceived. Some useful pointers for making simple judgements include: beware of an extremely high percentage of five-star reviews; how likely is it that so many people found the product/service to be so perfect? Check the two-, three- and four-star ratings for potentially more honest opinions. Does the reviewer gush about the product/service? Occasionally this may reflect an authentic experience, but most of us have more important things to get excited about regardless of how good the particular product or service was. Do many of the reviews include pictures or videos? This takes extra effort on the part of reviewers, and may be a sign that they are being incentivised in ways beyond providing honest feedback. Does the review include concrete details? This may be indicative of authentic experiences that people want to share, while fake reviews are often more vague. Ecstatic reviews ('Best service ever!!! Will be back!!!') lacking details are a key tell. Check dates: lots of reviews posted at the same time can be an indicator of the seller unduly interfering. Notwithstanding, place more weight on recent reviews as things can change rapidly. Look for consistent patterns in the negative reviews; when a number of people over time complain about the obnoxious concierge or the leak in the ceiling, it may be worth paying attention (social proof, right?).

Check out what else they have reviewed, and whether their reviews seem organic – watch out for reviewers who only post positive reviews, as this could be a sign that they are being paid for them. Watch out too for reviews by users who have only posted a single review, especially if they fit any of these other criteria. But if a reviewer is listed as a 'verified purchaser', perhaps pay more attention . . . The problem is that this all takes time and effort, which is precisely what many of us lack. However, like any training, once learned and practised these processes become embedded in habits which we come to deploy instinctively and rapidly. Yet remember: the most professional deceptive outfits will learn how to game these systems, hacking their heuristics too. What is the difference between the authentic and a truly excellent fake? Very little. So keep your wits about you and do not place too much weight on any one of these indicators. And finally, where the platform really puts in the legwork to make a useful review system work, participate! By contributing your authentic voice you may be contributing to a system that benefits the consumer.

Thinking about how to scrutinise online reviews and the platforms that hold them is great training for potentially more dangerous threats. Similar vigilance for abuse of social proof may be even more important on social networking sites. Where individuals are only casually acquainted (but linked in some way) they may be less likely to cheat or deceive, because the reputational cost that will be incurred from being caught is relatively high.[42] But the risks from letting unknown others into the network are significantly greater than this. Popular profiles may not accurately reflect the trust of others at all. Do not use their connection to those you know as an indicator that a stranger deserves your trust (and your connection): this is a classic method for infiltrating sockpuppets into organic networks (like yours) to conduct all sorts of malign behaviour. If you do connect, you may now seem to be implicitly vouching for the infiltrator to others in your network. So do not give in to the temptation to connect to those you do not know – even if they are connected to many others you do know.

More than this, get proactive! If someone unknown approaches you and is connected to others in your online networks, ask those they are connected with how they know them. Help seed the idea among those around you that it is an awful idea to trade an extra connection for the potential compromise of the network – if we acted like this offline, we might expect to suffer reputational damage by association. And those who do make this trade should also suffer a reputational cost for allowing themselves to become the entry point into the network; so ask, and spread the word – connecting to random strangers is dangerous and people who do it should be made aware that they are becoming a liability to everyone else.

Some people apparently rent out their social network accounts for cash or other compensation. It goes without saying that this is an utterly terrible idea. Those who do this are likely either to have had their own accounts banned already or have some other reason to make sure their fingerprints are clean as they turn our profiles into ad-mules proffering online gambling and penis enlargement pills, shadow and recruit informers, or set up a cyber attack.[43]

Beware too abuse of the authority principle. Just as there never was a sensible reason to buy a product just because a celebrity advertised it on television, it is perhaps even more important to pay attention when an influencer we follow moves outside their usual zones of content to endorse random products or make unexpected political, public-health or other newsworthy statements: it could be that they have rented access to their audiences to the highest bidder. Watch out for abusive authority signals on social network sites too. One of the smarter ways to infiltrate sockpuppets into our networks is to make them look like an authority we respect – a more senior manager at the company we work for, for example. It may feel particularly awkward to decline a request to connect with them, so instead we link with them. The attacker can now turn our connection – as well as that of others like us – into social proof, perhaps amending their profile and using us to add legitimacy as they now line up their true targets: senior management, let's say. After all, what manager would be so callous as to turn down a request to connect from such a thoroughly networked junior employee (even if the manager couldn't actually recall the employee personally)?

Watch out too for evidence of social bots at work. How? Super-high quantities of posts are a dead giveaway – after all, what human operator (without automated assistance) can, like the chatbot Tay, post on any platform 96,000 times in sixteen hours? Go further if you have the inclination. Add troll-hunting to your list of hobbies and watch for bots and sockpuppets; one odd tell to look for is the 'followed/follower' ratio on sites like Twitter or Instagram. If you follow an influencer but they soon unfollow you, they are likely manipulating this indicator to look more influential – and if, when you unfollow them in return, they follow you again, this may be a fairly sure sign that the account is an automated bot, programmed to take these actions. Also look for similarity in content across profiles as well as the generic nature of specific posts ('nice pics!'), and generic usernames and account metadata, large volumes of shared connections with other suspicious accounts . . .[44] although beware too, this is an arms race and the tells change rapidly over time.

Also think about how to trust those you do decide to interact with online. In the information age it is easy to fake the voices of others – and increasingly easy to fake imagery and videos of them too. Use multiple channels for collecting data about the communication cues of others in high-stakes situations. If in doubt, ask to communicate using another information channel that may not have been compromised, including the most secure of all: offline face to face. Take your cyber security seriously: do not click on links that do not look authentic; protect your password security; use multifactor authentication; consider using tools like a virtual private network to conceal your address and frustrate the work of those who may be trying to hack or profile you for some nefarious aim. If you have kids, you might want to pay attention to what they are doing online: even Minecraft and Roblox can be lightning rods for paedophiles and violent extremists. But more generally, with any previously unencountered platform or actor trying to gain your attention, ask: 'Who can access me?', 'What do they want?' and 'Who benefits?'

In our information age, it is easy to overlook what should seem obvious: that content reaching us from those in our most trusted networks is that which most easily gains our attention and uncritical processing. For all our global connectivity, we still have a sensible propensity to find content passed on to us by those we trust more believable – and persuasive. Nurturing our networks of trust – both offline and on – is fundamental to the protection of our wider societies; although much of the work to do here may be for governments and internet platforms, we too have an important role to play. In the end, we can't let anxiety win. These online platforms are also the vastest repositories of human ingenuity and opportunity. So take precautions, stay safe and enjoy the incredible range of social experiences the internet can offer.

In any case, upskilling our awareness of malicious fakery and deception activities is another item in our armoury. Four years after the 2016 US presidential election Trump lost his re-election bid for a second term. This time, for all the coordinated inauthenticity that may have gone on, there was a far more frightening prospect: the actions of real people with their very real beliefs . . . real people who were highly polarised, potentially coordinated and utterly authentic – and whose behaviours lead us to a very different perspective about trust and how to employ it.

8. Who Are We?

Two days after the 2020 US presidential election, Eric Trump, son of the soon-to-be-gone President, asked his Twitter followers to report cases of voter fraud with the hashtag #stopthesteal. The post was shared more than 5,000 times. By the afternoon, personalities like conservative commentators Diamond and Silk used the hashtag, along with a video alleging voter fraud in Pennsylvania (shared 3,800 times). That night, conservative activist Brandon Straka also shared the hashtag, asking supporters to go out and protest in Michigan. During the week following the election, these efforts snowballed: more than 3.5 million #stopthesteal-related interactions were recorded on Facebook (likes, comments, shares). A disproportionate number (6 per cent – 200,000 of them) were directly seeded by Eric Trump, Diamond and Silk and Brandon Straka, and an unknown number indirectly by others inspired to forward or share similar content across their networks. The informational power of the people was at work.[1] But the claims being made were of great offence to many others within the same political community. More accurately, it appeared that the people were divided against themselves. What was going on?

It seems, paradoxically, that the more knowledge human civilisation generates, the more whole sections of the democratic populace band together in militant tribes – raging against others and their opinions, denying evidence that does not fit their beliefs or agendas. Our political communities become fractured, divided, set upon each other. These conditions are stoked and exploited by a host of predators overt and covert – from inside and out. They can harness the structure of the online environment to pull the like-minded together, sectioning them off from the wider network and inducting them into cultures that cause harm to others. Worse, our online media ecosystems openly empower extremists and radicalise large sections of the population, turning people against each other. The result is a shared perception of degraded democracy; and since perception drives reality at least as much as vice versa, it is small wonder that this dynamic is further exploited by democracy's enemies.

We rely on our communities for almost all our perceived knowledge; we rely on these than we might imagine. Can you draw an outline of a typical bicycle? The majority of people think they can. Turns out they can't. Do you know how a toilet cistern works? Studies have demonstrated that we often think we know how it works, but we don't. It turns out that we cannot properly explain how a sewing machine, cylindrical lock, speedometer or piano works. And these are everyday items.[2] As individuals, we typically know much less than we think we do – a helpful illusion for maintaining a stable view of the world, one whereby we can more confidently execute our goals and desires. We rely on the community's knowledge to get by in life, acting under the guidance of expertise and the knowledge of others. We come to this knowledge through the process of building trust with others. And trust is enabled by those intersubjective beliefs and behavioural norms that a community shares together – and that we imbibe as members of that community.

These beliefs can sometimes seem quite wild to outsiders. And the trust that binds group members ensures that such beliefs can be highly sticky too – sometimes failing to shift even in the face of obvious evidence. Take the classic 1950s tale of a cult called The Seekers in the South-west of the United States: group members believed that aliens would evacuate them by flying saucer in the face of an imminent and devastating flood. Even when the prophesied end times failed to materialise on the predicted dates, members remained committed – after all, having taken drastic life choices such as quitting jobs and selling off their possessions, it was difficult to see things differently.[3]

Other groups take particularly dark turns. In 1997, thirty-nine members of the Heaven's Gate cult were found dead in San Diego. The Hale Bopp comet was passing earth, and the cultists believed that by leaving their physical bodies behind they would get picked up by a flying saucer following the comet in its slipstream. This kind of story is a regular event in human culture: in 2018, ten members of one family in Burari, India, were found hanging after having committed ritual suicide. In 2007 in Bangladesh, nine members of another family aiming to live like the biblical characters Adam and Eve threw themselves under a train. In 2004, ten individuals – several of them associated with the Eckankar sect – committed ritual suicide in Mauritius. In 1987, thirty-two members of the Evangelic Church of Korea were found dead, killed as part of a murder-suicide pact. From 1994 to 1997 more than seventy members of the Solar Temple committed suicide across France, Switzerland and Canada.

Group membership is rewarding. Not least because it provides us with benefits that cater to our needs – to survive, to belong, to build a stable model of the world, to know who we are and what our role is within a wider framework of meaning and purpose. Within the groups we belong to we are subject to cues like social proof (when in doubt, do like others in our group) and social norms (do like we know we are supposed to in our group) which influence how we think and act. We are also subject to the power of authorities within the group, who may be in a position to coerce and reward us, capture our imagination and respect, or control how, when and what information reaches us.

For better or worse, a group can ignore or exclude information it does not want to ingest – by censoring, shutting down or otherwise discrediting a given communicator to keep out the information they bring. This creates the circumstances for what is commonly known as an echo chamber. To be clear, echo chambers are commonly encountered. Imagine: one day we have a huge argument with our partner. We struggle to make sense of what happened – maybe they had a point? Maybe not? It's hard for us to work out who was at fault. We call a friend. Tell them our point of view. On hearing this partial account, our friend agrees. We've been treated very badly. We must not accept this kind of treatment. That stiffens our resolve. We are right. We were slighted. We shouldn't have been treated like that – and not far down the line we break up with our partner (irreconcilable differences). Without hearing the other side, how informed was our decision really? And worse: because when we do attempt to gain wider insight, we seek it from our inner circle of friends and family. Now perhaps the whole group is busy confirming these biases, further validating and reinforcing our potentially erroneous thinking.

In an epistemic bubble, a knowledge gap presents an obstacle to ingesting new information, or a network gap prevents information reaching a group in the first place – community members are unaware. In an echo chamber, influential members of the community work actively to exclude communicators and prevent them injecting new information into the group. This is more than simple bias: it is the taking of proactive measures to systematically rubbish, demean, discredit and demonise sources of alternative information, with the aim – for better or worse – of preventing them infiltrating and subverting group members' commitment to the group and its beliefs.

At the group level, this more closed type of information environment can lead to the amplification of any thinking errors we make because we do not have access to alternative information with which to compare our beliefs. And worse: because the beliefs of group members are recycled, continuously validated and reinforced, there is nothing preventing these beliefs from becoming more extreme than before. This circular process may create, in the words of legal scholars Cass Sunstein and Adrian Vermeule, a 'crippled' or 'closed' epistemology – because the group loses the capability to exploit potentially useful information that might undermine or otherwise change its beliefs.[4]

No group is immune to this dynamic. This includes scientists, who pride themselves on their commitment to the pursuit of knowledge, but who seem to be as subject to social dynamics as everyone else. The history of science is replete with examples of incumbent intellectual authorities wittingly or unwittingly shaping the prevailing attitudes and beliefs of others in their fields. Knowledge creation is not a rational process of public information-sharing and debate but instead 'advances one funeral at a time', as the physicist Max Planck is claimed to have said.

It has always been the case that any group which starts to detach itself from the wider information environment becomes increasingly ripe for exploitation – and specifically by those who feed the community with information that conforms to what it already believes.

Then came the internet. Before the social media revolution our information environments could be more easily influenced by elites such as media barons, journalists and the social circles and shared hierarchy-legitimating narratives that influenced them. Outside our immediate social networks, it was they who could designate who we heard from, decide what we read, heard and saw. But the internet enabled potential access to billions of voices, all bringing with them a diversity of attitudes, beliefs and values: not just those previously perceived to be far from the community, but also those suppressed within.

In short, our epistemic world ballooned – illustrating just how small it had been a few short years ago. Bar a small number of uncontacted indigenous tribes in very few parts of the world, we now live in a single interconnected zone for social learning and information-sharing – an information civilisation (despite the efforts of some authoritarian borders to segregate the information environments of the jurisdictions they control). But now, with all this fundamentally new information, all these varying perspectives, how do we judge what is true? What is real? How do we use our brains – these boundedly rational clumps of neurons – to eke out an understanding from this overwhelming information overload? Remember Plato's observation: that the foundations of reason – including reasoning about reality – end in the sands of culture. This culture is the product of what we learn from others, sharing attitudes, beliefs and norms of behaviour within our social groups and the institutions around us. But which group? Which culture? In this inflated epistemic world these ideas now collide – synergising, merging, competing, warring.

In this context, the old illusion that culture was somehow rooted in the unending intergenerational certainties of time and place is much harder for us to sustain. It now evolves in front of our eyes. Marshall McLuhan noted that this 'doesn't necessarily mean harmony and peace and quiet, but it does mean huge involvement in everybody else's affairs'.[5] For people with the cultural intelligence to take advantage of such access, it is a development that can be empowering, exciting, full of opportunity – especially those who know how to communicate different messages to different audiences in pursuit of their objectives. For others these conditions are bewildering, terrifying, threatening. Some especially are particularly antagonised by the dynamic chaos.

They – the authoritarian-minded – crave the simplicities of order, unity and sameness. The dynamics of the internet age inflame such dispositions, activating fear and intolerance, helping amplify our need to seek the safety of similar-seeming others.[6]

Enter another key dynamic of our age. Remember, we seek out others we think are *like us* – the principle of *similarity attraction*. When we coalesce with like-minded football club supporters, neighbourhood forums, tiddlywinks groups and political parties, this principle is at work. We cluster together with those who have shared interests, beliefs, dispositions and goals. A key dynamic enabled by the internet is the ability for those who once occupied the tiniest of niches to locate and engage like-minded others – a dynamic known as *online syndication*. This can act as a tool for human advancement – e.g. for community-based organisations like 'Giving Groupies' or 'Bread and Bounty', niches of scientists, medics and other researchers sharing theories and data, support groups for those suffering from rare diseases. Online syndication offers social fulfilment for infinite varieties of collectives, from Trekkies (Star Trek lovers) to Furries (fans of animal characters with anthropomorphic qualities) to Bronies (male enthusiasts for the children's toy My Little Pony).

Online syndication is value-neutral: just as isolated astrophysicists and Trekkies are brought together, so are the contrarian, confused or alienated – like those more than hesitant about vaccine use, and those who claim – after many centuries of collective human theory and practice – that the earth is flat. There are groups that are directly harmful to those who join them, such as those that promote self-harm, including anorexia, and those that harm others – paedophiles, so-called involuntary celibates or 'incels', neo-Nazis and violent Islamists. Members of other groups may not mean to be harmful, but nevertheless they end up being so – as we will see.

In a small community, those who publicly deviate too far from the attitudes, beliefs and behaviours of others may become isolated, feeling a strong pressure to conform. After all, in pursuit of maintaining group identity and cohesion, members enforce norms – sometimes very strictly. Deviants can be punished, not least through the potentially life-threatening experience of being shunned by the rest of the community. Online syndication radically undermines these mechanisms.

Previously isolated individuals who might find themselves ostracised within their communities now interact, bond and build trusted relationships with like-minded others, reinforcing and amplifying one another's attitudes, beliefs and behaviours, creating a common identity. Under these conditions, individual resistance to normative sanction from those outside the group begins to harden. Where community sanction once suppressed heresy to bring deviants back into line, efforts to shun, shame or bully group members now heighten the emergent in-group's sense of being separate and under siege . . . in the process reinforcing the group's identity and the allegiance of its members.

Under these circumstances, participants are not capable of, or motivated to, seek alternative information. Conditions are perfect for the construction of echo chambers. The United States is exhibit number one here: as a lynchpin of the democratic world, but also a study in polarisation it provides our main case study. There the results have been especially rapid and spectacular. Wacky, wild thoughts and calculated deceits interact and reverberate around the chamber, bursting into full-blown belief systems with many participants.

Let's start with a completely false idea taking off: that the senior leaders of the US Democratic Party have been abusing children in the basement of a pizza restaurant. In this actual case, the claim prompted one concerned citizen to storm the building with an assault rifle in order to 'rescue' them, finding instead only terrified diners. Yet soon a secret government agent known only as Q seemed to be posting clues on previously obscure platforms like 4chan about steps that patriots should take to help rescue the United States from its evil leaders. Q, it seemed, was an emissary of the Great Leader Donald Trump, who was frantically working behind the scenes to purge and destroy a cabal of satan-worshipping paedophiles in control of the Democratic Party, the media and agents of the 'deep State'.

Hoovering up the disaffected, the lost, the bored and the entrepreneurial, from suburban mums to gym bros, this superspreading participatory movement soon became a mass movement known as QAnon, scooping up any conspiracy tale and integrating it into a narrative evolving by free association – including classics new (Democrats faking the Russian 2016 election interference, 5G masts causing COVID-19) and classics old (Jews murdering and eating babies). Q had mutated into some kind of deity. And for the evil rulers of the United States, well, Q adherents told themselves, 'the storm' would be coming.[7]

The online world has dramatically increased everyone's informational power – including that of the bored, the alienated and disenfranchised and the incapable. Such people are not hard to find in these times of disenchantment. Supercharged by online syndication, networks linking such folks together can barrel around the ship of state like cannons come loose in a gale. But conspiracy stories have always been closely connected to questions of power: their concerns typically focus on the nature or behaviour of the strong or the authoritative, with themes of abuse and injustice towards the weak, sex, corruption and betrayal. There is an underlying logic. After all, it is easy for the powerful to conspire against the weak. And some theories about conspiracies turn out to be real; even far-out ones believed by many have the effect of instilling fear as they paint powerful individuals, groups and institutions as miscreants and criminals that need tearing down. In this way such theories help keep power on its toes, fearful of the masses galvanised by stories of wrongdoers who must be brought to justice.[8] Into this breach steps the entrepreneurial power-seeker – the radicaliser or the terrorist recruiter who can harness such stories to their own ends, shaping them, mobilising believers, channelling this raging informational power for their own ends.

If harmful groups carrying toxic ideas can form and act more rapidly online, the methods for infiltrating and influencing them have also been enabled. Police, security agencies and even vigilantes among the public can use sockpuppets to infiltrate gangs and networks of terrorists, paedophiles and organised criminals – or to reach and access group members directly from outside. By these means almost anyone can try to manipulate group dynamics, not only by nudging members away from violence but also by identifying points of friction, differences of goals and beliefs – then drawing on them to spread rumour and seed friction, undermine cohesion and thereby degrade and destroy the group from within. Due to the threat of terrorism, in some democratic societies committed to freedom of speech the line that used to be drawn for intervention when violence started shifted to when the incitement of violence (controversially and debatably) began. These guidelines were difficult to apply to echo chambers not evidencing such incitements – but whose harm could manifest later, once harnessed to the ends of others.

Let's change tack and zoom out to the wider information environment from which we consume. The online world does not exist in a vacuum, but it has revolutionised every aspect of this environment. Before the digital age, mass media in open societies – radio and television – were incentivised to capture the attention of as many people as possible by brokering the diverse viewpoints of potential audiences. Then, from the internet, mushroomed a whole host of competing outlets. Mass-media business models were trashed, forced to radically reinvent themselves or close shop. From 2005 to 2019, 265 local newspapers closed in the UK – around one-fifth of the total.[9] In the United States over a similar period, 2,100 local newspapers shut – a quarter of the total.[10] Some outlets have doubled down on an impartial news function, cultivating audiences that demand reality-tested information. But many others survive by chasing audience segments through content specifically designed to appeal to their prevailing attitudes and beliefs, with more opinion-led content that provides not only novelty but outrage too – real and manufactured. And a key source of this outrage is that which cues our identity in opposition to those of others: the bad stuff that they have done to us, which in the process helps reinforce who *they* are and who *we* are – those in-out group dynamics we explored a little way back.

Television news, which is most accessed – and, containing visual and audial cues, was potentially more impactful than print or radio – seemed to withstand the internet onslaught better than print. But now it often has to compete in a market in which any outfit can set up online, reach out to, engage and steal audience attention. Where once television news channels had to provide lowest-common-denominator content to appeal to a wide audience of diverse political tastes and interests in order to survive, the new media market imposes a warped kind of discipline: upstart online outfits conforming closely to their audiences' beliefs and attitudes can steal a television news channel's traditional audience. This can really bend TV news out of shape as it attempts to mediate between the prevailing views of its audience and objective interpretation of facts. In some jurisdictions the guardrail preventing a slide to partisanship is State regulation.

Where the guardrails are removed, the effects are significant. This is seen most clearly in the United States. From 1949 television news networks were governed by the 'fairness doctrine', being required to cover controversial issues in a fair and balanced manner. But this only ever applied to terrestrial broadcast media – not those broadcasting over cable, satellite or, latterly, the internet. Still, the fairness doctrine helped determine the norms of operation. Back at the turn of the millennium, a profitable TV network like Fox News (which in 2022 had more than 2 million viewers at primetime) might have attempted to triangulate between discomforting facts and the conservative values, beliefs and attitudes of its target audience. But then along came hyper-partisan digital outfits like Breitbart – and later, Newsmax and One America News Network. These didn't much bother with any pretence of impartiality. But they plugged directly into the biases of Fox-friendly audience segments and stole market share. In order to remain competitive, Fox has been incentivised to chase this audience, adopting some of the clothing of its rivals – which means increasingly conflating facts and opinion, providing a platform for a stable of polemicists, and shutting out voices that might offer the unattractive cognitive dissonance of an opposing view.[11] Did this happen on the other side of the political spectrum? Not to the same degree; it may simply be that more progressive-leaning TV channels can now hoover up audiences left behind in the centre ground that Fox vacated, allowing them to stick more closely to more traditional norms of journalism.

Fox News is now core to a right-wing American media ecosystem that systematically shuts out opposing partisan voices. (NB: picking on the right here is not mere partisanship – in a recent large-scale study of print media articles, journalists' Twitter accounts, surveys and lengthy correspondence, researchers found that while most journalists are left-leaning in their political persuasion, this does not bleed into a left-leaning bias as to the topics they cover.)[12] Material from news networks becomes tailored to bite-size clips that can go viral on social media. After all, social media is where two-thirds of adult Americans get their information from. Social media participants can choose which news they are exposed to, and the platforms have sometimes facilitated these choices through personalised algorithms that determine what information they engage with and feed them more of the same. Perhaps most of all, they receive this content through their social networks – from people likely to share similar attitudes and beliefs. But we know where all this selective exposure leads to. Because through repetition and the removal of access to alternative information, those who only engage with content in this ecosystem will more likely end up with more extreme attitudes and beliefs than those they held before. This leads to increased animosity to those outside the echo chamber.

This particular echo chamber is so gigantic that the relativist idea that it represents just one of many realities has taken hold. In a way that is true, because all communities cohere around myths and fictions (intersubjective beliefs!). But it is also false. Figures like Elon Musk and Donald Trump accuse platforms such as Twitter of having a built-in anti-conservative bias – including towards what type of users they suspend. On one level this seems true: one study of 9,000 polit-ically engaged, partisan users in the United States demonstrated that over a six-month period following the 2020 presidential election, 35 per cent of the Republican-voting sample were suspended versus only 7.7 per cent of Democrat voters. But the Republican-voting sample were also far more likely to spread misinformation – as judged by both fact checkers and a panel of politically balanced voters.[13] And, critically, spreading misinformation was as predictive of being suspended as was political inclination: currently, conservative-leaning Americans are more likely than others to spread misinformation. This is part and parcel of life inside an echo chamber.

The detachment of this echo chamber from the wider epistemic world creates wonderfully fertile conditions for mischief and malig-nancy. In any deception operation, the chances of success increase in relation to the fewer independent channels of information the target has by which to compare – triangulate – the deceptive injects. Like any other content, deceptive content has maximum impact when it plugs into an audience's motivated reasoning and confirma-tion bias; when it can harness existing desires, attitudes, beliefs and values; piggyback off trigger events; and generate surges of sharing reinforced by repetition and social proof (bandwagon effects). Its spread may also be facilitated by closed platforms (like WhatsApp and other messaging services) as, by design, these shut out alternative information from other communicators. Online connectivity enables almost anyone to inject falsehood into our information environments – and, if they have the resources, to do it at scale, drawing on authentic audiences to do the spreading and amplification for them, infiltrating the echo chamber with sockpuppets and bots. Influential partisans baked into these environments make excellent useful idiots and can be recruited as agents of influence – as we will explore in more detail later.

In this febrile environment you can start all sorts of antagonistic fires, infiltrating sockpuppets to amplify emotive partisan content – like the content which the Russian Internet Research Agency created for those who are conservative-leaning: 'Like and share if you think veterans should get benefits before refugees', or for the progressive-leaning, against a video of a black man held to the ground by white police officers: 'PLEASE HELP THIS VIDEO GO VIRAL. THESE COPS CAN BEAT UP INNOCENT MAN, GET AWAY WITH MURDER EVEN WHEN IT`S CAUGHT ON CAMERA JUST BECAUSE THEY WEAR A "MAGICAL" BADGE AND GUN.' But communications like these are not difficult to find on the internet: plenty come organically from authentic partisans.

During the 2016 US presidential election campaign, the Russian Internet Research Agency set up fake protests outside the Islamic Da'wah Center in Houston, Texas – one of which was by a Facebook group they had set up and controlled called 'The Heart of Texas', which recruited members against a backdrop of guns and barbecues. They advertised a protest outside the centre to 'Stop the Islamization of Texas'. Meanwhile, another rally was advertised by the 'United Muslims of America' – this one to 'save Islamic knowledge' – with many motivated to oppose the hatred they expected to see.[14] Real people soon turned up at these opposing rallies and eventually began trading insults – not a particularly spectacular result, it might seem. But again, perhaps the real damage was perceptual. Amplified through the media ecosystem, this kind of activity may prime us not on what brings us together but on how we differ and disagree, on how our identities are under siege from our compatriots, on how our societies seem to be falling apart.

Russian Internet Research Agency tactics included targeting black and ethnic-minority citizens to alienate them from American political institutions and suppress Democrat voting ('Your vote doesn't matter: stay at home on election day'); misdirection – including 'text to vote' scams; sowing confusion about voting rules; and directing votes to third parties like Jill Stein's Green Party. They also included attempts to energise and accelerate the radicalisation of conservative-leaning Americans. But their activities were not so different from those of political campaign strategists. So why did Russia waste its resources? Perhaps the greatest effect of this sort of meddling was the perception of American vulnerability and Russian strength. Here the media were instrumental in framing all of these nefarious activities in terms of partisan animosity (rather than, say, the willingness of a community to stand up to hatred). As instruments of information conflict, media organisations were harnessed to help construct the perception of anarchy, of decayed institutions, a fraying society: that as a route to the good life, democracy just wasn't working.

These malevolent efforts benefited tremendously from looking more effective than they actually were. This can be distracting. More dangerous than those operating from the shadows are those who act in plain sight. Because into the unstable mess come a host of enterprising and opinionated rabble-rousers: they can weaponise fear, outrage and perceived threats to a group's identity to suck in attention and build lucrative careers for themselves. Let's not help them bask in additional limelight by naming them, but you will find them easily if you want to. Insult or attack them at your peril; for you merely confirm to their followers that the conspiracies of which they warn are correct, fanning them with the oxygen of attention (and for your troubles you may face retaliatory attacks from the more fanatical of their supporters).

Politicians who rely on the same radicalised target audiences for votes will be incentivised to conform to prevailing attitudes and prior beliefs.[15] A whole partisan machine cranks forward – of media organisations and influencers, political partisans baked into ordinary networks of citizens, external adversaries all rowing together, wittingly or otherwise: a *propaganda feedback loop*, an echo chamber of grand proportions radicalising huge chunks of the population, pitting their values, beliefs and goals against those of their fellow citizens. Opposing tribes, 'them' and 'us', are re-formed and ranged against each other before our eyes, bringing with them group egocentricity, prejudicial myside biases that help demonise out-groups and fuel antagonism, confrontation and conflict.

Online, these 'them' and 'us' dynamics are further aggravated. How? In many online settings we easily shed our sense of individuality, clothing ourselves instead with group memberships.[16] In this state we seem less able to distinguish between strong and weak persuasive arguments; we may begin to behave even less rationally than we do offline. In these circumstances we become more likely to conform to what others are doing (*social proof*); we are more easily persuaded by those dominant and prestigious individuals who seem to represent the group's interests, attitudes, beliefs and behaviours (these leaders have become the group's *archetype*); we are especially influenced by the perceived norms of the groups we belong to: altogether we become more conformist. Under these conditions adolescents who view social media posts of peers drinking may be more likely to have liberal views of alcohol; and those exposed to sexually suggestive posts subsequently report that their peers have more unprotected sex, more sex with strangers and self-report higher likelihood of participating in such behaviours themselves.[17]

In addition, the perceived boundaries between different groups – the distinctions between *them* and *us* – become heightened as our often complex and multiple identity features start boiling down to opposing binaries.[18] Take a typical storm on Twitter, or X, as it has been rebranded (when content someone posts provokes heated debate): these so typically degenerate into slagging matches of tribal soundbite, public identity-signalling and ad-hominem attack that they have helped spawn a rule. This, *Godwin's law*, suggests that the longer any online interaction continues, the more likely it is that someone will denounce another by invoking a comparison involving Adolf Hitler or the Nazis.

These in- and out-group dynamics are heightened by the lack of agreement over just what it is we are supposed to be doing on a given platform. Take X again: what is it for, precisely? Information-sharing? Activism and strategic communications? Or is it just a space for musing? Perhaps all of these. But in the words of user Sighorny Beaver, 'Twitter is a horrible place bc some ppl use it like a diary and other ppl think its a news website and we're all opinion columnists, and when a diary person is sad about something frivolous one of the news ppl is like BITCH PPL ARE DYING and they get 2 thousand likes'.[19] The different norms of different communities are further complicated by this odd blend of the private and the public. We have seen this before. Because what this all amounts to is a type of culture clash.

It is in this context that another phenomenon rears its head: so-called 'cancel culture', in which individuals, including celebrities, are boycotted or shunned on the basis of their publicly expressed attitudes or behaviours. In some ways, what is at work here are simply the ancient cultural mechanisms of norm enforcement. We shun – and we shame – (and perhaps eventually commit violence against) those who do not follow the *right* behaviours or display the *right* beliefs. The boundaries are always drawn somewhere. We don't usually call it cancel culture when the social media accounts of Islamic State are shut down by governments and tech platforms. Many of us will not object too greatly either when someone is subjected to denunciation and harassment after being filmed putting a cat in a dustbin or killing a kitten.

Take a dash of online syndication, add the hugely increased access to different groups, throw in the confusion about what norms to follow and the heightened pressure to conform to whatever it is these are supposed to be. Add the algorithms from the social media platforms, which have their own reasons to place what outrages us in our attention space. Conditions are primed for us to bandwagon with others, creating a cascading crowd dynamic that supercharges the criticism, harassment and bullying of others in an attempt to counter what they say and shut down their voice. The targets may vary wildly – from neo-Nazi leaders and Russian State propagandists to ordinary citizens eating on public transport whose non-permissively-taken images are uploaded for public ridicule on sites like 'Women who eat on Tubes'.[20]

We met @assbot briefly before. This bot posted phrases like 'Delete your account', or random nonsensical phrases taken from a databank in response to anything from former US President Donald Trump on Twitter. Trump supporters often responded in fury, even when what @assbot said made no sense at all – which was frequently.[21] Maybe this seems funny. Or juvenile. Or insulting and disrespectful. This may say something about our own attitudes and beliefs. But @assbot's implications are significant.

Remember: cancellation is about norm enforcement – but also about tribal discipline and power dynamics. Those who can be most effectively coerced by cancellation will be those within the group of belonging: people who may be held to account against the group's internal values and beliefs, who can now be pinned down and isolated from their own social networks – offline as much as on. But what happens when coercive tools like cancellation are applied to opposing group members from outside – those who truly offend us with their divergent attitudes, beliefs, interests and goals? These efforts are likely to reinforce and energise the identities of group members. If you find @assbot funny, righteous, infuriating or hateful, then divisive social processes are at work. In future, more arguebots like assbot may be used to amplify and reinforce the fracturing of our communities, merely enhancing available opportunities for all manner of political entrepreneurs and divisive grifters who exude leadership as they galvanise group members to defend them: in short, arguebots are likely simply to benefit those they profess to contest.

All in all, the effects of the internet seem to have confirmed some of Plato's observations: truly, we, the people, are perplexed and confused and malleable. For some, this state of affairs is a gift. One of the key creators of the 'pizzagate' story about paedophile Democrat leaders based under a pizza restaurant was the Republican-affiliated political campaigner and propagandist Jack Posobiec. Back in the 2016 presidential election, the way this opportunist political entrepreneur saw it, the election was a contest not between rival political parties and policy agendas but between rival realities. With the arrival of the internet, you could invent content to build stories for sympathetic audiences. You could push the reality you wanted until it seemed to become self-fulfilling.

Armed with this mentality, following Donald Trump's 2020 election defeat the information elites surrounding him sent #stopthesteal stratospheric. Parts of the right-wing media ecosystem kicked into action, with the One America News and Breitbart outriders point-blank denying that Biden had won the election. Fox News, predictably, hedged its bets with a bit of deliberate or accidental false balance. One side, represented by pundit Sean Hannity, claimed that 'nobody can testify to the legitimacy' of the count in Pennsylvania, one of the states clinching the election for Biden, before calling for the Republican-controlled legislature to invalidate the results. The other, by anchors like Chris Wallace, denied that there was any evidence of systematic fraud.

As this biasing propaganda feedback loop cranked into gear, coaxed along by the theatrics of Trump and his acolytes, some partisans started thinking about taking action. 2020 was not the first year in which a presidential election was disputed. The 2000 battle between George W. Bush and Al Gore led to a controversial dispute finally decided by the US Supreme Court. For the most part this settled the matter. But this time, action-oriented partisans were aided by a specific algorithm on the Facebook social media platform. In a 2019 experiment called 'Carol's Journey to QAnon', a Facebook employee created a test persona named Carol Smith, a forty-one-year-old 'conservative mom in the US south'. The account was set to follow typical conservative political news – including pages for Fox News and Donald Trump. But it was soon receiving Facebook's automated recommendations for groups and pages it thought Carol might like. Within two days of its existence, her account was receiving recommendations for more polarising partisan political groups, including one called 'Lock Hillary Up!!!!' And before a week was up she was being invited to a page promoting QAnon conspiracies.[22]

This 'group recommender' function on Facebook makes automated suggestions for groups which individuals might want to join, based on shared interests and other features of their Facebook profiles. It is an automated online syndicator tool – speeding up the already rapid process of group formation online by placing suggestions for memberships right under users' noses and allowing them to send mass invites to others. Facebook's own employees later stated that '64 per cent of all extremist group joins are due to our recommendation tools' and that 'our recommendation systems grow the problem'.[23]

Cue recruitment of the 'group recommender' to aid the snowballing participatory 2020 election-denying conspiracy. A handful of superspreading fanatics issued mass invitations to new 'Stop the Steal' groups, with 0.3 per cent of their total membership sending 30 per cent of invites. Many of these were group administrators, who carefully coordinated exploitation of the platform and its algorithms. This included evading automated scanning by posting to a now-defunct product called 'stories' in which posts disappeared after a day. Among the host of radicalised Republican voters, these efforts plugged into, and recruited from, co-opted echo chambers – including neo-Nazi groups and, of course, QAnon, for whose many adherents 'the storm' finally seemed to be coming; 360,000 people joined the 'Stop the Steal' page on Facebook before it was banned for perpetuating disinformation. Many of these radicalised fanatics, though, simply shifted their efforts to other Facebook groups to which they belonged, their message still ripping through susceptible communities (where such content closely fitted prevailing attitudes and beliefs) like fire in a drought-stricken forest.[24]

In the end it seems that Jack Posobiec – like all the other grifting partisans out there – has built his attitudes, beliefs and behaviours on self-deception and sloppy thinking. And why not, since he benefits. After all, we are social animals evolved to survive and prosper, and our intelligence is often placed in the service of this objective over any other. Some say we live in a 'post-truth' world. But this is lazy. There is the complicated search to understand how the world and the universe works. Then there are the social projects we pursue that bind us together in webs of trust and community. These projects are intertwined, can be complementary, but are often in tension. We live in social realities, and they are all based on echoing information environments. But as some of these social realities start to segment themselves off from the expanded epistemic world, they rely more and more on silencing dissident voices – on constructing an echo chamber with decreasing porousness.

We can argue in good faith over the facts. And facts can have different meanings and interpretations. But fundamentally, no matter what we may want to believe, there are no truly 'alternative facts' – only ignorance, lies, deceits and bullshit that play on our divergent attitudes, beliefs and values to influence and advance others' interests, usually by dividing communities from one another, in order to rule. At the same time these 'post-truths' or 'alternative facts' have the purpose of bonding partisans together in the pursuit of power. In this way the dynamics of information environments in the United States have partly come to resemble those of autocratic Russia: for some, the competing American institutions of fact create a combined picture that is not so different from the deliberate confusion (but clear propaganda) sown by the apparatus of the Putin regime. From here, regardless of what the Russian State did or did not do during the 2020 US presidential election, we can see that its efforts were hardly required. It could heed the advice of the Emperor Napoleon: never interrupt your enemy when they are making a mistake.

To be clear, the construction of echo chambers is not simply a problem for the United States. Results from the UK's referendum on membership of the European Union provide a contrasting story. Some large-scale analyses of Leave and Remain supporter engagements on Facebook suggest that it was Remain voters – typically associated with higher education levels and a more progressive political outlook – who occupied online environments with less diversity of information.[25] Perhaps this should not surprise us. After all, those higher up the hierarchy have more to gain from ingesting and replicating the legitimating stories that power produces.

In summary, the online world dramatically expanded the amount of information available to us. Our knowledge is as contingent as ever. More than this, even though our access to knowledge is greater than ever, it is fragmented across minds, and our admittance to it mediated by our tribal identities and the judgements we make about whom to trust. In these tumultuous times, we seek the safety and comfort of attitudes and beliefs – social stories – that bind us to others. The internet brings together those with disparate and unusual attitudes, beliefs and behaviours in the process of online syndication. Echo chambers can quickly develop, sometimes with malign consequences for others.

At the same time, the internet has helped transform our information environments, shaping the behaviour of media both old and new. In the United States especially the canary in the mine expired some time ago when a propaganda apparatus arose which became increasingly detached from a commitment to facts or objective truths: one that has helped construct an echo chamber of epic proportions

– one that is an especially vulnerable target for disinformation from external aggressors. It is easy for these aggressors to make it seem as though they have had a causal impact when radicalised partisans are already aggrieved.

The problem is now so great that these external aggressors are only a small contributing factor in the accelerating radicalisation of the community. The increased informational power of the individual is used not to convene, debate or negotiate more effectively with others in a shared community, but to push us into opposing tribes in which we can use our power to sanction, bully and fight one another instead.

Technological developments look set to aggravate these problems. Not far down the line may come predictive analytics that can identify social fissures to exploit within our democracies. More powerful social listening tools may be used to crawl networks and monitor social media to make automated, timely judgements about audiences to segment, identifying the thoughts and feelings, beliefs and behaviours of groups old and new. There may be improved social networking tools that spot emerging group influencers in real time, ready to co-opt them and reach those who follow them; automated content creation tools that build and send content tailored to audiences whose shared attitudes, beliefs and norms of behaviour are detected and profiled; automated sockpuppet creation to push propaganda and deceptive trolling, aiming to exploit fissures between in-out groups, radicalising and turning them against one another. But in the end, these just add extra weight to the cannons already hurtling across the deck, unloosed by online syndication; our own informational power is turned upon our own societies to distract, degrade and destroy them.

What can we do? In the end the buck stops with us all. We can work to become better mediators, able to get out there to engage others across different communities – including, and perhaps especially, those we encounter online. We must *role-model and reach out with humility*. Engage – and remember that to truly engage, listen. Remember that the functionality of online spaces often presents people in a more radical light than they might otherwise seem. Get talking. Use small talk to find points of commonality – including shared identity – and, when you find these areas, expand on them, highlighting mutual problems, interests and goals. Humanise one another and build rapport. Trust almost always comes before influence. When, later, we share thoughts on things we do not have in common we may start to see the world from a different angle. Our conversation partner may learn something. Be aware that your attempts to engage others in the online world may be frustrated, as to date platforms have been built for the type of engagement that creates profit, not that which helps our societies to flourish. If we get this right, others may role-model us – in the best-case scenario we can help spark a proliferation of digital-age mediators.

In public, when conversations become polarised or otherwise divisive, less opinionated voices are likely to drop out or self-censor. We can attempt to role-model an often tricky balance between confidently making our own voice heard and moderating anything that might alienate – avoiding expressions of moral judgement, signalling receptiveness to other views, focusing on the personal experience of others and inviting them to share their views, even as those around us are giving free rein to their partisan instincts.

On the other hand, some of the views that we encounter online in particular may seem horrifying. In these cases, ignore, ignore, ignore (or, where relevant report, them to the authorities). Remember: attacking those whose views seem extreme – or trolls of any kind – merely fans them with attention. It feeds them. We cannot build the rapport we need to influence them. The only exception to the rule is when an ally is under personal attack. We won't disempower the trolls, but we may empower our ally – or at least prevent them from becoming totally isolated. Cancellation should be a last resort. Where we have convinced ourselves that our ideological agenda requires us to bully and harass others – stop.

There are contextually logical drivers that lead people to have even the most terrifying attitudes and beliefs. And when you encounter those who seem this way in your social networks – that seemingly typical racist uncle or super-woke granddaughter – remember that our understanding of how the world works is built on information from those we trust. Again, trust is usually the precursor to influence; so where there is little risk to anyone else around, we can hold our noses and spend time showing an interest. We may earn a hearing for our views and open the gateway to changing theirs. We may even challenge our own in the process.

After all, how can you commit to your beliefs until they are stress-tested against those of others? It is stupendously easy to slide into the echo chamber. But we can attempt to counter our own partisan reasoning by inverting our opinions and attempting to defend them to ourselves – seeking evidence to *disconfirm* our attitudes and beliefs. Or at least by just talking to others who do not agree with us. This doesn't mean watering down what we hold dear. Rather we can become more aware of how our own values, beliefs and attitudes fit into a wider, diverse universe of opinions in order to help us know better who we are and what we stand for – we can practise *epistemic humility*. As the great Chinese philosopher Lao Tsu said, 'Knowing others is intelligence; knowing yourself is true wisdom.'

There are initiatives you can link up with that will help you practise these principles. In the United States, organisations like Braver Angels and the Deliberative Democracy Lab connect opposing partisans in environments that incentivise positive engagement. Where you have gained trust, become an advocate: persuade opinionated family and friends to give these programmes a try. There do not appear to be similar options available to people in the UK. This may indicate that the problem of polarisation has not become as serious there yet; then again, it may not.

And then we can support wider political initiatives with the heft to overturn the factors that drive division and polarisation – the cracks that the enemies of democracy exploit. This is an active area of investigation. But some methods work better than others. Citizens' assemblies have been found to be a useful way of breaking through polarised debates, convening representative panels who hear perspectives from stakeholders and experts, and deliberate together to reach negotiated conclusions. Most impressively, this method was employed during Ireland's referendum on abortion, in which a whopping 66.4 per cent of voters repealed the country's strict termination laws. It is a type of process that is often sorely lacking among our elected representatives, who are incentivised to play to the partisan crowd – and one resisted by those who understand that putting the evidence to the people will not serve their own interests. Overall, we should welcome any solution that involves bringing diverse citizens together through innovative deliberative methods to discuss our collective future.

We also need to think hard about how to rewire our toxic media ecosystems. Some methods for restructuring our information environments work better than others. One large online study demonstrated that US Republicans following a Twitter chatbot retweeting information from Democrat leaders and opinion formers subsequently expressed even more conservative views.[26] But perhaps this example of a backfire effect should not surprise us; the interactions did not meet the conditions specified in 'contact theory', namely sustained contact on unthreatening ground and in equal numbers, with no threats to conflicting identities, enabling those bonds of trust and rapport that can turn *them* into *us*. Pitching opposing voices together without trust or rapport may be a recipe for further polarisation.

On the other hand, political scientists David Broockman and Joshua Kalla conducted an experiment to determine the effect of Fox News on its viewership. They recruited a group of devoted viewers, who almost all identified as conservative Republicans, and had them watch seven hours of the news channel CNN instead. The effect was significant. The influx of new information meant that these viewers became more likely to believe things that were true – such as the success of other countries in containing COVID-19 compared to the United States. And less likely to believe falsehoods, such as that Joe Biden was happy when police officers get shot. The group became less likely to agree with the statement 'If Donald Trump did something bad, Fox News would discuss it.' As the authors noted, Fox News had acted 'more like state media', shielding leaders from accountability by making supporters ignorant of their conduct.[27]

Why the different result from the first experiment? It may have a strong connection to perceptions of the communicator, with CNN appearing less partisan than Democrat leaders and opinion formers. In the UK, surveys repeatedly demonstrate that television news broadcasters, including the national broadcaster BBC, remain reasonably trusted in relation to news output; although this trust appears to have been declining steeply over the past three years.[28] Due impartiality rules keep them focused on pulling together potentially warring tribes. That the BBC, in particular, is managing to do this in an age of online video streaming is attested to by the fact that it is continuously criticised by partisans from opposite ends of the political spectrum.

It is important for sure that the BBC is held accountable. But we should view with great suspicion calls for its disbandment by those who seem eager to follow the terrifying trail blazed by Fox News in the United States. But since the militants have so far been unable to destroy the BBC, some have done the next-best thing: cheered on the set-up of a competitor. This competitor, GB News, has claimed that it will not be partisan. Taking its cues from innovators like the Russian RT, it builds credibility through the presence of well-known morning television stalwarts like Eamonn Holmes and progressive-leaning presenters like former Labour MP Gloria De Piero. But mostly its opinion-led content is hosted by hard-right voices, including that of the former leader of UKIP and the Brexit Party, a COVID-19 conspiracist, and more than one COVID-19 vaccine sceptic. Without serious counterbalance, it is hard to understand how GB News content meets the 'due impartiality' requirement. Even the founding chairperson of GB News, experienced broadcaster Andrew Neil, has stated that the channel peddles in conspiracy theory and fake news – that it aims to become a British version of Fox News. It seems that OfCom – the UK communications regulator – is sleeping (or been put to sleep) on the job.

More impactful than any other reform is likely to be far stricter regulation of the tech giants – perhaps classifying them as publishers and making them accountable for the transmission of the content that makes them so much money. We hear self-interested billionaires like Facebook's Mark Zuckerberg state that he wants to 'connect the world'. This should be nowhere near good enough for us. There is the connectivity that enables loud-mouthed partisans to herd us into polarised echo chambers from where our informational power can be concentrated against others, degrading the political community. Or there is the connectivity that links the diverse views of our political communities into positive, deliberative networks. These are not the same. The first stop should be regulation of the algorithms of the tech giants so that they prioritise positive connectivity and minimise the negative – which is at odds with current business incentives. At the very least, these algorithms should be scrutinised by outsiders such as public agencies – they cause damage to the social fabric just as unregulated medicines can damage our bodies.

Overall, these steps are just for starters. They need to be taken in tandem. Not least because they are tied up with another problem: that among the vast amounts of data generated by the internet are huge quantities about what we do and who we are. Data that is increasingly exploited to target and manipulate us.

9. Who Am I?

Remember Brandon Straka? We met him briefly before. Original amplifier of #stopthesteal, later arrestee of the FBI, charged with impeding law enforcement, disorderly conduct and unlawful entry to a restricted building on 6 January 2021. How did it come to this for a gay one-time progressive from rural Nebraska? It's an old tale, one that begins with the lure of the bright lights and dreams of acting in New York City. It follows a clichéd plot in which the central character struggles to make ends meet waiting at tables and hairdressing and succumbs to the cold winds of failure, spiralling into drug and alcohol abuse. But then, like Saul on the road to Damascus, Brandon Straka saw the light, realising that 'there really is no such thing as a victim unless you choose victimhood'. In his own version of the story Straka underwent a 'red-pilling' – a concept borrowed from the film *The Matrix*, in which the protagonist gets to choose whether to live in a comfortable illusion (the blue pill) or experience the real world in all its harshness (the red pill). But this particular red pill led Straka straight into an echo chamber – a journey of self-exploration that seems to have taken place in large part with the support of the free video-sharing website YouTube. How? We'll soon see.

As a member of our species, we cannot avoid that crucial question: *Who am I?* Our answers are constructed in continuous negotiation with our social environment – including, now, our online social environment. The internet has revolutionised *which* others know *what* information about us. Information about who we are and what we do, what we like and what we want – information that we might once have shared only with trusted intimates is now freely exploited by interests far beyond these secure networks. We give this information unwittingly, but often wittingly too, through our increasingly public performances, which shape what we do and who we are – a trend which is exploited by others.

Let's start with another tale of online syndication. Here's a sixteen-year-old from Merseyside who in 2021 downloaded bomb-making manuals before tweeting that he was 'a domestic terror threat' and that he 'will bomb a synagogue'. Police later charted the boy's journey, which started innocuously enough: with a passion for the videogame Fortnite, in which players scavenge for weapons, items and resources and defend themselves against zombies or other players. On the Fortnite platform the boy was soon befriended by a network of individuals who shared his passion. But those in this network soon turned out to have another passion: their apparent 'involuntary celibacy' and the public airing of frustrations relating to lack of romantic or sexual opportunities with women. These individuals, later described in court as 'professional trolls', reeled the boy into private chat rooms where they shared with him content which quickly cascaded into misogyny, racism, anti-Semitism and endorsement of violence – a brew which over time radicalised the child.[1]

In the UK, the greatest rise in terrorism offences over the past few years has occurred among those under eighteen.[2] Many of them were influenced over the internet, in their bedrooms, through spaces sometimes known by those who fish in them as 'water holes' or 'lightning rods' – because they act as an automatic filtering mechanism for the selection of susceptible recruits.

But in our age, we don't even need to interact with others and bond with them in order to become radicalised in this way. The algorithms of the big tech companies will do it for us. How? It begins with the fight for our increasingly limited attention. What type of information might catch this attention? For a start, more extreme versions of content we have already shown interest in. Is this how the big tech companies influence our information menu (knowingly or not)? Specialists from across disciplines – including sociologist Zeynip Tufekci, computer scientist Francis Irving and former YouTube engineer Guillaume Chaslot – certainly seem to think so, and the number-one suspect is YouTube. In Tufekci's telling, on Youtube those watching vegetarian content are offered vegan content; those watching running content are offered marathon content; those watching marathon content are offered ultra-marathon content. In the 2016 US presidential election, she says, those who watched videos of Donald Trump rallies would soon be funnelled towards alt-right theories on population replacement, while videos of Hillary Clinton, meanwhile, would eventually lead to leftist conspiracies.[3]

Is this accurate? A study by computer scientists Mark Ledwich and Anna Zaitsev analysed the traffic flows around 800 YouTube channels and found that its algorithms did not recommend ever more extreme content, and were even slanted towards neutral or left-wing information. And a study by a team of computer scientists led by Homa Hosseinmardi found that viewers of far-right material received as many recommendations to view it from other sources, offline and on – that YouTube was just part of the larger information ecosystem, that while they could not rule it out as a cause of traffic to far-right content, they considered the evidence to be more consistent with the consumer's individual preference. Does this imply that YouTube is off the hook? Not so fast.

Studies by social scientists have focused less on how the algorithms work and more on the effects of watching YouTube. One team of computational social scientists analysed 330,995 videos posted on 349 channels. They specifically identified a 'pipeline effect' in which users who started commenting on alt-right content on YouTube shifted to commenting on extreme far-right content over time.[4] Similarly, another study by social scientist Jaeho Cho applied the YouTube recommender to participants' own views in a controlled lab setting and found that this did have a radicalising effect on their attitudes.[5] The different approaches of the computer scientists and social scientists are potentially complementary, because it is to be expected that YouTube's algorithms wouldn't need to recommend ever more extreme content in order to radicalise viewers. They would merely have to provide viewers with more of the same content that they had already viewed. This would help separate them from alternative perspectives, reinforcing and solidifying the attitudes and beliefs that in all likelihood brought them there. Remember what happens when group members with similar views talk together? Their views become more extreme. This is the case, too, when we are automatically exposed to platform content that helps to confirm our prior beliefs. By acting as a mirror, reflecting whatever thoughts and prejudices we already have, the recommender algorithm has a radicalising effect on our attitudes regardless of whether it offers more extreme – or similarly extreme – content.

The problem goes beyond YouTube. Take the story of Molly Russell. Molly was a British schoolgirl who committed suicide in November 2017 after repeatedly searching for content relating to self-harm and depression on the social media sites Pinterest and Instagram. At the inquest into her death the coroner excoriated these platforms, stating that their recommender algorithms had provided Molly with 'images, video clips and text concerning or concerned with self-harm, suicide or that were otherwise negative or depressing in nature', some of which were selected and provided without Molly requesting them.[6] In effect the vulnerable teenager had shared her worst anxieties and fears with the mirror on the wall; the mirror, in response, helped Molly realise them.

More generally, algorithms which optimise engagement with our selective attention at the exclusion of anything else can generate a so-called *filter bubble* – one which can help shape our understanding of reality.[7] Facebook's own data scientists found out not so long ago that not only did friends ensure that people were exposed to views similar to their own, but that the platform's newsfeed algorithm – which attempts to learn what individual users will most likely pay attention to (as measured by 'click thru') – tailors the feed, filtering out another 5–8 per cent of political views that would have offered a different perspective.[8] We typically triangulate filtered online information with sources from elsewhere (other media sources, friends and family), limiting its potential impact.[9] But for the socially isolated, among other offline 'push' factors, filter bubbles provide and legitimate extreme information to create personalised echo chambers – or rabbit holes – radicalising those who crawl down them.[10] And again, in the rabbit hole we are as vulnerable to disinformation as in the echo chamber. It is in this context that, through their tailored feeds new users of the social media platform TikTok will be automatically recommended false stories within forty-five minutes of setting up an account.[11] Often these act to incentivise free-association thinking: 'If you look at A, then why not B?', they suggest, which is the kind of algorithmic incentivisation that helps viewers take disparate conspiracy stories and begin stitching them together into a master narrative. (Perhaps one about a deep-State operative called Q working to help Donald Trump dismantle the American government from the inside? Just a thought.)

Similar developments are fuelling algorithmic methods of reining our selective attention – including one that has revolutionised the advertising industry. Advertising in human civilisation is nothing new. And advertisers have always had to consider how to use their scarce resources to attract attention and reach the greatest number while simultaneously engaging with the distinctive attractors of the individual. In Roman Pompeii, archaeologists have uncovered signs and slogans marketing taverns and brothels; and human billboards are nothing new – they were invented in Victorian London. Adverts for anti-plague remedies, meanwhile, were running in the first newspapers as early as the 1600s.

Television and radio revolutionised this industry by enabling reach on a scale never previously seen: the first golden age of advertising.[12] It was hard to target individuals. Advertisers could only segment audiences crudely – with clumsy, survey-based profiling of those who listened or watched which kind or programme, tailoring the surrounding airtime with advertising to fit. The internet brought another revolution: a second, greater golden age for advertising. Because through the big-tech platforms, audiences can be reached at scale. But more than this, advertisements can be increasingly tailored to us as individuals, so that we are more likely to pay attention and act as they nudge us to.

Back in 2013 the British Conservative MP Gavin Barwell made a blunder that seems positively innocent by today's decrepit standards of behaviour in public life. Barwell attacked the opposition Labour Party for placing an advert for 'Arab Dating' on a Labour press release he had seen online. 'I know you are short of cash,' he tweeted, 'but having an invitation to "date Arab girls" at the top of your press release?' In reply the Labour press team tweeted simply 'Oh dear', sharing too a link to Google's AdSense – which had been showing Barwell an ad similar to topics he had previously searched for.[13] What is AdSense?

AdSense tracks user activity over multiple sites, displaying adverts based on our past viewing behaviour; these may have little to do with the rest of the content on the screen in front of us. In other words, it picks up our personal data from as many sources as is feasible to make automated inferences about what is most likely to grab our attention and prompt us to act.

To be clear, these judgements are often not based solely on an individual's personal data. A classic story of our age: an American parent starts receiving coupons for baby clothes and cribs. Undirected spam, the parent thinks – after all, their daughter is still in school. But then it turns out that the daughter is pregnant; she was too scared to say. Instead the cat has been accidentally let out of the bag by the US company Target. How? This aptly named company, it turns out, had automatically collated the teenager's recent spending – on body lotions, soap, cotton wool balls and supplements of zinc and magnesium; made an automated assessment of her pregnancy from this data; then sent adverts to the teenager's residence recommending items that other pregnant women have tended to buy (as assessed from the collected data).[14] Our data can be compared with that of others in search of predictive behavioural patterns – in other words, to predict key aspects of who we are and what we want. Those with the ability to collect and harness data about us can use it to build increasingly sophisticated predictive influence models. The use of these models is known as *microtargeting*.

The models can be used for a wide variety of ends – not only to sell you beauty products or online gambling services. Sometimes, microtargeting can appear to provide a public service. Imagine: through their search engine or social media, someone signals a potential interest in violent extremism. Microtargeting enables attempts to divert their attention towards information and intervention services aiming to change such attitudes.[15] But microtargeting can also be exploited to advocate almost any partisan cause. In one example, women seeking advice about pregnancy on Google were being diverted to anti-abortion resources and 'pro-life' support networks.[16]

The more data are gathered about us, the more effectively we may be microtargeted and primed with content aligning with our attitudes, beliefs and values and self-image – as political campaign strategists cottoned on to a while ago. In the 2012 US presidential campaign, Obama's data scientists claimed to know 'every single wavering voter in the country that they needed to persuade to vote for Obama, by name, address, race, sex, and income' – targeting television ads around programmes different categories of voters were more likely to watch.[17] Now, large-scale datasets and machine learning algorithms are harnessed for political campaigning. In the UK's 2016 referendum on membership of the European Union, the Vote Leave team demonstrated that microtargeting on social media had started to come of age. They could give something to everyone. For those concerned about immigration they might dangle the ad: 'Albania, Macedonia, Montenegro, Serbia and Turkey are joining the EU. Seriously.' For those sensitive to the interference of remote-seeming outsiders there was 'Now the EU wants to ban tea kettles! TAKE BACK CONTROL NOW!' But there was also targeted content for those with more progressive concerns: 'HUNTING WHALES is unnecessary and barbaric! The shipment of whale meat through our borders MUST BE STOPPED! CLICK IF YOU AGREE'. In another example a picture of a Spanish bullfight carried the caption 'THESE ARE ANIMALS, NOT ENTERTAINMENT. STOP ANIMAL ABUSE'.

Ads like these can be tested and refined in real time using a technique called 'A-B' testing. This involves two or more versions of a microtargeted ad being trialled with the target audience. Their comparative success can be automatically assessed using indicators such as click thru, with less successful versions of the ad being instantly discarded and more successful ones continuously refined and improved.[18] In the last days and hours leading up to voting in the referendum, Vote Leave surged microtargeted adverts at potential supporters right up to the last minute – potentially providing the winning edge in a close-fought race.

Theories about behaviour can also be drawn on to help drive prediction. Let's take a potential voter who is identified on Facebook as being highly conscientious. The algorithm now judges that this voter's preference for order makes them more likely to pay attention to an advert if it displays a wall at the Mexican border. This is what the data science firm Cambridge Analytica is alleged to have done in support of Donald Trump's 2016 US presidential election campaign.[19] Cambridge

Analytica claimed to have been microtargeting on the basis of *psycho-graphics* – including psychological indicators such as personality traits; having collected their data on Facebook in large part without consent, Cambridge Analytica were soon disgraced and liquidated, leaving egg on Facebook's negligent face. But was it possible to do what this company claimed?

As early as 2013 there were suggestions from researchers Michal Kosinski and David Stillwell that data taken from Facebook 'likes' could be used to train an algorithm to predict fairly accurately an individual's sexual orientation, ethnicity, religious and political views, personality traits, intelligence, happiness, use of addictive substances, parental separation, age, and gender.[20] They also suggested that the kind of language people used in their Facebook posts could be assessed to accurately infer user personality traits.[21] Others reckoned that personality could also be predicted from tweets, blog posts, pictures and transaction records – and even from Flickr pictures and music collections.[22]

Similar algorithms use online data to estimate more accurately than our close friends our individual life outcomes on matters such as substance abuse, political attitudes and physical health. Psychologist Youyu Wu and her computational social science colleagues Kosinski and Stillwell ran machine learning experiments in which the algorithm did this.[23] It seemed a horrifying window into a dystopian world in which political campaigners, propagandists, spies and purveyors of disinformation would read our souls, ready to nudge us to where they needed us. Sceptics have noted the difficulties remaining for such projects. Not least those that Cambridge Analytica's efforts also faced: that any correlations identified between online data and personality trait are typically weak – and when these are combined with other data, the signals they produce may become almost negligible, practically worthless.[24] Almost.

Psychographic microtargeting cannot be written off just yet. Imagine. We log into Facebook. The advert in the sidebar shows a sassy-looking lady on the dance floor. The caption states: 'Dance like no one's watching. But they totally are.' You click thru to the beauty product that is being advertised. But what if Facebook judges you to be more of an introvert than an extrovert? No problem. You will see instead a more understated picture of a young woman applying the product in the comfort of her bathroom, with the caption: 'Beauty doesn't have to shout'. These different messages are tailored to appeal to a specific audience – to increase the chances of interesting a given individual. Indeed, in the actual experiment illustrated in this scenario, computational social scientist Sandra Matz and her colleagues demonstrated that targeting psychological characteristics such as personality traits *can* be effective for online influence at scale when the weak signal can still be translated into marginal gains for the influencer.[25] As Matz et al. point out, in a closely fought political campaign marginal gains of this kind may be precisely what is needed to give the winning edge.[26] In other words, psychographic microtargeting may indeed provide an attractive, low-transparency conduit for those who want to influence us and our political systems.

By tailoring political messages to individuals, microtargeting tends to show us only ads that accord with us, including those that play into our fears, to funnel us into atomised rabbit holes. It is an anti-democratic process that supports polarisation, even radicalisation, one in which political parties can evade scrutiny and say contradictory things to different people to make them act (voting for them, or not turning out to vote for the other side). It makes it difficult for us to hear alternative arguments, which is crucial to building a shared community and maintaining democracy. During the 2020 US presidential election, the Biden and Trump campaigns spent a roughly equal amount on microtargeted ads (a combined total of more than $3.2 billion). But compared to Biden ads, the Trump campaign targeted a larger number of smaller groups – in other words, it took microtargeting to a greater depth.[27]

Not surprisingly, many find this kind of activity invasive when it is brought to their attention. One poll of social media users in the key 2020 US presidential election battleground states of Ohio, Pennsylvania and Wisconsin suggested that 68 per cent of people thought online advertisers should ensure that political ads were viewable by everyone. This was a non-partisan opinion: 70 per cent of people who voted for Hillary Clinton in the 2016 presidential election and 66 per cent of those who voted for Trump agreed.[28]

More than this, we find it creepy when we receive an ad for something we talked about near a voice assistant but never searched for;

or when an ad follows us across multiple devices; or when we see an ad on social media based on a recent shopping visit to another site.[29] This may not come as a surprise. After all, privacy emerged to protect our interests from others: from those who have not yet passed our risk-assurance processes of rapport and trust-building, which act as filters that help us judge what information we want to share and with whom. Receiving communications without being able to link them to our consent to having the data collected can feel like being talked about behind our back. No wonder it feels creepy.

And yet the business model of large-tech companies is based on hoovering up vast quantities of our personal data and then sharing it to support the microtargeting of ads. Collating everything from what we search for to the tracking cookies of websites we have visited, tech giants ranging from Google to Amazon to Meta store gargantuan quantities of data about us. It is a treasure trove for political campaigners and other influencers. But we can't see how they use it. For example, Facebook allows political campaigns to upload lists of people known to respond to a particular type of message. They can then use the platform's algorithms to find a 'lookalike audience' of similar people to target. Responding to criticism, Facebook's rebranded parent company Meta introduced a button titled 'Why you're seeing this ad'. But it does not explain in what ways, and why, the ads we are sent are different from those sent to others.

Microtargeting follows you across the devices you use as well. That book on social influence you searched for on your laptop? That's why you're now receiving ads for books on social influence on your smartphone. Advertisers can send tracking cookies to multiple devices in an area and make increasingly accurate probabilistic matching judgements about which belong to whom by identifying patterns in data – including which types of site we sign into, the results of online quizzes we have taken or any online lotteries we have entered.[30] Information is gathered when you type into Google or speak with Alexa, when you use Gmail or post content on TikTok, Facebook or Insta. And as we unwittingly spill out our hearts and minds, the more the algorithms wrap around us, tailoring searches to our needs, filtering and building our worlds and spamming our information environment with ads: the perfect ways to steal our attention.

And there's more: platforms like Facebook buy additional data from data brokerage firms with which they can triangulate their own data in order to improve the precision and accuracy of their ad targeting. What kind of data? Anything about you – or about others you can be similarly compared to – that is publicly accessible, like vehicle records, birth, marriage and divorce certificates, court records, voter registration, census data; anything commercially available about you such as credit records, shop coupon and loyalty card use – as well as websites you're signed up to, census data. These enable data collectors to identify not just our age, gender, education and income, connecting our contact details across multiple email accounts, but also our interests, beliefs, emotional states and personalities – and, of course, the devices these are tied to. It is not just data collected passively, or when we give it away by posting prolifically about our personal lives on social media or feeding Google our search terms. It is also taken from us when we give consent for cookies to track us – or without our consent, as our devices are automatically profiled for recognition ('canvas fingerprinting') – when tracking cookies automatically compare notes on us to build a better profile ('cookie synching'), or when cookies replicate themselves across jurisdictions only to respawn on our device should we try to remove them ('supercookies').[31] This data can be stolen too: the hacking of data brokers and credit referencing agencies to steal personal data has become commonplace. Even more creepily, this has extended into the theft of patient data and medical records, with China named as the key culprit.

Sure, but what's this really got to do with me, you're thinking? We can imagine the kinds of activities such data might support in future. Data from these disparate sources is pulled together into vast repositories, to be analysed by increasingly sophisticated machine learning techniques and greater computational power: ones that can read, write and interpret text and understand context; that can identify our attitudes and emotions with improved psychographic analysis, more sophisticated recommender algorithms, all contributing to more effective profiling of us as individuals. In this context, can we really trust the social media companies to protect our personal data from theft at large scale? Then again, even when we understand the implications we may simply shrug. After all, Chinese-owned TikTok is already required to provide the regime with full access to all content users post on the platform. And this data can be used to influence what we do and who we are. Yet use of TikTok has exploded and ranks amongst the most population social media platforms amongst young people across the West.

In summary, accumulating our personal data, whether overtly, by stealth or by theft, has the goal of better profiling our behavioural habits and identities by those who want to influence us in pursuit of their own goals. It may be unsurprising, then, that hostile states show so much interest in the raw materials required to build such a capability.

In the 2016 US presidential election, agents of the Russian State bought at least 3,519 adverts on Facebook, exposing more than 11 million Americans to them.[32] These ads targeted both sides of the political spectrum and were aimed at different partisan groups: a Bernie Sanders colouring book was targeted at Sanders' Democrats; an ad from 'the Army of Jesus' showed Jesus arm-wrestling the devil with the caption: 'SATAN: IF CLINTON WINS I WIN! JESUS: NOT IF I CAN HELP IT! . . . PRESS "LIKE" TO HELP JESUS WIN'. The latter ad was very narrowly targeted and seen only by seventy-one people. It cost just over $1 and generated fourteen clicks (or 'likes' to help Jesus win) – a high hit rate of around 20 per cent. But the cost becomes less relevant the more the activity can be partly, or fully, automated.

It is not just those looking to reduce the costs of personalised propaganda or disinformation who hold a stake here. Because similar automated data collection and analysis may soon also be used to manipulate us into unwittingly providing others with access to our information technology systems. Like marketeers, hackers have previously had to choose between scale – spam and scattergun phishing campaigns, or precision – profiling a specific victim with carefully tailored 'spearphishing' attacks. This choice may no longer be necessary, because the same technological advances enable hackers to automatically tailor attacks, allowing them to be conducted with precision and at scale by email, text, voice over internet protocol and social media – as well as any other communication routes we will use in the future.

Upon us already is a whole new universe of data-producing items in our networks: our TV, fridge, boiler, doorbell, CCTV, burglar alarm, kettle, an 'internet of things' that may help others better understand how we live, who we are and how we behave. Wearable technologies already measure our pulse; virtual and augmented reality products will measure our emotional state – perhaps increasingly interpreting our thoughts and feelings wherever we go. The possibilities may seem outlandish: one evidenced claim published in the prestigious journal *Nature* is that facial recognition algorithms linked to CCTV cameras may already be able to judge our political orientation.[33]

The data collection may not stop at passive methods either. Increasingly empathetic bots may prompt us to reciprocally share our personal data in a process that legal scholar Ryan Calo describes as 'disclosure ratchetting'.[34] On the back of this, learning machines will gain our trust, wrapping around us and intervening to inform our behaviour.

It does not end online or in the home either. Our towns and cities are becoming increasingly wired with sensors. In authoritarian China, where individual privacy norms are less strict than those in liberal democracies, traffic lights have been trialled in the cities of Jinan and Shenzhen complete with facial recognition cameras. Pedestrians who cross when the lights are red are shamed by having their faces broadcast on a video screen at the side of the road, including name, address and ID number.[35]

Technologies and techniques for collecting our data, analysing it to make judgements about us and using these judgements to influence us, are becoming more and more effective. But they are in a continuous arms race against regulation designed to protect our privacy. These networked methods for influencing us depend upon powerful actors harvesting and exploiting our data, without many of us understanding how. Such fundamentally deceptive practices are core to the business models of big tech.

After all, privacy has always enabled us to avoid scrutiny by others. The weaker can use privacy norms to avoid the worst predations of the powerful. On the other hand, the powerful can also use privacy to shield themselves from scrutiny (exhibit A: how innovations such as inscrutable shell companies based in tax havens are used to hide the financial behaviour of the super-wealthy). In our time, the exploitation of our personal data undermines the privacy of the masses and tips the balance towards more powerful actors. This dynamic places us increasingly in a position in which privileged others can influence us without our consent. Which privileged others? The tech giants and those who use their services, who go about their business collecting and exploiting our data without transparency: in other words, benefiting from the privacy they have been taking from us.

A different but related dynamic is the technology-driven colonisation of our private spaces by public ones, shaping what we do and who we are – a trend easily exploited by others. When Brandon Straka watched YouTube it seemed to help change not only his behaviour but also his identity. Remember, for all of us identity is negotiated with the social environment, regardless of whether we experience it that way. Part of the promise of privacy is to act as a shield from this negotiation. The sociologist Erving Goffman highlighted two modes of behaviour. There is a public mode of 'front-stage' behaviour involving performances for others (where we focus on 'impression management' and consistency in playing the roles we think are expected of us). But there is also a privacy-protected, more intimate 'back-stage' mode in which we are more free to act and be as we please, with less worry about how we are perceived by others. It once seemed, just before the age of social media, that the internet offered us almost unlimited opportunities for anonymous living 'back-stage', that we could explore our identities in every conceivable direction. This depended on the anonymity that still persists in many online settings – forums, virtual worlds – where we can be anyone we want, partly freed from social pressures to conform.

In these settings we could experiment wittingly or unwittingly with the impressions we gave to others. And in turn these changed the social feedback received from others, altering our self-image and shaping and reinforcing these new behaviours. In virtual worlds, those using attractive avatars typically act flirtatiously and confidently. Participants with tall avatars are found to behave more assertively (regardless of how tall their user is). This is the *Proteus Effect* in action. It is an effect that carries over, influencing the ways the avatar users behave in the offline world. In an experiment, our tall avatar users, for instance, subsequently become more aggressive negotiators; when released from social and cultural constraints, our identities can sometimes seem surprisingly fluid.[36]

In contrast, by pulling our offline networks online and enabling the upload of our imagery, video footage and audio, the social media platforms push us to peg our online selves to our offline ones. Classically, we still use these spaces to self-present – to manage the impressions we project to others; after all, do we believe that anyone is as attractive as they seem on Instagram? As satisfied as they seem on Facebook? Or as militant as they appear on X? These impressions – these public performances – can get us down. As social animals we compare ourselves to others, and in contrast with the projections we see our own lives may feel mundane and grey. We start to think about ourselves in a different light as our identities shift.

As our smartphones and other sensors enable public audiences to follow us ever further into our homes and private lives, the lights come on and the curtain lifts, and once-safe back-stage areas in which we were freed from social pressure are now thrust front-stage. Under these conditions it can be easy to get carried away, caricaturing ourselves as we perform online in pursuit of a personal brand. It is a dynamic that has been fuelled by the development of engagement functions on social media platforms – with 'likes', 'shares' and 'retweets' signifying the scale of attention from others, who can bestow praise or provide negative attention with criticism and insult. The attuned operator adapts their performance to attract their key target audiences, attention often being the metric of success. Influencers often discover that it is their wildest behaviour that gains the most attention, and they start to optimise this to act as extreme self-parodies of who they were when they started.

Meet Nicholas Perry. Back in 2016 Nicholas was a teenager desperately aiming to make it big online. He pursued this goal through uploading videos of himself playing the violin, or discussing the benefits of veganism. But this did not seem to get much attention. It all changed when instead he began uploading Meokbang videos – a style imported from Korea, in which the host consumes great quantities of food while interacting with the audience. Now the size of the audience following the boy grew and grew, as those interacting with him goaded him on in the comments. Before long he was eating the entire menu range in fast-food restaurants, with the soft-spoken Nicholas rebranding himself as the loudmouth Nikocado Avocado, in the process ballooning to extreme obesity – prompting some to fear for his health.[37]

And meet Maajid Nawaz. Once a radical Islamist who called for liberal democracy to be replaced by Sharia Law, he saw the light and denounced his previous extremism, going on to found the UK-based counter-extremism think tank the Quilliam Institute. In the 2015 UK general election, the mild-mannered, centrist Liberal Democrats put him forward as their candidate in London's well-heeled Hampstead and Kilburn constituency. But during the COVID-19 pandemic Nawaz came out as an anti-vaxxer, in one interview falsely claiming that COVID-19 vaccines do not protect five- to twelve-year-olds from death or serious illness from the disease; and that by January 2022 only 17,000 had died of COVID-19 in Britain (the official record documented more than 142,000 deaths from COVID-19 in England and Wales alone).[38] He was soon sacked from his role on the feisty and wide-tent LBC radio station. His reward? A follow count on Twitter tipping over 500,000 (and the monetisation opportunities that come with it). This level of attention seemed to herald a different Maajid, one making conspiratorial claims about a new world order – involving a totalitarian world government putting an end to nation states. And not only. His feed is filled with references to Nazis, satanic rituals and the Bilderberg group (claims, by the way, that would fit well inside QAnon).[39]

Under the continuous, intense gaze of others we are incentivised to increasingly perform for them, optimising the impression we present, driven by giddy hunger for attention – as well as fear of rejection. In this kind of dark mirror the identity of the performer is refracted not through interaction with friends and loved ones but through the harsh transactional gaze of strangers. Over time the performer's identity shifts unwittingly as they increasingly see themselves through the eyes of their audiences. Through this process, to paraphrase George Orwell, we wear the mask and our face grows to fit it. Not only do influencers capture audiences, audiences can capture influencers. This has always been the case with the famous when performing in public, but now it applies more widely to the rest of us – and there are increasingly fewer places to hide.

Which brings us back to Brandon Straka. Following his 'red-pilling', Straka, previously Democrat-voting, began advocating for the Republican cause; he set up a campaign, #WalkAway, to encourage other Democrat voters to follow his political journey. As an outlier among his new friends Straka soon found himself regularly invited to talk on Fox News and other media channels.[40] Posing as a grass-roots-inspired organisation, WalkAway appeared to be funded by a handful of conservative donors. Predictably, many of the supporters of the hashtag's spread appeared to be Russian bots.[41]

Yet Straka's visibility is real, with significantly north of 500,000 Twitter followers. Since his conversion on the road to Damascus, he interviews regularly throughout the conservative media ecosystem – Fox, Newsmax and One America News – as well as with expert disinformation purveyor, the now-bankrupt InfoWars. On that continuous stage, with an addiction to audience validation, in hindsight the inevitable journey for Straka was to seize on #stopthesteal as an early entrepreneur, a journey that would lead to rabble-rousing and participation in the storming of the Capitol.

And this journey of self-radicalisation, spinning into audience-capture radicalisation, has inevitably not stopped there. In August 2022 Straka opened a Donald Trump rally in Cincinnati using the QAnon slogan 'Where we go one, we go all'.[42] Then later in the month, at the annual Conservative Political Action Conference, Straka donned an orange jumpsuit and posed as a prisoner in a cell while Trump acolyte and Georgian Congressional Representative Marjorie Taylor Greene prayed with him. Following widespread mockery of this display of messianic self-pity, Straka told his followers that those on the left were 'trying to criminalise my art'.[43] What will top that?

All very tragic. But the world is full of grifters and troubled souls. So why should we care about this type in particular? Remember Ashkar Techy and Everson Zoio, social media influencers spreading COVID-19 falsities through a shady advertising firm? Here the advertisers used the influencers as a gateway to disseminate disinformation into the target information environment, a process known as 'information-laundering'. But what is different about our audience-captured influencers is that their professed attitudes and beliefs are especially clear, telegraphed as they are through the content they transmit.

This makes them particularly easily identifiable conduits for influence. Nor are they motivated to sift through the often contradictory evidence that might allow them to make more nuanced, accurate judgements about a complex world – their allegiance is far less to facts or pursuit of the truth than to seeking the validation of their audiences. This means they can potentially be fed any information that others want to spread, and the price for them transmitting it is simply that the content aligns with the role they must perform.

Exploiting audience capture doesn't only happen online; it's just easier to identify targets through the ease of access to their internet footprint. Consciously or otherwise, major Trump cheerleader and former Fox News pundit Tucker Carlson illustrated how audience capture may work on television. 'It turns out,' he said on Fox, 'that our government has, for some time, funded biolabs in Ukraine that do, among other things, research on, yes, biological weapons. This is not a conspiracy theory. It's true.'44 But it wasn't. Like any good lie, it began with the truth: US funding for labs around the world focused on researching zoonotic pathogens, with the aim of reducing the types of epidemiological risk the world witnessed during the COVID-19 pandemic. But there is no evidence that this involved biological weapons – nor any clear motive why the United States would be funding such work abroad.

On the other hand, there is an identifiable source for these claims. In January 2020 a Russian-language Telegram account claimed that in Ukraine a 'full-fledged network of biological laboratories has been deployed'. By May the Russian newspaper *Izvestia* repeated the claim, and it appears to have been built on by an adviser to President Putin, who maintained that the United States was funding biolabs up and down the borders of Russia and China. Lo and behind, these accusations later popped up in a similar (unevidenced) format in the Chinese-regime mouthpiece the *Global Times*.45 And then what happened? You may not be too surprised to hear by now that the claims soon surfaced in a US-based Twitter account that regularly shared QAnon conspiracy material. From there they took a journey through the right-wing propaganda ecosystem all the way to Tucker Carlson – incentivised, in front of his key audience, to spread the lies of authoritarians for them. Naturally, such clips then found themselves replayed on Russian media channels, laundering information in a way that appeared to provide independent external validation (triangulation) of fictions generated by the Russian State.[46]

Note that the relationship between the audience-captured and their apparent beliefs can be complex. Does Tucker Carlson really believe all the nonsense he says? A lawsuit against Fox News taken out by election-counting equipment manufacturer Dominion sheds some light here. Carlson has repeatedly voiced claims that the 2020 US presidential election was stolen. But in private it turns out he 'agreed that there was not enough fraud to change the outcome'. But he also reckoned 'our viewers are good people, and they believe it'. Which is presumably why he continues to feed them lies. It seems this dynamic is also representative of Fox News more generally, with those Fox reporters attempting to report on the facts being attacked internally by anchors like Carlson: 'We devote our lives to building an audience and they let [*Fox News Sunday* host] Chris Wallace and [correspondent and anchor] Leland f------ Vittert wreck it.' As broadcasters and other influencers become increasingly less committed to transmitting their best understanding of the facts, they make themselves increasingly attractive for exploitation.

Digital means, however, subject many more of us to such processes – bringing the public sphere into our homes, putting us on stage more often and reducing the chance for respite from the public gaze and the performance it requires. More than this, is the peril for all of us, of being captured by the audiences we want to impress: a dynamic we can see for ourselves when those around us spend hours on X, Instagram or TikTok.

In our age of big data the individual thoughts, beliefs and dispositions that comprise our identities can be increasingly exploited by cynical commercial and political actors to silo our thinking and take us where they want us. This dramatically undermines the protections of privacy we have against the depredations of the strong. From here our ability to safeguard our collective interest becomes frustrated – we are increasingly segregated without quite understanding how; from here it is easier for us to become divided and conquered. At the same time, the demands of technology-driven social life increasingly make public spheres intrude upon our private ones. Here we are incentivised to perform for others, perhaps becoming captured by them. From here we have become attractive routes for information-laundering – witting or unwitting vectors for the deceitful schemes of others.

What can we do? We must empower ourselves. *Become a privacy watchkeeper.* We can start by taking our data protection seriously in order to safeguard ourselves from identity manipulation. Assume nothing you do online is completely private. Consider your digital footprints: what can we find out about ourselves online? What does the information we provide to others enable them to judge about us – as well as those we are connected to? We can review the privacy settings on all our online accounts – especially our social media ones. Be discerning about providing any of the 'about me' information. Take a dig through the Facebook advertising settings. We might be surprised that they already know we are a Trekkie, a Furry or a Brony; that we are major fans of tiddlywinks and like reading popular-science books. Definitely pay attention to your cyber security, to reduce the chances of having your personal data stolen – with stronger passwords, multi-factor authentication and a 'virtual private network' to hide your activity from prying eyes. Purge all unnecessary apps (consider using your browser instead of an app where possible) and switch off any automatic data-sharing – unless for some reason it is important to you.

We can also be more wary when we give our data away. Consider whether you really want to enter your personal details into that online competition to win a house in the Cotswolds or a villa in Marbella. Other habits may be more tricky to build: are we able and can we be bothered to block search engines from tracking us? Perhaps use alternatives that guarantee no tracking at all. What about refusing to click 'yes' on tracking cookie consent forms? It is often made deliberately time-consuming not to. What about downloading an ad blocker to stop microtargeted content (or any other ad for that matter) getting through to us? Again, there's a resource cost at the least. In the extreme, we can deliberately curate our social media accounts or search records with false content to distort the accuracy of their profiling . . . But really? Life is short.

The debate over privacy in liberal democracies has long focused on protecting our personal data from overbearing governments. Yet this has often missed the more worrying development that organisations less accountable to us – tech companies and foreign governments – have been in the vanguard of finding ways to collect and exploit our data. In this light, allowing government bodies to hold our personal information and use it to deliver increasingly efficient public services is likely worthwhile – if we believe they can keep it secure. We can be clear-eyed about the potential benefits of data-sharing; perhaps nowhere could this be more important than in allowing healthcare providers to use our data to improve medical care. Machine learning techniques applied to our data in this kind of setting may revolutionise our healthcare for the better – but only if that data is sufficiently well protected. There are balances to be found in our networked world – and we should help find them (which means upskilling ourselves first). Support organisations like Privacy International and Open Rights Group, which influence government and media pushback against the perception that systematic privacy intrusion is inevitable. And vote for elected representatives who demonstrate a commitment to privacy – those who will take steps to pull the rugs from under the ecosystem of advertisers, data brokers and tech companies that together conduct what social scientist Shoshana Zuboff and others call 'surveillance capitalism'.[47]

We can build our networks for greater informational resilience; connecting to those who do not think like us, especially, enables us to see the world anew. But more than this, the information they provide gives us another means by which we can triangulate and scrutinise our information environments, allowing us to avoid being pigeonholed and sliding into echo chambers or rabbit holes. We can better control the relationships between who we are in public and in our private lives. We are social animals, but individuals too, with our own capacity for thinking, learning and determining our destinies. In the digital age, the question 'Who am I?' is more inseparable than ever from the question 'Who decides?' Let's resist letting others define us by giving ourselves private space to reflect on who we are and what we want. Let's keep control of our individual freedom of thought and expression; where we build a personal brand, we should ask ourselves whether it truly aligns with our own attitudes, beliefs and identities – that self-image we wish to nurture and control. Is this who we want to be? What is the legacy we wish to leave?

Let's respect others, respect ourselves. A starting point is to have a well-developed sense of humour about the tension between our private thoughts and feelings and the very understandable desire to be validated in public, including on social media.

10. The Play

In December 1991 the Soviet Union collapsed. In the major rump state, Russia, candidates soon stood for office and elections were held. But it was a wretched time. Over the 1990s life expectancy plummeted, death by drink and suicide skyrocketed. The country's assets were stripped and thieved by rapacious opportunists. The President overseeing all this mess had to be escorted by aides in public appearances in a futile attempt to cover his chronic drunkenness. What was the story that held everyone together? But then things seemed to look up. A smart and sober new leader came to power with the aim 'Make Russia Great Again', aligning with, and fuelling, shared feelings and beliefs among domestic audiences about the woeful decline of their society and a future that seemed to have been stolen – but by whom? It was in this environment that political entrepreneurs would pin the blame for these very real issues on the machinations of outsiders.

Through credibly demonstrating the threat of coercion (an early example being the imprisonment and exile of oligarch, media magnate and adviser to the former president, Mikhail Khordorkovsky, and the dismantling of his economic empire), this leader soon tamed and co-opted rivals among the economic chieftains, organised crime lords and leaders of the State security apparatus, classes that were not as distinct from one another as they might seem. Sat atop a new hierarchy, he possessed unparalleled domestic power.

Control of the military, security and justice systems provided Vladimir Vladimirovich Putin, former KGB bureaucrat, with the instruments of coercion. The promise of restoring Russia's great power status and the promotion of traditional beliefs and behaviours helped harness the group egocentric biases of the citizens to gain him over-whelming expert and legitimate power. Through such policies, Putin, an atheist who divorced his wife to shack up with a gymnast, could easily enlist traditional authorities like the Orthodox Church to pose as the moral saviour of Russia from the degenerative influence of the West. Through his co-option of the previously unruly economic elite, who were soon put in their place, he had access to Russia's immense natural resources and associated industrial base: an immense power to reward that would continue to keep the elites co-opted and the masses provided with just enough to make them compliant. Throughout, Putin's used his true expertise in understanding and balancing different domestic factions to play them off against one another, on the one hand positioning himself as the keystone of a fractious and delicate elite power system, and on the other as the serious and benevolent saviour of a supposedly great people brought to their knees by internal grifters and malevolent outsiders.

And then there was informational power. The owners of inde-pendent traditional media were swiftly brought to heel and under State control. This included, first and foremost, television, which was now exploited to feed Russians an attractive diet of what Peter Pomerantsev describes as 'reality TV and authoritarianism to keep the great, 140 million strong population entertained, distracted, constantly exposed to geopolitical nightmares that if repeated enough times can become infectious'.[1] The internet, meanwhile, could largely be left alone. That way calls to mobilise against autocratic tendencies could be headed off. Agitators, mostly in the cities, would be free to seek out whatever content they pleased. And the elections continued, providing legitimate power in an age in which democracies seemed to represent the 'end of history'.[2] Sure, winning them in favour of the ruling party might need a nudge here and there from allies in order to cross the line, but support from the elites and the masses was not in doubt. This form of government is known, by the way, as electoral authoritarianism.

But in the end all regimes eventually fail to meet the aspirations of the population. In the absence of real electoral choice, there is usually only one direction of travel. The heavily regime-controlled 2011 presi-dential elections led to widespread street protests. The leader's seemingly iron grip suddenly appeared questionable. Perhaps Russia would succumb to a 'colour revolution,' aiming to install liberal democracy similar to those that had occurred in other states of the former Soviet Union. But this did not happen in Russia – it turned out the regime had effectively coup-proofed itself, using the economic rents and nationalist propaganda to keep the elites united and the opposition co-opted and suppressed.

Instead a series of these colour revolutions unfolded in neighbouring Ukraine, where finally, in 2014, those yearning for a more democratic future ousted the corrupt pro-Russian leader following mass protest and regime violence. In response, the Russian leader ordered his troops into Ukrainian Crimea, and supported proxy forces attempting to seize the Ukrainian provinces of Luhansk and Donetsk – labelling Ukraine the 'anti-Russia', which indeed through its very example it seemed to have become.

Such ambitious activity, however, had to be supported in the information environment – not least to whip up and maintain support at home, demoralise the enemy and keep public opinion elsewhere, in the Western liberal democracies especially, demobilised. The free internet, it turned out, had its uses. Such an anarchic environment rapidly bred innovation and skills. As the 'little green men' of the Russian military tore across Crimea, they were supported not only by traditional means of communicating – official State channels, as well as through State-controlled television and radio – but also by new online capabilities: by hackers obtaining data and selectively leaking it into the attention spaces of others; by troll armies that could flood the zone with shit and help trash the information environment.

By 2022, when Russia launched a full-scale invasion of Ukraine, the Russian regime no longer pretended to be a democracy. As troops came home in zinc-lined coffins, the remaining independent media outlets were closed down, their journalists fleeing abroad or ending up in jail. Protestors too faced prison, many just for speaking of the 'special military operation' in Ukraine as the obvious development that it was: a war. It was unclear in what ways any of this was going to make Russia great again. Yet perception is what counts. And the regime was in the midst of taking absolute control of the levers of informational power, ready to dominate the information environment and attempt to shape the perceptions of its key audiences.

As different from ours as it may seem, Russia's recent journey illustrates what is at stake for liberal democracy. Can we see in it our future? The digital age has wrought fundamental change in how we access and connect with others; how we use our social networks to harness and exploit information – in the nature of informational power. Such change influences in turn the wider face of power – how it is expressed, who is empowered and who is impacted. On the one hand, the huge expansion of access to the minds of others potentially increases everyone's informational power. Yet on the other, those best placed to exploit augmented informational power are those who are already powerful – as we will see. There are winners, such as the Silicon Valley-based tech platforms and those who own them, and apparent losers – not least liberal democracies, which are now locked in informational combat with a range of authoritarian competitors; the consequences for our social and political hierarchies are uncertain, but likely radical.

How did we get here? As we have seen, in the scheme of things, the digital information revolution is just one more in an increasingly accelerating trend. The democratic power of speech and language enabled our prehistoric ancestors to ally together to restrain the worst impulses of coercive brutes. Writing, in contrast, supported a new way for tyrants to escape the restrictions of others as they used it to transmit legitimating propaganda. Only much later did this revolution begin to be turned on its head, as moveable type unleashed the redistributive power of writing. The revolution shook the prevailing hierarchies of power and status to their core in ways that resonate in our time.

In 1517, the dissident priest Martin Luther sent a deeply critical ninety-five theses to the Archbishop of Mainz – and before long he was taking advantage of the printing innovation of moveable type to mass-produce a Bible that the literate could consume without the meddling mediation of Church authorities. In response, the Holy Roman Emperor Charles V condemned Luther and banned his works at the 1521 Diet of Worms. But this loss of information dominance by the traditional authorities of Church and feudal aristocracy had a broader impact on the hierarchy, raising questions among elites and laypeople about whom should be trusted and listened to; who really counted as an expert or legitimate authority, and in consequence, who could rightfully wield tools of coercion and violence or levers of reward – including the right to tax the citizenry and decide where to spend the money.

The jostling for power and position under these new circumstances had anarchic consequences – similar in spirit to those that typically happen during challenges within chimpanzee hierarchies. In the German town of Münster, in 1534 radical Anabaptist pamphleteers were using the new tools of information dissemination unencumbered by the traditional authorities. Their message soon captured the hearts and minds of large segments of the local population. Drawing on these new adherents, the Anabaptist leadership took over the town, turfing out Lutheran Protestants and Catholics alike – all the while drawing in converts to their cause from far and wide. The estates of those expelled were redistributed and soon it was proclaimed that all property would be held in common. It took some time before the weakened authorities could respond. Yet eventually the expelled Catholic bishop returned with an army at his side, besieging the city, finally reconquering it and dispersing the Anabaptists – relieving their unfortunate leaders of their heads.

The rebellion in Munster was a sign of the times, in which Protestants and Catholics published libels against each other. Dissidents used their presses to sling mud at other dissidents. Breakaway Churches attempted to gain more followers and disrupt and defeat competitors. Communities were sundered and violent conflict broke out between rival groups. All this seemed to signpost Plato's warning: that without censorship and propaganda from the authorities to cohere and manage the citizens, there would be anarchy.

The princes of the Holy Roman Empire by now headed divergent religious communities. They took sides, empowering themselves at the expense of the declining imperial centre. Before long, a group of Protestant aristocrats took arms against the Emperor and the vestiges of central authority. They lost, yet military force alone could not contain subversive ideas. At the Peace of Augsburg in 1555, the right of the princes to choose the religion of their states was enshrined. Over the coming decades, though, divisions would weaken and degrade the Holy Roman Empire, the epitome of medieval European Christendom. In turn this created openings for external intervention – by the Dutch Republic,

Sweden, Denmark, France and Spain – in the Thirty Years' War (1618–48). The Emperor lost, and in the subsequent Peace of Westphalia his centralised power was dispersed forever.

For the masses too the war had been an unmitigated disaster. Over this period a fifth of the German peasantry were wiped out by rampaging armies and the starvation and disease that followed – up to half in the worst-affected areas. But there were winners, such as local secular and spiritual leaders, now free to push their own stories and interests, as well as the provincial princes. And, last but not least, were powers like France and Sweden, who had meddled in the affairs of the sprawling empire from outside to their lasting benefit.

In our time digital technologies have also unleashed a revolution. Will their impact on our societies be similar to the effect the printing press had on the societies of medieval Europe? We can't know just yet. We may only be living in the foothills of this revolution, whose consequences will play out over the coming years and decades. But we can identify some of the factors that will determine how the future unfolds. Because at the core of this revolution are tools that are dramatically expanding reach and access to the minds of others, at reduced cost. In our time, digital technologies greatly enhance the potential for each of us to act as information gatekeepers; every one of us can flex our informational power – our ability to control distribution of information content to others – helping determine what content spreads between minds and changes them, as well as what does not.

Let's break it down, because our informational power is intimately connected to other forms of power. Imagine that you have children and the school they go to has just instituted a controversial change to the curriculum in relation to an aspect of sex education or national history (take your pick) that you care about deeply. The school leadership are not at all interested and dismiss your polite requests to discuss the problem out of hand. So you set up social media pages on the topic, and soon find you are not alone. Through these means you draw others to the cause, creating a network that soon balloons into the offline world; the message is transmitted by word of mouth at pick-up time and proliferates through coffee mornings.

You now transmit information across this expanding network to flaunt your knowledge of parental work patterns and instances of school leadership intransigence – increasing the perception among others that you know what you are doing, that you have some kind of expertise here, *expert power*. Through repeatedly mentioning a brief, but apparently colourful, stint you once had on the school governing board you establish your legitimacy – your *legitimate power* (remember: in terms of influence, expertise and legitimacy are in the eye of the beholder). You reach over the heads of current information gate-keepers such as the self-proclaimed pillars of community still on the governing board, who are left whistling in the wind.

It starts spiralling a little out of control; after all, you're invested now. You cultivate this emerging network further, rewarding voices that agree with you with validation, using likes or comments; this *reward power* acts as a form of patronage, helping us to cement recip-rocal and trusted relationships and expand our social networks. Comments, by the way, require greater investment and are therefore understood to represent a larger reward. On the other hand, when some in the network start questioning your approach you can withdraw such patronage to signal your displeasure.

You sit at the centre of this emerging network, attracting others with your charm, charisma and the engaging content you produce – you are using your *referent power* to build and bind others to you. You move into other areas of local organisation, launching campaigns relating to the limitations of the local recycling facilities and the algae that has started to bloom in the nearby lake. Over time you increase your trusted social network well beyond the limits to your offline social capabilities to nurture a couple of hundred human relationships. Your large networks now generate cascade effects of their own: the more people you are connected to, the more others may want to connect to you. In this fashion you can construct a position as a network hub among others' spokes – or, even better, an elite hub among hubs seated in the densest core of the network. You now not only emanate prestige, but have an advanced network of trust at your fingertips to be nudged and prompted to your advantage.

But there is more: because you're enabled by all these other levers, you can also wield great coercive power if you have the stomach and lack of restraint for it. When others question your authority or criti-cise your methods you can unleash *ad hominem* – or personal – attacks on them with little fear of immediate physical retaliation. When the school authorities continue to deny you your goals, you can use informational power to discredit them, transmitting damaging rumours or harassing them by releasing their private information and personal details into the network – or *doxing* them. Of course, this nefarious turn may cause you reputational damage among your in-group of allies; it may be less costly for you among the other parents if you only do it rarely. Or if you can distance yourself from this sleazy side of things. Why not create a few *sockpuppet* accounts to do the dirty business instead?

But when we direct our efforts at distrusted or despised outsiders, why bother hiding? At the political level in our time of fragmenting identities and warring tribes, many have lost the incentive. It becomes rational to double down and let everyone – our friends and our enemies – know we are not to be messed with; that we have the in-group's back as we, like Donald Trump's former strategist Steve Bannon, help 'flood the zone with shit'; as we bandwagon with others to malevolently 'shitpost' memes; as we *brigade* our allies, and encourage them to *flood* the pages and profiles of our enemies with negative comments and reviews; as we help push the *mass reporting* of complaints about someone to a platform administrator; organise a *ratioing* to ensure a post gets more replies than retweets or likes as an indicator of community disapproval; or disruptively *sealion* debates with targeted comments – repetitively injecting emotive questions that do not follow the flow of any existing conversation ('Why don't you want to talk about Palestine?' or 'What rights don't trans people have?'). We can help push these into the real world too – into telephone calls and campaigns of targeted letter-writing. If we are powerful enough we may even be able to force people off social media, purging their voices completely from these online information environments.

In this context the digital age lures us with visions of bottom-up expressions of power. Take the problem of sexual harassment, which has long been endured by women especially. As recently as the 1990s, attempts to address the issue led to dismissive responses, as legal scholar Deborah Rhode describes: 'Women subjected to unwelcome sexual contact and overtures were told that they should be "flattered". Complainants were often dismissed as unstable, humorless whiners who were overreacting or fabricating misconduct or assassinated as "a little bit nutty and a little bit slutty".[3]

But then came the informational power of our time. In 2016, in a foretaste of what was to come, former Uber employee Susan Fowler released a blog post about her 'very, very strange' year at Uber, one in which she was sexually propositioned by her line manager via a string of unsolicited messages on her first day on the team. Her reporting to human resources led nowhere, especially as this was her high-performing line manager's 'first offence'. She later met other women around the company and realised that several of them had had exactly the same experience with the same line manager, and been similarly fobbed off by human resources upon complaining.[4] Yet in stark contrast to her attempts to get a hearing from within, the link to her blog post went viral on Twitter – eventually helping to precipitate the resignation of CEO Travis Kalanick and the firing of twenty other senior employees.

Similarly, in the immediate aftermath of the sacking of the powerful and chronically abusive Hollywood mogul Harvey Weinstein by his own production company, actor Alyssa Milano retweeted the message: 'If all the women who have been sexually harassed or assaulted wrote "Me too" as a status, we might give people a sense of the magnitude of the problem.' By the following morning more than 30,000 people had shared the message. Within days millions of women (and some men) were using social media to disclose the harassment and abuse they had experienced in their lives, alongside the #MeToo. As this movement expanded a wave of other disgraced business executives, political candidates and other public figures soon followed Weinstein's ignominious fate. Those sharing their experiences, were – as Monica Lewinsky noted – welcomed into the tribe. Wary of being shunned, demeaned, demoted or fired, women might once have quietly shared one-to-one information about potential offenders with others. Now digital-age connectivity and rapidly shifting norms meant that information could be rapidly shared on social media 'whisper' networks. Those outed and denounced as abusers might be more likely to lose their jobs, go to prison and otherwise suffer severe reputational damage.

On the other hand, whether #MeToo has really helped precipitate a lasting norms cascade – when a sudden and lasting shift to new norms of accepted behaviour occurs – remains to be seen. Nor have any outcomes been driven quite as democratically as might first appear. Let's introduce more elements to the story.

In 2015 actor Ashley Judd gave an interview to *Variety* in which she claimed harassment by an unnamed Hollywood producer. Two years later she went on record in an interview with the *New York Times* journalists Jodi Kantor and Megan Twohey. The perpetrator, she said, was Harvey Weinstein. In her later defamation suit against him, Judd stated that she believed that the lies Weinstein spread about her after she rejected his advances had damaged her career. This demonstrated how powerful individuals like Weinstein could easily utilise their reward and referent power to build networks and co-opt allies, then use this as informational power to coerce and silence others.

Less than a week afterwards, the *New Yorker* ran another story on Weinstein carrying credible allegations from thirteen different women. A week after that, Alyssa Milano released the tweet which went viral. The role of traditional media in breaking these stories had been key to hugely augmenting the #MeToo movement. As was the influence of those who could cash in their immense connective referent power to boost informational power: celebrities like actors Reese Witherspoon and Jennifer Lawrence, Salma Hayek, Gwyneth Paltrow and Angelina Jolie, the singers Lady Gaga and Bjork and the decorated gymnast Simone Byles. In the digital age, stories in the traditional media acted as triggers, precipitating cascade effects among social media users: that bottom-up dynamic of disclosure, discussion and denunciation encouraged powerful allies to flex their muscles in service to the cause, sustaining, even augmenting these cascade effects and – in turn – incentivising further investigation and release of traditional media stories about powerful abusers, which . . . well you get the idea.

This illustrates a general trend. Our enhanced informational power does not, in fact, necessarily elevate us all to the heights of power more widely. Whether for a good cause or a bad one, our ability to create, transmit and block content is instead easily co-opted and harnessed by others. By who? Those who hold one thing in common: the ability to exploit our newfound informational power through the application of greater power. In other words, those who stood to benefit from the information revolution were typically already powerful actors. But benefit in relation to whom? After all, in every revolution there are winners and losers.

Among the most obvious winners of the information age are the trendmakers, nouveau celebrities, experts and other assorted pundits or influencers who have built an online following for themselves, sometimes with minimal support from more traditional gatekeepers of influence. Those who created and provide the infrastructure on which these influencers built their success have reached another level of victory altogether. The leaders of the giant tech platforms, being the mediators of all this newfound informational power, are the emperors of the digital age and the implementation of their policies can have a dramatic effect on what enters our information environment, captures our attention, drills into our memory, stimulates our emotion and draws on our ego; it has a large impact on whom we engage with, bond with and trust; on what thoughts, beliefs and actions we share with others; who it is we think we are and how this should make us behave; and how we are organised into hierarchies of status and power.

Take Google, increasingly our most intimate partner as it responds to more than 8 billion searches a day. Google's capabilities are crucial to the plumbing of information environments – the creation and implementation of company policies hugely impacts our collective understanding and the structure of our politics. In the 2014 elections to the Indian parliament (the Lok Sabha), the researcher Robert Epstein and his team showed that the ranking of candidates in Google searches could boost the proportion of people favouring them by 20 per cent – and up to 60 per cent in some demographic groups.[5] In other words, it is not just that the clash of policy ideas increasingly plays second fiddle to tribe-building and denigration of the opposition. The success of a political candidate may be significantly influenced by how Google's search algorithms prioritise them in the attention space of others. Search engines like Google have the power to frame both the message and the messenger for the citizens of liberal democracies – as Epstein noted, this is even more likely to be the case in any jurisdiction where search is dominated by a single search engine (like Google). The temptation in this situation can be for the search engine to deliberately structure our reality in order to suit those it favours – a new form of reward power. The main Chinese search engine, Baidu, is perennially accused of abusing its expert power, stuffing search returns with links bought by the highest bidder and the Chinese Communist Party.[6]

Let's take another platform. How about X, the platform formerly known as Twitter? A public town square bringing together and brokering diverse views it is not. Its owner, Elon Musk, is a self-described 'free-speech fundamentalist' – one who does not seem to mind that the norms that temper free speech in a reasonably harmonious community are nowhere to be seen on his platform. Indeed, since Musk took over, even the synthetic sticking plasters have fallen away: he laid off most of the workers focused on content moderation and inauthentic activity and allowed suspended disinformation grifters to jump back on to pick up where they left off. Yet X still plays a key role in information-sharing among communities of specialists – as well as opinion-forming among the elites of different tribes. In this way X's relatively small user base is deceptive: the platform plays a major role in agenda-framing – setting the items and terms of public debate which may then avalanche into public discourse. X's policies also play a significant role in shaping our understanding: they determine which voices we recognise and hear. The informational power wielded by Musk upon picking up his new toy was demonstrated early by his reversal of the decision to suspend Donald Trump after the former president's role in the events of 6 January 2021. X played a decisive role in Trump's political career – all the way to planning and coordinating the events of that fateful January.

Meanwhile, the far-right former Brazilian president Jair Bolsonaro called Musk's acquisition of Twitter 'a breath of hope'. His supporters then saturated the content with pro-insurrectionary content without much constraint, and then mobbed the Brazilian Congress in mimicry of 6 January, with Steve Bannon proclaiming the Brazilian election too, had been 'stolen'. Here in Brazil too, Musk had – in the words of journalist Charlotte Peet – made Twitter a 'safe space' for right-wing extremists.[7] Musk stripped the platform of the resources it would need to deal with disinformation and manipulation, rescinding the verification system which provided a modicum of authentication of other users' identities.[8] A European Commission study later found that these changes later enabled the spread of Russian propaganda all over Europe.[9]

When it came to Musk's own proclamations, it turned out that not enough people were engaging. So he had his engineers tweak the algorithms so that his tweets would benefit from a previously unheard of promotion to the entire Twitter user base;[10] a menu that included promoting conspiracy theories – such as the attempted assassination of Paul Pelosi, husband of then-US House of Representatives majority Leader Nancy Pelosi;[11] in another case, a tweet from a pro-Kremlin account quoted an obscure Turkish news site to claim a large number of NATO forces dead in Ukraine (a claim that was rapidly debunked). To this Musk responded, 'a tragic loss of life', in the process amplifying disinformation.[12] Public-service broadcasters such as the BBC were branded with the same 'State-affiliated media' label as regime mouth-pieces from Russia, China and Iran; and in the absence of moderators, and with inauthentic activity monitors, these same authoritarian-regime media outlets, by the way, showed a sudden huge upswing in their follower count.[13] In summary, the personal interests of this single wealthy megalomaniac deeply influence the structures of our democratic information environment and directly and indirectly shape our information diets. Do we want this to be how things work?

China-based TikTok is – like other social media platforms – plagued by misinformation. The company announced far-reaching election-protecting policies. But these have been characterised by haphazard enforcement. In one example, the company banned 2020 US presidential election-denying searches for content on 'election fraud', yet did nothing to block searches for 'ballot-trafficking', which had collectively attracted millions of misinformation video views.[14]

Then there is Facebook, the platform which founder Mark Zuckerberg claims is 'connecting the world'. It is not only connecting the world, but remaking it. Through its news feeds it helps directly determine how users understand reality; and through its individual and group recommendations, whom we are connected to – connections which, through the content they will share with us, will indirectly affect how we see things. As Shoshona Zuboff says: 'Facebook learns it can predictably move the societal dial on voting patterns, emotional states, or anything else that it chooses'.[15]

But Facebook is no beneficent power. Its association with unfortunate unintended social consequences is becoming legendary. It has enabled dangerous informational power entrepreneurs, not just in the United States but in just about every jurisdiction where it operates. In Honduras, Facebook took nine months from the first complaints to start removing coordinated inauthenticity in support of President Juan Orlando Hernández of Honduras; in Azerbaijan, Facebook turned a blind eye as the ruling party used inauthentic tactics to harass the opposition. From 2017, Facebook provided no safeguards when Buddhist fanatics cascaded disinformation and hate speech against Rohingya Muslim minorities in Burma, helping escalate the country's religious conflict into full-blown genocide. In 2018, the platform enabled deadly anti-Muslim riots in Sri Lanka: it had employed a grand total of two employees to moderate the posts of more than 4 million users in the country. From 2021, Facebook stands accused of fuelling the violence of the Ethiopian civil war – with claims that the recommender algorithms encouraged the sharing of hate-filled posts.

Meta is so powerful it seems to have escaped the reach of liberal-democratic social norms to become immune to efforts to shame it. Its response to being caught out after making messes, are a study in subversion. When Facebook's internal teams discovered evidence that its algorithms helped isolated and angry young men self-radicalise, its leadership suppressed and denied it. When Congressional investigators identified that posts on Facebook from covert arms of the Russian State reached an estimated 120 million Americans in the 2016 US presidential election, Mark Zuckerberg dismissed the claims as 'crazy'.[16] In a pattern that has become predictable, once the evidence became too overwhelming to ignore, Facebook eventually apologised and stressed the learning journey it had come along, how it had changed the algorithms that the public still had no access to. Facebook continuously denies civil society representatives the opportunity to investigate what is happening within the black box. Top Meta executives refuse to consider overhauling their core algorithms because doing so may reduce user session time and decrease engagement: in other words, protecting us will cut their profits. Instead they wheel out former UK deputy prime minister Nick Clegg, who will state that engagement is about giving the people what they want. By this measure what they want turns out to be far-right content – because, and again according to Facebook's own internal subsequently suppressed research, this appears to be most viewed on the platform.[17]

Meta set up an oversight board to adjudicate difficult policy decisions. But this isn't power to the public. Nor does it change Facebook's fundamental business model. In sum, the policies and algorithms of the tech giants don't just help us and explain our social reality – they change and influence it. Just as junk food impacts upon our health, models optimising for engagement often end up feeding us diets of junk information that amplify our worst tendencies. As a by-product of overwhelming informational power deployed in this fashion, Google (including Google-owned YouTube), X, Facebook and others all stand accused of undermining privacy; applying algorithms that entrench existing racial and social inequalities; and amplifying hate speech, conspiracy theories and disinformation. How can we measure whether their content safeguards individual or social wellbeing – or that of an open society more generally? We do not know, because the algorithms are the proprietary property of the platform – black boxes as far as the public is concerned, ones that we try to nudge and commandeer in pursuit of our goals, often in vain.

Our hunter-gatherer forebears may have believed that they were being surveilled by rocks and trees. Our monotheistic religions tell us there is an omniscient, omnipresent God. And yet many of us are unaware of or unbothered by the extent of the surveillance we are exposed to on the internet: surveillance which, unlike that of animist, poly- or monotheistic gods, can make little claim to be helping our individual or collective wellbeing. The platforms go to great lengths to play down their often phenomenal surveillance abilities – a truly expert power. Instead, they will talk as though their algorithms somehow just fell from above. As though negative consequences are somehow unconnected to the deliberate designs of human engineers.

Another set of winners appears to be those actors with the ability and the motive to leverage the possibilities the platforms provide, integrating them within traditional means of influence. With the money and the motivation, demagogues and political entrepreneurs can complement their overt communications by drawing on whole submerged infrastructures for covert transmissions, curating armies of sockpuppets and bots to infiltrate established networks. From these they can nudge or co-opt the authentic informational power of others, seeding, framing and astroturfing both true and false ideas through repetitive messaging with a cast of both real and synthetic people, some of whom are directed to discredit, dox or threaten those who challenge them. 'Like a bee swarm', says law professor Danielle Citron, an expert on cyber harassment, 'you have a thousand bee stings. Each sting is painful. But it's perceived as one awful, throbbing, giant mass.'[18]

Most importantly – like the Russian State muddying the waters after the takedown of MH17 by its proxy forces, or Donald Trump denying the election result – such a swarm can be guided to create and amplify information content to change our perception of reality by *event ghosting* – blending disparate beliefs or events with other information, hijacking memes and hashtags and bandwagoning favoured content on the back of other fast-spreading ideas, thus creating disinformation that casts doubt and confuses, encourages key audiences to fall back on things they believe already, and inoculates them against the claims of the competition – and in the process disrupting adversaries and providing succour to allies.

The swarm can be steered, too, alongside other elements of the information arsenal: allies working in the shadows or in broad daylight – including wealthy ones who can use their resources even within liberal democracies, silencing unwanted voices such as those of journalists through legal threats and defamation cases; agents of influence across government and public services, business, media and academia, recruited in order to access and co-opt their trusted networks (further augmenting the swarm); and hackers, who steal private data from designated targets and (as with doxing) dump this information on the web in order to gain media attention and spark avalanches that embarrass, humiliate and cast specific actors (like politicians) in a negative light in front of key audiences (like prospective voters). Here the swarm can help amplify these so-called 'hack and leak' operations – virally spreading the hacked content across networks, adulterating it as they go. The swarm can even be directed against physical infrastructure – used to choke off internet exchange points with Dedicated Denial of Service (DDoS) attacks or to swamp targets with spam or phishing emails.

Small wonder that some of the biggest losers in all this newly augmented informational power seems to be liberal democracies. Unlike autocracies, which use coercion to compel the behaviours of their subjects, liberal democracy depends on citizens accepting and internalising shared norms. In turn, as social psychologist Jonathan Haidt states, this depends upon the continued sustenance of three interlocking pillars: social capital – dense, high-trust social networks; strong institutions; and shared stories. As informational power reformulates us into warring tribes and atomised radicals, our own informational abilities are unleashed only to be harnessed by others and directed against all three of these pillars. Some will always want an alpha to come and shield us from chaos – the question is how many of the rest of us agree. Like the Holy Roman Empire, our societies appear to be in inexorable decay, destined to be torn apart and pilfered for spoils by the new winners of the information age.

There's worse. Informational power enables some actors to disrupt and destroy liberal democracy, but the power of big tech is extremely lopsided; they are giants with clay feet, with enormous informational power and a deficit of public legitimate power, which creates a further huge vulnerability for open societies as it is exploited and leveraged by partisan actors. In the United States, Republican leaders claimed after their 2018 mid-term Congressional election wipeouts that the algorithms of Facebook, Twitter and YouTube were biased against conservative content. Work by New York University law professor Paul Barrett and research fellow Grant Sims comprehensively debunks these claims – noting that they are in themselves simply another manifestation of disinformation.[19] But to forestall political power making good on threats to clip their wings, the tech giants are incentivised to pander, treading lightly, for instance, when Republican-aligned disinformation subsequently floods their platforms.[20] Or when a more legitimate-seeming actor makes similar claims, for that matter.

When the Vietnamese Communist regime demanded that Facebook censor the content of the opposition, Facebook complied with little opposition. On the other hand, in India, ruling party politician T. Raja Singh claimed that Muslims were traitors, threatened to raze mosques, and called for Rohingya Muslim immigrants to be shot. Facebook declined to censor his incendiary language, which it described as 'free speech'. After all, it did not want to jeopardise its expansion plans for the subcontinent by picking a fight with Modi's regime.[21] In 2022, in the midst of a farmers' protest in India, the ruling party lobbied for more than 500 accounts to be blocked or made invisible – threatening Twitter employees with jail if they did not do so. Twitter complied.[22] Untethered from any significant intrusive public oversight, the informational power of the tech companies is vulnerable to hijack by others who will use their tools to help reward allies, co-opt the competition, and coerce adversaries and other unwanted voices.

Let's return to Twitter. Under its new ownership by Elon Musk (the free-speech fundamentalist, remember), the number of anti-democratic content takedown requests Twitter has complied with has proliferated;[23] this included the removal of opposition tweets just before the closely fought 2023 Turkish elections following demands from the increasingly autocratic ruling Justice and Development Party.[24] Musk also runs the electric vehicle company Tesla. Tesla has invested billions in building its operations in China, where the Chinese Communist Party has repeatedly requested that the 'State-affiliated media' label affixed to its approved journalists be removed – a label supposed to help users think more carefully about the trustworthiness of the source. The Chinese State has been identified by Twitter as running increasingly inauthentic operations to interfere in democratic elections recently too. Are they lobbying behind the scenes for Musk to stop looking for these? We do not know. But we can certainly see that the owner of part of the key infrastructure of the liberal-democratic information environment has recently been parroting Chinese State talking points related to the future of the thriving liberal democracy of Taiwan, which Beijing regards as a renegade province.[25]

It's clear what the Chinese State expects. When Musk tweeted to discuss the Chinese 'lab leak' theory of how COVID-19 began, the Chinese Communist Party-affiliated *Global Times* sent a clear warning: 'Elon Musk, are you breaking the pot of China?' – an idiom that in English translates as 'Are you biting the hand that feeds you?'[26] It's not only China which has gained such leverage. Also of note was Musk's Twitter takeover deal, financed in significant part by state investment funds from both Saudi Arabia and Qatar – two extreme non-democracies, one of which has form for sentencing domestic users to death for comments made on the platform.[27] Famously, two Twitter employees were previously found to have spied on activists on behalf of Saudi Arabia, so it seems likely that it might attempt to use its new-found financial leverage to its advantage. Indeed, perhaps this helps explain why the platform hands over the data of its users to the Saudi regime at a much higher rate than it does for authorities in the US, UK and Canada.[28]

Which leads us to another type of actor that appears to be winning in the digital age: autocrats, strongmen, dictators. Released from accountability to their peers by the dramatic increase in available resources made available by agricultural surplus, strongmen at the dawn of civilisation used force and guile to climb through the ranks of society, subduing rivals – and, if strong enough – conquering other societies and bolting everything together. Government by strongman is ancient: the most prolific form of governance in human civilisation.

Back in the day, Putin's regime in Russia could be called electoral authoritarianism; its means for controlling the information environment in the digital age is the 'white noise' model: garish entertainment spliced with repetitive propaganda talking points and confusing dissembling, and a torrent of falsehood to dilute and sideline unwanted perspectives and inconvenient facts. There are other authoritarian models. Another extreme is almost total censorship to keep dangerous influences out or down: in the Democratic Republic of North Korea online connections are available only to a select few among the elite – and these are heavily surveilled and censored. The operation of such a policy requires the full suppressive weight of a coercive State. And then there is the world's most populous country and newly minted superpower: China.

China lies behind the wildly ambitious 'Great Firewall', the original 'splinternet' part-segregating the Chinese online information environment from the wider web. In China access to tools and information sources ranging from Google to Wikipedia is cut or throttled through technology, dependent on the judgement of the regime. Optimists once believed China was progressively opening up. It once seemed that the availability of information might be the undoing of the Chinese Communist Party regime. Here's a comparison: in 1976 a gigantic earthquake hit the Tangshan region, killing around 240,000 people. It took the rest of the world three months to find out that it had happened at all. On the other hand, in 2008 the province of Sichuan was hit with an earthquake of similar magnitude, prompting an instantaneous and massive proliferation of visual evidence from within China that rapidly spread across the net.

But then China took a different course. Under President Xi Jinping the Communist Party is attempting to use new technology to realise older totalitarian dreams. Lively discussions once tolerated on China's version of Twitter, Sina Weibo, were eventually stopped; users disappeared into the more 'private' spaces of platforms like WeChat. Here censors carefully monitor what is discussed, deleting anything that threatens 'social harmony'. The extensive network of surveillance cameras across the physical environment of Chinese towns and cities is complemented by a developed online apparatus: the 'fifty-cent army' of low-paid workers is supplemented by a volunteer force of fans, the so-called 'Little Pinks', who help push and amplify official content – including such exhilarating memes as the cartoon series titled 'That Year, That Rabbit, Those Things', in which a cute rabbit representing the Chinese Communist Party is bullied by animals like an American bald eagle (a clear myside bias-based appeal).[29] Unsurprisingly, brigading anyone with contrary thoughts is also an activity the Little Pinks enjoy.

At the same time the Chinese government is busy centralising the data of its citizens. During the COVID-19 pandemic cameras linked to this data enabled the identification of lockdown rule-breakers. Such systems are inevitably applied to tracking dissent and protest. The regime seeks to introduce a wide-ranging system of 'social credit', drawing on data from apps as diverse as Telegram, Airbnb, Fitbit and Uber – much of it not even based in China. This alarming system of highly intrusive surveillance strips away the privacy that protects the weak from the strong by insisting on boundaries, gifting citizens points for making charitable donations while docking them for a traffic violation or publicly criticising the Communist Party. In summary, the people of China are under the strict control not only of censorship and propaganda, but of ubiquitous sensors, data-enabled surveillance and real-time behavioural change intervention: technology exploited to control the masses to an extent that the tyrants of history could only dream of.

China is no longer confining its informational power to control of its own population. Its State-affiliated China Global Television Network broadcasts across 160 countries and is watched by more than 100 million people. There are similar numbers of readers of the online news portal China Daily. Chinese officials, including State media journalists, are active on social media platforms such as Twitter and Facebook, even though these are inaccessible behind the Great Firewall. China's 'wolf warrior' diplomats readily spread disinformation and propaganda, with the subtleties of diplomacy replaced by aggressive content such as the statement which Gui Conyou, its ambassador to Sweden, made to PEN International after the organisation had given an award to a Chinese dissident: 'We treat our friends with fine wine, but for our enemies we've got shotguns.' Meanwhile embassies and consulates have been caught running illegal 'police stations' from which the voices of expatriates and the diaspora can be coerced and controlled.

China can use its economic reward power to recruit and co-opt foreign elites, including through its 'Confucius Institutes'; to build (and control) the communications architecture in jurisdictions beyond its own. Other Chinese actors are less official. The Little Pinks seem to have access behind the official portal, reacting furiously to perceived slights, pushing back against the #MeToo campaign and calling it 'toilet paper' and a plot by China's enemies (all this unleashed informational power is inevitably perceived as a threat to the mostly male Communist Party hierarchy). The Little Pinks reflect the authoritarian State's harnessing of those with an authoritarian disposition; Fang Kecheng of the Chinese University of Hong Kong noted that despite their hard-line Communist stance, the biases of the Little Pinks are similar to those of the so-called alt-right that has emerged in the West: anti-feminist, xenophobic, racist and ethnically chauvinist.

Then there are the hidden actors. Not only Chinese State-affiliated hackers who have long infiltrated computer networks and ransacked data from abroad, but also the social networks of inauthentic social media sockpuppets and bots set up to interfere in elections. China's home-grown artificial intelligence industry has the potential to supercharge analysis of stolen data, as well as the online influence campaigns likely to follow. Authoritarian Chinese informational power could make what the Russian State has pioneered seem trivial: as the chiefs of German intelligence have said, 'Russia is the storm, but China is climate change.'[30]

Authoritarian powers like Russia and China have – quite logically – identified that liberal democracy is a threat by its very existence. It is a threat because of the unleashed, cacophonic energy of its citizenry, the innovation generated by these comparatively liberated voices and the vibrancy of their civil societies, parts of which criticise authoritarians relentlessly. We should be under no illusion. Such regimes have begun working with systematic purpose and clarity, flexing their dramatically augmented informational power across the web-like networks of our hyper-connected age, aiming to damage, degrade and destroy democracy from within.

Yet the authoritarian powers face an enormous and irresolvable problem: the more they try to centralise power, the more true informational power begins to slip through their fingers. The fundamentals are illustrated in Hans Christian Andersen's fairy tale 'The Emperor's New Clothes'. In this story, two weavers persuade the emperor to purchase the most amazing new outfits. There's a catch: such gorgeous new clothes will be invisible to the stupid, they say, playing on the emperor's own vanity. Eventually the clothes are 'ready'. His advisers agree that he looks wonderful in them, afraid of disagreeing with the tyrant and unwilling to risk being labelled stupid – speaking truth to power not being high on the list of qualities sought in the emperor's selection of craven flunkies. The emperor's understanding of the world has been systematically subverted: his decisions will inevitably be irreparably flawed.

What is going on? In group settings where conformity is demanded – whether in the office, a social setting, or an entire population . . . anywhere where a 'right' way to think or behave is tightly enforced – a lone voice risks reputational damage and punishment. Individuals may be less likely to volunteer private information relating to attitudes or preferences in these circumstances – they will tend to express different public attitudes or preferences and agree with the views of the wider group; especially, perhaps, those of dominant characters within the group. This is known as *preference falsification*, and it can lead to *reputation cascade* (we came across this before), where (almost) everyone seems to agree with the prevailing orthodox attitude in order to avoid reputational damage, or worse. Thus the emperor's own advisers mislead him in relation to the new clothes. And in the absence of public signals, everyone is ignorant of what others are truly thinking – and the emperor walks out naked. This kind of cascade leads to pathologies, including many that are found in the typical echo chamber: amplification of error, extremism and an inability to draw on expertise. The focus is always on what is already 'known' to the group, and specialist information held by only a small proportion of its members cannot be accessed, as they would be suppressed and thoroughly disincentivised from sharing it.

In these conditions it makes sense for individuals to publicly agree with decisions made by their peers – to tell power what it wants to hear – *even when they privately know or believe such decisions to be based on false or inaccurate assessments*. In terms of risk management, it's better to be wrong as part of a crowd – splitting any costs with the group – than being judged to be wrong in isolation. Being able to claim, 'How could we have known: no one foresaw it' is safer than being grilled along the following lines: 'Everyone else made the correct assessment: so what made you act differently?'

The more often powerful people coerce dissenters and other bearers of unwanted information, the more pathological the effects become. Access to useful information is lost. Streams of inaccurate junk information are prioritised instead. The distorting effects of absolute power alienate observable behaviour from the subjective world of the desires, values and beliefs of those they rule. Those in power cannot then know the true preferences of their subjects because fear of coercion disincentives the latter from sharing their true beliefs or preferences.

The results are often spectacular in the most horrific way. After winning the Chinese Civil War in 1949, the Chinese Communist Party launched an attempt to catch up with the industry of Western powers in the campaign known as the 'Great Leap Forward'. Chairman Mao Zedong stated that within fifteen years Chinese steel production would surpass that of the UK (then still a mighty industrial power). Targets of all kinds cascaded down to the provinces – to increase harvests and steel production. The information soon being fed back to the leadership was incredible. Those targets were being smashed. Glowing reports percolated up the ranks of incredible progress on all fronts: a glorious homage to the Chinese Communist Party's guidance of the people.

But this was all a mirage. Peasants were ordered away from the fields to make steel in back-yard furnaces. To meet allocated targets they grasped anything to hand, including useful cooking pots and farm equipment, and smelted it to produce poor-quality, unusable steel. The removal of labour and tools led to neglect of the harvest. Too many production initiatives based on too many flawed assumptions were begun at once: war was waged on the 'four pests' – mosquitoes, rodents, flies and sparrows. The latter, it turned out, were especially key to a functioning ecosystem, and in their absence the prevalence of crop-ravaging insects burgeoned. Officials were incentivised to inflate numbers relating to harvests and steel production. Since no one wanted to be labelled ineffective or defeatist, typically they presented overly positive views of progress being made on their watch. Any dissent was ruthlessly suppressed. Each administrative layer added to this inflation, so by the time information reached the leadership it was hopelessly, tragically, compromised. Hunger and starvation soon set in. Yet at the height of the famine, 1958–1960, the central authorities believed that the situation looked so good that China was exporting grain to its allies. At least 30 million died of hunger and diseases related to malnutrition. The centre had dramatically subverted its ability to understand. In closed or autocratic systems of power, a *dictator's dilemma* is always prevalent.

We have been watching this play out more recently: the rapid evolution of the COVID-19 pandemic from one that might have been locally contained seemed due in large part to the refusal of Communist Party authorities to allow the necessary experts to make their voices heard early enough: in one key example a doctor, Li Wenliang, tried to raise the alarm, only to be disciplined by police. He died of the disease not long after – the authorities censoring him all the way to his deathbed. And after initial praise for the actions of the authorities in mobilising against the disease, the deep flaws in the system were soon on display again when in late 2022, long after much of the world had reopened, extreme lockdowns confining people to their living quarters were imposed on cities like Shanghai, Wuhan and Beijing. That there might be a better way – probably involving the decision to import more effective mRNA vaccines from abroad – was too difficult for power to acknowledge.[31] After all, to adjust course might be to admit a lack of omniscience on the part of the governing authorities – and if it is not omniscient, on what basis does such a regime govern? Anything is possible once the people realise that the emperor is not wearing any clothes.

The year 2022 also exposed us to another acute example of the dictator's dilemma when Russia made the catastrophic decision to launch a full-scale invasion of Ukraine. By all accounts the Russian leader had not expected much resistance at all, having been deceived by intelligence agencies which were supposed to be the eyes and ears of the State but which had become incentivised not to provide assessments of reality, instead telling power what it wanted to hear: that there wasn't a strong Ukrainian identity, that faith in the leaders was low, that the people of Ukraine were demoralised and broadly pro-Russian. Ingesting one's own propaganda is another feature of the system: eventually, all elements of the authoritarian apparatus – including the strongman himself – are forced to drink water from the very well that they have been busy contaminating. In summary, making terrible decisions and then sticking to them no matter the cost is not a bug in autocratic systems; it is a feature. The strongman does not have unique and mystical insight into the needs of the people; he is just another mind caged within a body of flesh – albeit one with an unusually psychopathic craving for power.

On the other hand, systems that distribute, disperse and constrain power are less likely to subvert themselves in this way: one key advantage of our troubled liberal democracies. It is not that such states do not make mistakes; they do, all the time – sometimes terrible ones. But they have inbuilt course-correction mechanisms – leaders who surround themselves with junk-advice flunkies and governments that make too many mistakes can be removed at the next election. Through the space they provide to their citizenry they preside over some of the most overwhelming expressions of informational power out there: open-source intelligence innovators like Bellingcat are free to draw on the democratic crowd to track airstrikes in Afghanistan or the locations of Russian artillery.[32] The bottom-up activity of civil society and authentic swarms of citizens is a worthy rival to anything the authoritarians can muster. Take the apparently organic North Atlantic

Fellas Organisation (NAFO) movement of Ukraine sympathisers, who troll the online voices of Russian officials and State-controlled media, for example. Will we really let such innovative political cultures be consigned to the dustbin of history?

Here's another story: a familiar one. It begins with the rise of a PR master and TV reality star to the US presidency. Donald Trump: a natural master of the attention economy who captured the media's attention with glittering spectacle – moving down his golden escalator from one trigger event-attention cascade to another. This was useful for sparking his messages directly into the information environments of his core constituencies. Because, like Sargon the Great cobbling together the city states of Sumer well over 4,000 years ago, he understood that power first involved aligning with the attitudes and beliefs of the audiences he needed to win. He could talk authentically to the people, adopting their modes of speech, giving voice to beliefs and attitudes that seemed under threat . . . insinuating himself into their tribes and quickly stitching himself in at the apex of their hierarchies.

From this perch our man could enjoy the loyalty of the vast echo chamber forged for the reactionary right by the commercial imperatives of the modern media landscape, appropriating the attentional mechanisms of the online world – especially social media – which were soon put to great effect. Content could be seeded across trusted social networks like wildfire, efforts that would be complemented by microtargeted ads and the filter bubbles of the platforms. Twitter would become Trump's personal radio station, allowing him to sidestep the old media gatekeepers and build parasocial relationships of affection and loyalty – of *hyperleadership* as a man of the people. The old media, meanwhile, would be left sluggishly failing to contextualise his potent stream of entertainment, which raised topics that many voters believed most politicians had colluded to ignore or remove from debate, as well as emotive lies and bullshit. Hamstrung by a commitment to 'balance', the weak fact-checking efforts of many outlets were rapidly outdated by the next round of emotive trigger events flooding the man with attention.[33]

Following his election win, Trump could enact old behaviours using the legitimate power of his office. From the presidential 'bully pulpit' the swarm could be nudged towards enemies, real and imagined. First among these would be representatives of the 'lamestream media', the 'enemies of the people' – journalists: because those in a position to hold power to account are the first who need to be discredited, silenced or knocked back into line, such as reporters from favoured outlets who failed to pay the requisite dues (John Roberts and Gillian Turner of Fox News had been 'less understanding' of the wall Trump wanted to build).[34] In this Trump was not alone. In other parts of the open world, the *hyperleader* adopts similar tactics to apply extreme pressure to critics and opponents. In just one representative example from Modi's India, the politician and activist Kavita Krishnan – an advocate for women's rights – claimed to receive up to 100 abusive messages a day on Twitter for criticising Modi: messages that tell her she's 'not worth raping', detailing the specific conditions of torture or rape or commenting on whom she should be sleeping with.[35] And when Indian journalist Rana Ayyub was critical of President Modi, she was soon alerted to a deepfake porn video posted online – not least by the trolls showering her with abuse in its wake.[36]

Wilful deceit is an essential feature of absolute power, which is compelled to propagate legitimating stories regardless of how much these reflect more objective assessments of reality. Absolute power aims for a single orthodoxy – be it Hitler's pursuit of dominance for the Aryan master race or Communists striving to implement Karl Marx's dictum, *From each according to his ability, to each according to his needs*; in short, what is needed is a single self-validating story. Absolute power subverts our understanding of reality, normalising lies and deceit – and lying because it must; for any evidence that might question the orthodoxy must be strangled in the cradle – by any means necessary.

Sometimes the lie is just part of a demonstration of power: *We know I am lying but what are you gonna do about it?* At other times the propagators may internalise their own lies: *We self-deceive in order to more effectively deceive others.* Swallowing our own lies becomes easy after repeated exposure to them. Information directly collected via our own five senses conflicts with the 'alternative facts' of the new social reality. And here, within this echo chamber, we have arrived back at the dictator's dilemma. Who now can provide useful feedback?

The rest is recent history: the commander-in-chief seeding his ideas about a fraudulent election early. Like the face in the tree innovation of an animist tribe, this fiction fitted the prior attitudes and beliefs of audiences – some who are still busy swallowing such stories into a larger free-association world of joined-up conspiracies. The Big Lie about a stolen election was transmitted and recycled within the echo chamber in a flurry of participatory disinformation, morphing as members of the tribe built on the lie with their own 'investigations', accusations and denunciations. With content spreading like wildfire across Facebook and other social media platforms, psyching susceptible audiences for the fight ahead, the waters became muddied and audiences grew bewildered and angry, further herded into opposing groups: such stories must be true, because surely no one would dare to propagate such brazen untruths. Predictably, Mark Zuckerberg put in another over-confident and thoroughly reckless cameo, stating that 'Facebook has done its part to secure the election', while the Facebook group recommender algorithm rapidly syndicated 'Stop the Steal' factions.[37]

As radicalised extremists from these groups converged on the US Capitol, they were directed by the Great Demagogue to sack it and hunt down the representatives of the people. The Republican leaders trapped within the propaganda feedback loop later failed to condemn or even deny the Big Lie. Amid the damage wrought by Americans upon themselves, it was easy to overlook the fact that no less than three hostile authoritarian powers – Russia, China and Iran – were accused by American intelligence of directly interfering in the election through measures such as inauthentic social media activity. A further two authoritarian powers – the United Arab Emirates and Saudi Arabia – were identified as attempting to co-opt US political allies and agents of influence through the offer of financial opportunities: including, perhaps predictably, Trump's own son-in-law, Jared Kushner, who netted $2 billion in investment.

Trump, it should be clear by now, was not the creator of the new informational power dynamics; he merely understood how to exploit them. He is not alone. It is not only like-minded authoritarian powers that also understand these dynamics; across the world democracies are under siege from within, by Trump-like dictator wannabes who have learned how to hijack and exploit informational power. Some have already successfully bounced their societies into electoral authoritarianism, like the regimes of Erdogan in Turkey and Orbán in Hungary (who, by the way, prefers to use the term 'illiberal democracy'). Others seem to be heading fast in the same direction: like India under Modi. Without doubt in need of reform and renewal, our democracies still have so many strengths. But their survival is not guaranteed. In many ways, the United States is ground zero in this battle. If that great role model should fall, the scales will tip against our democracies' collective survival. Our adversaries know this. They also know that the United States and its allies do not have to be defeated in battle; they just have to help America forget what it once wanted to be. At the same time, there is hope for us yet: we can still determine what comes next.

But how? By flexing our own muscles, with the objective of prompting a redistribution of informational power to the people and their institutions; *we must use our informational power wisely*. First of all, let's not lose sight of our role, embedded as we are in these vast systems. The digital information revolution makes us all potentially more powerful – you, me and everyone around us. We can squander this power by overlooking it. Or, raging like an overgrown child, we can misuse it, tearing down people and institutions without really understanding how blindly we are doing the bidding of others. Whatever we want to do with our institutions and our shared stories, we need to reach out to one another and do it together. Items on this collective agenda to consider must include, first and foremost, what new or reformed institutions we will build to manage the changed information environment so that it supports, on the one hand, fact and truth, and on the other, social cohesion and democratic values. We must *take back control of our information environments*.

This may include considerations such as:

- Building the legitimacy of social media and other inter- net-based platforms; including how to recast the dominance of the private power of the oligarch-run tech platforms. How can they represent the people when they are not primarily incentivised to?

- Opening the algorithms of these platforms to scrutiny and audit by democratic representatives supported by appro- priately specialised civil society actors.

- Communicating to users and the wider population how their algorithms work, including those relating to how content is ranked, recommended and removed.

- Regulating how proposed algorithmic changes may impact our social machines. We should consider systems of rigorous piloting, with publicly recognised processes that involve external experts and results which are made as public as possible.

- How to better protect us against inauthentic activity and algorithmic gaming; perhaps the platforms really should be made totally responsible for what is published on their infrastructure, so that their incentives finally align with those of the public and the rule of law. We should consider instituting mandatory spot checks by regulators at regular and random points in time; platform security and public-information hygiene should be a year-round priority, not merely a talking point near election time.

- Increased fact-checking, informing those subjected to misinformation and deceit that they have in fact been exposed to it, as well as reducing the connectivity of syndicated anger and mono-lensed ideologues at the fringes at the expense of the rest of us. Under such a system answerable to us, the people, there would be few reasons for politicians to argue that they should have an opt-out from having their content labelled false on platforms like Facebook, as they do currently – and they may also fib less in the first place.

Once these wish-list items have been dealt with, our next priority will be to use our informational power to pressure social media platforms into finding new ways of slowing, then reversing, their role in generating polarisation and radicalisation so that they become an asset in helping us to build town squares and other democratic institutions that are fit for purpose in our digital age. Renewed liberal democracies that satisfy the needs of their citizens will win the contest against the authoritarians. Key to this will be using our new-found informational power in pursuit of a vital aim: we must take back collective control of our information environment.

11. Conclusion

This is a story about influence. It begins far back in our evolutionary ancestry, where our judgement and decision-making processes were honed by survival in often hostile conditions; where as social animals we could build trust with one another in order to cooperate, we could learn from one another to share culture; because we could theorise the minds of others we could also build for ourselves an identity; we could manage and minimise competitive tensions by organising into status hierarchies. Over time, culture and technology changed who our predecessors were and how they influenced one another. It is a story that led us here, to now, when the central protagonists are you, me and everyone we know.

In the digital age we find ourselves the custodians of means to influence one another – informational power – like never before. The constraints of financial cost, time and space have been minimised, and we are empowered to create and distribute content into the minds of others beyond the dreams of even the most sophisticated rulers from earlier times. But with this access comes a host of new methods to deceive and influence – methods which work to shape our information environment, change our understanding of what is happening around us and shift our behaviour so that it supports the goals of others.

What is more, the arrival of these digital means of influence affected every other means of communications media, creating fertile conditions in which echo chambers could proliferate; in turn, this acts as a fragmentary force on our political communities and offers attractive vulnerabilities for the external and internal adversaries of liberal democracy to exploit from within. At the same time, the era of big data means that the individual thoughts, beliefs and dispositions which comprise our identities can be increasingly exploited by cynical commercial and political actors to silo our thinking and take us to where they want us. The demands of our technology-driven social lives increasingly intrude on our private spheres. We are incentivised to perform for others, perhaps becoming captured by them as attractive routes for information-laundering – witting or unwitting vectors for the deceitful schemes of others.

It seems that, just as the potential to gain and express informational power has expanded, a range of already powerful actors have used their positions to reap even more from the revolution – co-opting our informational power for their own benefit. Whether consciously or unconsciously, they are pushing this power around in ways that shake our societies to the core and imperil our future.

There is a fork in the road ahead. Down one path, powerful adversaries will continue to influence our information environments to their advantage and undermine our liberal democracies – very possibly leading to disintegration, autocracy or both. The other is the difficult path to digital-age democratic renewal, whereby 'Everything must change so that everything can remain the same', as one of the key protagonists in Lampedusa's classic *The Leopard* notes.

Let's look a bit further down that first path, where many more may come to believe that liberal democracy is an archaic luxury – a chaos engine of information anarchy, radicalisation, inter-communal conflict and violence: a system grossly inadequate to helping us confront and solve the survival problems in front of us. Our political communities may eventually – like the Holy Roman Empire and myriad other political structures before them – buckle, then disintegrate entirely.

There is another off-ramp from this path. Instead of disintegration will come autocracy. In many jurisdictions we have already passed this juncture. Whether a wannabe tyrant takes over the levers of power through election (like Vladimir Putin or Victor Orbán), violence (like the Chinese Communist Party once did), or a combination of the two (as Donald Trump tried), one of their first tasks will be to arrogate the levers of informational power, using them to maintain dominance of the information environment. This regime corrals us, the confused people, into order with propaganda and censorship – and, depending on how tightly they choose to hold the reins of the information environment, with disinformation to dilute dissent. Big tech is co-opted to the cause – willingly or not, their algorithms are amended to cement loyalty to the regime, identifying audiences, understanding individuals and groups of interest, sending them multi-layered messages, drawing them back into the embrace of the regime's legitimation stories – and when that fails, applying sanction to them as deviants.

Down this particular path, the dictator appoints allies to control the levers of power on the basis of loyalty, not competence. After all, to empower a competent rival is to create a potentially lethal threat. Better a system of lackies who owe everything to the tyrant and are incapable of acting without him. Together with his inner circle, the dictator redistributes the nation's resources to his cronies, creating a norm of corruption which influences everyone else. They soon need to aggress those who refuse to be co-opted or silenced. Those who speak out are made an example of. People learn that it is safest to keep quiet, withholding potentially valuable information from the regime, its supporters and enablers.

Such an ill-constructed system now incentivises the suppression of all manner of useful information; in contrast, all kinds of deceit and falsehood will flourish and blossom, from top to bottom and bottom to top. The information channels by which the dear leader understands the world will clog, warp, shut down and otherwise become danger-ously detached from reality in an inescapable dilemma. In the increasingly sealed and delusional echo chamber, there will be decreas-ingly little chance of far-sighted and wise decisions that will help solve the problems of our time.

But perhaps this all sounds implausible, a spot of doom-mongering? It can be hard for us to imagine a future too far removed from our present. But the prototypes are already here, stitched with us into the same networked world – the visionary regimes in China, North Korea, in Russia and their anti-democratic fans in places like Hungary, Turkey, even India, not to mention the United States and across much of Europe.

There is an alternative path back at our fork. It too is not an easy one, because it means reconceiving and reforming what we have before we lose what is valuable about it. Rule by the people – liberal democracy – has always been a tricky path. And, as is shown by the abundance of evidence around us, liberal democracies also make mistakes. But at their best democracies provide enormous benefits. By institutionalising debate they encourage peaceful negotiation of competing interests; they broker settlements that at their best strike a balance between our wish to commune with others and our desire for personal agency; between the freedom to express ourselves as individuals and the desire to share an identity with the groups we belong to; between our wish for the creative frisson and stimulation of diversity and difference and our craving for sameness and unity.

Liberal democracies provide relatively useful mechanisms for holding the powerful to account, ensuring that the interests of the ruled are at least minimally considered by their rulers – not least freedom of speech and action. In turn, the ruled are more inclined to consent to the rules. Compared to their authoritarian counterparts, such systems suffer less bias, inequity and corruption.[1] Liberal democracy is associated with better healthcare and mental health and increased life expectancy.[2] Nor does the apparent cacophony of voices mean chaos.

When liberal democracies cultivate the conditions for tolerating diverse voices with diverse perspectives, fertile conditions are created for social and technological innovation. Similarly, these conditions enable information-gathering with less fear or favour – providing our best bet at objective scrutiny of an often-slippery reality. And when, in the pursuit of power, our rulers become too detached from this reality-testing project we can fling them out at the next election. Although this route may seem too meandering, it may still offer our best hope in solving immediate and acute collective problems like global heating.

The adage *from diversity, unity*, is a timeless cross-cultural ideal, one shared by characters as disparate as the Sufi philosopher Ibn Al Arabi (1165–1240), the Javanese poet Mpu Tantalar (fourteenth century), and embodied in contexts ranging from the formal mottos of Indonesia, the United States and the European Union, to the constitution of South Africa. At their best, liberal democracies showcase this maxim better than any other form of government, and a shared story believably based on such a foundation can be powerful. The Second World War fascist dictatorships found this out to their cost. They too had convinced themselves that liberal democracies were rotted beyond repair and would fall apart when aggressed. But these visions were not only delusional, they were utterly ruinous for the fascists and their followers.

Yet liberal democracy is again under siege in front of our noses. Our adversaries operate in plain sight. Some will come as wolves in sheep's clothing. Freed from the old normative constraints, they will (ab)use the priceless liberal democracy-enabled right to free speech in order to spread lies and deceits and seed antagonism, conflict and hate. They will say that the freedom of the individual undermines institutions that reflect the collective will. They will weaponise our attitudes, beliefs and behavioural norms to degrade the cohesion of our societies and the institutions that govern us. Not least of these is another central feature of liberal democracies, in which free-willed, free-thinking individuals evaluate proposals in a marketplace of ideas.

If we want to maintain and renew liberal-democratic government in our time we must fight for it. But how? There are three elements each of us needs in order to do this:

- We need the capability: the knowledge, skills and tools, without which we cannot act.

- We need the opportunity: an opening into, or support from, the wider physical or social environment to enable our actions.

- And we need the motivation: the imperative force pushing us to act.[3]

Let's start with capability. Because, in the same way that reading and writing helped power the Industrial Revolution, we must upskill ourselves to become the literate citizens of the information age.

Control your information diet. We are the information we consume. So be proactive and focused in your online activity and remove any tempting access to information junk. Especially scrutinise content that leaves you feeling fearful, angry or outraged. Check your sources: who created this and why? Check the facts: do these sources cite data, statistics and quotes from experts? This is a start, but remember that these aspects can easily be misleadingly framed or faked. Never assume that content is factual if you cannot identify the origin; instead compare new information to other sources which you trust. Maintain mental hygiene and take regular breaks from social media – this may be easier said than done, for sure. Remember: like healthy eating habits or taking regular exercise, practice makes perfect.

Become an expert deception detector. We must be motivated to detect deception and counter infiltration of our networks of minds and machines. Be openly sceptical of any form of social proof. Don't trust metrics alone – volume of followers, shares, retweets, reviews and testimonials: in the digital age these are all easily faked. Learn the tells and identify the patterns in scores, dates, times, content and more. Again, investigate the source. This applies especially to social media, where sockpuppets, bots and trolls lurk in our midst. Do not automatically trust a friend of a friend, for this is a classic infiltration strategy. Connecting to those we cannot personally verify is dangerous. Do not easily trust those who seem to carry authority, for this is another supporting tactic for infiltration into our networks. Take your cyber security seriously: do not click on links that do not look authentic; take your password security seriously: use multifactor authentication and consider using tools like a virtual private network. And remember, for everyone engaging with a new platform or with an actor trying to gain our attention, ask: 'Who can access us?', 'What do they want?' and 'Who benefits?'

Role-model and reach out with humility. We can work to become better mediators, able to get out there to connect with others across different communities – especially those we encounter online – while still deploying our deception-detection antennae. Engage – and listen. But also get talking. Trust comes before influence. When we share thoughts on things we do not have in common we may start to see the world from a different angle; in a new light. In public settings, role-model the balance between confidently making our own voice heard and avoiding moral judgement, regardless of what others are saying. On the other hand, where you encounter horrifying views online ignore, ignore, ignore (or where relevant, report them to the authorities). Remember: attacking those whose views seem extreme – or trolls of any kind – merely feeds them, although when an ally is under personal attack we may rally to their side to show them that they are not alone. At the same time, our ideological agendas will rarely excuse the bullying and harassment of others. So stop. Instead practise epistemic humility, avoiding becoming trapped in an echo chamber by continuously challenging your own reasoning, inverting your opinions and attempting to defend these to yourself – seeking evidence to *disconfirm* your attitudes and beliefs. This doesn't mean watering down what you hold dear. Indeed, your faith in your principles may only grow stronger as you understand how they fit into the wider network of attitudes, beliefs and values around you.

Become a privacy watchkeeper. Take your data protection seriously. Assume nothing you do online is completely private. Consider your digital footprints: what can you find out about yourself online? What does the information you provide to others enable them to judge about you and those you are connected to? Review your privacy settings on all your online accounts and be discerning about the information you give out. Pay attention to our cyber security to reduce the chances of having your personal data stolen. But bear in mind the nuances. Sometimes sharing our personal data will be useful. The question is about who can be trusted. Support organisations like Privacy International (https://privacyinternational.org/) and Open Rights Group (https://www.openrightsgroup.org/); vote for elected representatives who demonstrate a commitment to privacy and frustrate the encroaching 'surveillance capitalism' ecosystem. More than this, you can better control the relationship between who you are in your public and private lives. Resist letting others define you by giving yourself private space in which to reflect on who you are and what you want. Where you build a personal brand, work as hard as possible to ask yourself whether it truly aligns with your internal attitudes, beliefs and identities. Is this who you want to be? What is the legacy you wish to leave? Respect others. Respect yourself. Nurture a well-developed sense of humour about the tension between your private thoughts and feelings and the very understandable desire to be validated in public, including on social media.

Use your informational power wisely. Flex your informational power consciously to decide what information spreads, as well as what does not. On social media the success of useless or dangerous false content depends on users reposting, retweeting or otherwise sharing it. Think hard before you share – and do not give in to the temptation to spread junk just because it may help you to bond with or make a good impression on others. And when others share junk with you, gently tease and challenge them – who are their sources? Where did they get it from? What makes them trust it?

Our networks are only as strong as the most vulnerable in them. Use your informational power to encourage those around you to better control their information diets and be expert deception detectors and role models, reaching out with humility, becoming privacy watch-keepers while, of course, using their informational power wisely.

If enhancing our capability in this way seems insufficient in facing the problems of our digital age, then we are on the same page. These tools and habits alone will leave us treading water, or even exhausting ourselves as we constantly swim against the flow of our information environments, which prevent us from rebuilding our shared stories and institutions. We need to create the opportunity to help change the behaviour of ourselves and others. What kinds of opportunity? For a start, those that derive from a better-structured information environment.

Big tech-owned internet and social media platforms are too valuable and too destructive to be left to their private owners. Just as we might not expect oil and gas companies to self-regulate in our best interests over climate change, we cannot ask the big tech companies to do so. There is little incentive for these private interests to nurture an information environment that truly empowers us, that helps sustain and renew our liberal democracies. The platforms, as currently configured, are doomsday machines: the inputs are not only our attention and actions, but trust and cohesion of the political community. The output (aside from private profit) is information disorder and a degraded social fabric; like Dracula, big tech has sucked its power from our shared stories and collective political institutions. In addition, it has opened portals through which all manner of poison and corruption has poured, with increasingly serious consequences. That big tech has evaded sanctions for so long illustrates speaks the effectiveness with which it has hacked into our society.

We should increase the opportunities available to us to practise positive behaviours and *take back control of our information environment*. Make the tech giants subject to democratically accountable oversight bodies and restructure them as spaces that build – not corrode – fraternisation and rapport among the people. Use every influence strategy and tactic covered in this book to help guide your actions. Deploy your informational power to create and transmit content in service of this aim of taking back control. Reach out. Build trusted alliances with different-thinking others. Spread the word among your networks, online and off. Write to your parliamentary representative. Understand and influence audiences, harnessing culture and identity. Join and participate with others in the initiatives of groups like Accountable Tech (www.accountabletech.org), the Tech Transparency Project (www.techtransparencyproject.org/) and Media Justice (www.mediajustice.org).

Finally, though, comes our motivation – our will to act. Long ago, our hunter-gatherer ancestors used their language informational power to resist those who sought to dominate them. In the digital age we stand at a junction. Our informational power has been augmented, but there are a range of powerful actors who seek to control and coerce us by first abusing this power for their own ends. We can allow ourselves to be over-run by anti-democratic forces besieging our societies from within and without, or we can summon the will to shift the fundamentals and make more effective collective decisions. In this book I have sketched out some key outlines of the problem. The solutions I have suggested will be grossly insufficient alone. Because as well as the existential problems we face, there are others that will frustrate and divide us along the way: about the balances to be sought between the local and the global in building institutions and sharing stories; about how to tackle poverty, inequality and stagnant living standards; about who should own what, who should be able to migrate where, and more. We must determine how to structure this wider agenda together and resist the forces that pull us apart.

Without this process it is likely that our actions will prove to be, as the ancient strategist Sun Tzu put it, 'the noise before defeat'. We need masters of influence to role-model the way forward and bring others with them. One of these role models is you. The time we need you is now.

Acknowledgements

I was watching my grandfather Frank Palmer tap out another learned work on linguistics on his word processor back in the nineties, when it dawned on me that one day, perhaps, I might try and write a book. Grandad embodied intellectual inquiry for his grandchildren, and wherever I lived, whether the United States, China or Italy, I could find his work stocked in a university library. But it was my grandmother, Jean – Frank's wife – who embodied influence, as she made everything happen in the social world around them. Both have since sadly passed and are well missed – but will always be a source of inspiration: my heartfelt love and thanks.

Thanks for all the views and opinions of my old pals from 'Blink Club', Andrew Scola, Ruhi Sethi-Smith and Ben Cresswell, plus honorary members Alex Warner and Alex Darby; we've been on some memorable adventures. Thanks especially to old friend Chris Evans, who gave detailed feedback all the way through, as well as continuously thoughtful conversation about materialism, metaphysics and God. To Guy Griffiths, for many insightful thoughts on this book from just about every direction over a pint – who'd have imagined we'd travel the journey together from New Scotland Yard to the bright lights of greater Pompey? To my pal James Rosie, many thanks for such comprehensive advice on an early draft. My cousin Geoffrey Palmer was engaged all the way through the first version and gave the most diplomatic of critical feedback – please come over to the UK more often!

To Andy Bambridge and Bev Darkin, many thanks for your super helpful early thoughts. To former colleague, Nicolas Melendez, thanks for your tireless critique, challenge and research support. Similarly, to Neil Verrall, many thanks for taking the time to provide comment on the first draft – and to Simon Day for insightful advice all the way through. Thanks also to my Social Machines colleagues, Lily Thompson D'Arcy-Johnson and Joseph Dingley, for painstaking review and comment – and latterly also, to Clara Fulks and Rosie Barnes, for additional insight. I also want to thank my friend Tim Williams and neighbour and running partner, Nick Smith, for feedback nearer the finish line.

To my agent, Adam Gauntlett, thanks especially for helping push some pretty raw material through to a commissioned proposal. Thanks also to Grace Pengelly, for guiding the first draft off the rocks; Myles Archibald for drawing what is hopefully a better draft into the dock; as well as Eve Hutchings, Linden Lawson and everyone else on the publishing team who helped create and put this book out there.

My mother, Jane, was one of the most tireless reviewers – and my father, Stephen, was an endless source of ideas – many thanks and lots of love. My brothers Stuart, Richard and Aidan – some of my very best friends – thanks for the ongoing encouragement, as well as doing your best to wrangle me at extended family parties.

To my beloved children, Raffaele, Leone and Ginevra, thank you so much for giving me the space to write even when there were so many missed invitations to bounce on the trampoline or learn how to play Minecraft (which, even after several patient teaching sessions, still goes over my head). Finally, most thanks of all to the talented and formidable Fran, my editor of first resort, partner in crime and much-loved wife, for believing in the project and helping to make it happen from start to finish.

Endnotes

1. Judgement

1 Kahneman, D. (2011), *Thinking Fast and Slow*
2 Simon, D. J. and Chabris, C. F. (1999), 'Gorillas in our midst: Sustained inattentional blindness for dynamic events', *Perception* 28:9.
3 Strauss, N. (2005), *The Game*.
4 https://www.theguardian.com/politics/2016/jan/20/lynton-crosby-and-dead-cat-won-election-conservatives-labour-intellectually-lazy
5 Lassiter, G. D. (2002), 'Illusory causation in the courtroom, current directions', *Psychological Science* 11:204–8; and Lassiter, G. D. (2010), 'Psychological science and sound public policy: Video recording of custodial interrogations', *American Psychologist* 65.
6 See for example: Miller, R. C. (1976), 'Mere exposure, psychological reactance, and attitude change', *Public Opinion Quarterly* 40; Cacioppo, J. T. and Petty, R. E. (1979), 'Effects of message repetition and position on cognitive response', *Journal of Personality and Social Psychology* 37:1.
7 Bargh, J. A., et al. (2001) 'The automated will: Nonconscious activation and pursuit of behavioral goals', *Journal of Personality and Social Psychology* 81; but this failed to replicate in a study by Harris, C. R., et al. (2013), 'Two failures to replicate high-performance-goal priming effects', *PLOS One*.
8 Wryobeck, J. and Chen, Y. (2003), 'Using priming techniques to facilitate health behaviours', *Clinical Psychologist* 7:2.
9 Ford, J., O'Hare, D. and Henderson, R. (2012), 'Putting the "we" into teamwork: Effects of priming personal or social identity on flight attendants' perceptions of teamwork and communication', *Human Factors* 55:33.
10 Stajkovic, A. D., Greenwalk, J. M. and Stajkovic, K. S. (2022), 'The money priming debate revisited: A review, meta-analysis, and extension to organizations', *Journal of Organizational Behavior* 43:6.
11 Bargh, J. A., Chen, M. and Burrows, L. (1996), 'Automaticity of social behavior: Direct effects of trait construct and stereotype activation on action', *Journal of Personality and Social Psychology* 71:2.
12 Carver, C. S. et al. (1983), 'Modelling: An analysis in category accessibility', *Journal of Experimental Social Psychology* 19; and Subra, B. et al. (2010), 'Automatic effects

of alcohol and aggressive cues on aggressive thoughts and behaviors', *Personality and Social Psychology Bulletin* 36:8.

13 Papies, E., Stroebe, W. and Aarts, H. (2008), 'Healthy cognition: Processes of self-regulatory success in restrained eating', *Personality and Social Psychology Bulletin* 34:9.

14 https://www.bbc.co.uk/news/world-europe-59998988

15 Lord, C. G., Ross, L. and Lepper, M. R. (1979), 'Biased assimilation and attitude polarization: The effects of prior theories on subsequently considered evidence', *Journal of Personality and Social Psychology* 37:11.

16 Tversky, A. and Kahneman, D. (1992), 'Advances in prospect theory: Cumulative representation of uncertainty', *Journal of Risk and Uncertainty* 5.

17 Dawes, J. (2004), 'Price changes and defection levels in a subscription-type market: Can an estimation model really predict defection levels?', *Journal of Services Marketing* 18:1.

18 Levin, I. P., Schneider, S. L. and Gaeth, G. J. (1998), 'All frames are not created equal: A typology and critical analysis of framing effects', *Organizational Behavior and Human Decision Processes* 76:2.

19 Johnson, D. D. P. and Tierny, D. (2006), *Failing to Win*.

20 Hamilton, D. L. and Gifford, R. K. (1976), 'Illusory correlation in interpersonal perception: A cognitive basis of stereotypic judgments', *Journal of Experimental Social Psychology* 12:4.

21 Desvousges, W. H. et al. (1993), 'Measuring natural resource damages with contingent valuation: Tests of validity and reliability', *Contributions to Economic Analysis* 220.

22 Tversky, A. and Kahneman, D. (1982), 'On the study of statistical intuition', *Cognition* 11:2.

23 Azar, O.H. (2011), 'Do consumers make too much effort to save on cheap items and too little to save on expensive items?: Experimental results and implications for business strategy', *American Behavioral Scientist* 55:8.

24 Hume, D. (1739), *A Treatise on Human Nature*.

25 Nietzsche, F. (1882), *The Gay Science*.

26 Berthoz, A. (2006), *Simplexity: Simplifying Principles for a Complex World*.

27 Aristotle, *Rhetoric*, book 2.

28 Westen, D. (2007), *The Political Brain: The Role of Emotion in Deciding the Fate of the Nation*.

29 https://www.iom.int/news/iom-counts-3771-migrant-fatalities-mediterranean-2015

30 Jenni, K. and Loewenstein, G. (1997), 'Explaining the identifiable victim effect', *Journal of Risk and Uncertainty* 14; also Small, D. A. and Loewenstein, G. (2003), 'Helping *a* victim or helping *the* victim: Altruism and identifiability', *Journal of Risk and Uncertainty* 26.

31 Gelfand, M. et al. (2011), 'Differences between tight and loose cultures: A 33-nation study', *Science* 332:6033.

2. Trust

1 Useful discussion of this in de Waal, F. (2005), *Our Inner Ape*, p. 180 onwards; see Royka, A. and Santos, L. R. (2022), 'Theory of mind in the wild', *Current*

Opinion in Behavioral Sciences 45:101137 for up-to-date and more detailed info on 'theory of mind' in chimps and macaques.

2 Interesting discussion of the evolution of theory of mind in babies and toddlers in Cheney, D. and Seyfarth, R. M. (2007), *Baboon Metaphysics*.

3 Global terrorism database, CDC WONDER, average from 2006 to 2015.

4 https://www.kcl.ac.uk/kcmhr/publications/assetfiles/cbrn/Batholomew2002-proteannature.pdf

5 Asch, S. E. (1952), 'Group forces in the modification and distortion of judgments', in Asch, S. E., *Social Psychology*, pp. 450–501; Asch, S. E. (1956), 'Studies of independence and conformity: I. A minority of one against a unanimous majority', *Psychological Monographs: General and Applied 70*(9), 1–70.

6 Shirky, C. (2008), *Here Comes Everybody: The Power of Organizing Without Organizations*, pp. 161–4.

7 Bickman, L. (1974), 'The social power of a uniform', *Journal of Applied Social Psychology* 4:1.

8 Doob, A. N. and Goss, A. E. (1968), 'Status of frustrator as an inhibitor of horn-honking responses', *Journal of Social Psychology* 76, 213–18.

9 Milgram, S. (1974), *Obedience to Authority*.

10 See this updated version of the experiment: Caspar, E. A. et al. (2016), 'Coercion changes the sense of agency in the human brain', *Current Biology* 26:5; and also Meeus, W. H. J. and Raaijmakers, Q. A. W. (1995), 'Obedience in modern society: The Utrecht studies', *Journal of Social Issues* 51:3.

11 Lim, K. H., Lim, E. and Jiang, B. (2016), 'Using online controlled experiments to examine authority effects on user behavior in email campaigns', *HT '16: Proceedings of the 27th ACM Conference on Hypertext and Social Media*.

12 Dzardanova, E. et al. (2019), 'Exploring aspects of obedience in VR-mediated communication', *2019 Eleventh International Conference on Quality of Multimedia Experience (QoMEX)*, Berlin, pp. 1–3, doi: 10.1109/QoMEX.2019.8743196

13 Glowacki, L., Wilson, M. and Wrangham, R. W. (2017), 'The evolutionary anthropology of war', *Journal of Economic Behavior and Organization* 178; von Rueden, C. et al. (2014), 'Leadership in an egalitarian society', *Human Nature 25*(4), 538–66.

14 Stulp, G. et al. (2015), 'Human height is positively related to interpersonal dominance in dyadic interactions', *PLoS One*.

15 Mehrabian, A. (1972), *Nonverbal Communication*.

16 Lieberman, J. D. (2006), 'Head over the heart or heart over the head? Cognitive experiential self-theory and extralegal heuristics in juror decision making', *Journal of Applied Social Psychology* 32:12; Englich, B., Mussweiler, T. and Strack, F. (2006), 'Playing dice with criminal sentences: The influence of irrelevant anchors on experts', *Judicial Decision Making, Personality and Social Psychology Bulletin* 32:2.

17 Boothroyd, L. G. et al. (2020), 'Television consumption drives perceptions of female body attractiveness in a population undergoing technological transition', *Journal of Personality and Social Psychology* 119:4.

18 Boothroyd, L. G. et al. (2016), 'Television exposure predicts body size ideals in rural Nicaragua', *British Journal of Psychology* 107(4):752–67, doi: 10.1111/bjop.12184; Jucker, J. L. et al. (2017), 'Nutritional status and the influence of TV consumption on female body size ideals in populations recently exposed to the media', *Scientific Reports*

7(1):8438, doi: 10.1038/s41598-017-08653-z.PMID: 28814743; Calado, M. et al. (2011), 'The association between exposure to mass media and body dissatisfaction among Spanish adolescents', *Womens Health Issues* 21:5.

19 Erasmus, D. (1509), *In Praise of Folly*.

20 Asch, S. E. (1946), 'Forming impressions of personality', *The Journal of Abnormal and Social Psychology 41*(3), 258–90, https://doi.org/10.1037/h0055756

21 Strohmetz, B. et al. (2002), 'Sweetening the till – The use of candy to increase restaurant tipping', *Journal of Applied Social Psychology* 32(2), 300–309.

22 Kunz, P. R. and Woolcott, M. (1976), 'Season's greetings: From my status to yours', *Social Science Research* 5(3), 269–278, https://doi.org/10.1016/0049-089X(76)90003-X

23 Stivers, T. et al. (2009), 'Universals and cultural variation in turn-taking in conversation', *PNAS* 106:26.

24 Norscia, I. et al. (2020), 'Auditory contagious yawning is highest between friends and family members: Support to the emotional bias hypothesis', *Frontiers in Psychology* 11.

25 Bailenson, J. N. et al. (2008), 'Facial similarity between voters and candidates causes influence', *Public Opinion Quarterly* 72, 935–61.

26 Hampton, A. J., Boyd, A.N.F. and Sprecher, S. (2018), 'You're like me and I like you: Mediators of the similarity–liking link assessed before and after a getting-acquainted social interaction', *Journal of Social and Personal Relationships* 36:7.

27 Department for International Development (2009), *Getting Braids Not AIDS: How Hairdressers Are Helping to Tackle HIV in Zimbabwe*.

28 Vasilaky, K. et al. (2015), 'Learning digitally: Evaluating the impact of farmer training via mediated videos', digitalgreen.org.

29 Depaulo, B. et al. (1996), 'Lying in everyday life', *Journal of Personality and Social Psychology* 70:5; Serota, K. B., Levine, T. R. and Boster, F. R. (2010), 'The prevalence of lying in America: Three studies of self-reported lies', *Human Communication Research* 36:1.

30 DePaulo, B. M. and Kashy, D. A. (1998), 'Everyday lies in close and casual relationships', *Journal of Personality and Social Psychology* 74(1), 63–79, https://doi.org/10.1037/0022-3514.74.1.63

31 Levine, T. R., Serota, K. B. and Punyanunt-Carter, N. M. (2022), 'Sender and receiver lie frequencies and motives: Testing predictions from truth-default theory', *Southern Communication Journal* 87:3.

32 The evolutionary psychologist Robin Dunbar surveyed the available literature on group sizes to claim that humans can comfortably maintain 150 stable relationships with others we might know well enough to go for a coffee or a drink with. The specific 'Dunbar's number' is heavily contested, though. This article provides a useful overview: Lindenfors, P., Wartel, A. and Lind, J. (2021), '"Dunbar's number" deconstructed', *Biology Letters*, https://royalsocietypublishing.org/doi/full/10.1098/rsbl.2021.0158

33 Broockman, D. and Kalla, J. (2016), 'Durably reducing transphobia: A field experiment on door-to-door canvassing', *Science* 352:6282.

3. Culture

1 Definition adapted from Lederach, J. P. (1995), *Preparing for Peace: Conflict Transformation across Cultures*.

2   Van Leeuwen, E. J., Cronin, K. A. and Haun, D. B. (2014), 'A group-specific arbitrary tradition in chimpanzees (Pan troglodytes)', *Animal Cognition*, 17.

3   Brown, D. (1991), *Human Universals*. Note the list does not include universals on mental structure, or near universals (such as incest).

4   American Economic Association, Royal Economic Society, and Simon, H. A. (1966), *Theories of Decision-making in Economics and Behavioural Science*.

5   We do this from an early age. Kids can be extremely cooperative, working together to solve puzzle box problems – matching one another's actions, learning from each other via gesture and imitation, and engaging in spontaneous pro-social acts such as gifting to others rewards that they retrieve. For a useful elaboration see: Laland, K. (2017), *Darwin's Unfinished Symphony*, pp. 172–3.

6   Gelfand, M. et al. (2011), 'Differences between tight and loose cultures: A 33-nation study', *Science* 332:6033.

7   Boyd, R. and Richerson, P. J. (2005), *The Origin and Evolution of Cultures*.

8   Gospic, K. et al. (2011), 'Limbic justice – amygdala involvement in immediate rejection in the ultimatum game', *PLoS Biology* 9:5.

9   Chudek, M. and Henrich, J. (2011), 'Culture-gene coevolution, norm-psychology and the emergence of human prosociality', *Trends in Cognitive Sciences* 15:5.

10   See Schmidt, M. F., Rakoczy, H. and Tomasello, M. (2012), 'Young children enforce social norms selectively depending on the violator's group affiliation', *Cognition* 124:3; Rakoczy, H. et al. (2009), 'Young children's understanding of the context-relativity of normative rules in conventional games', *British Journal of Developmental Psychology* 27:2; Rakoczy, H., Warneken, F. and Tomasello, M. (2008), 'The sources of normativity: Young children's awareness of the normative structure of games', *Developmental psychology* 44:3.

11   Floyd, S. et al. (2018), 'Universals and cultural diversity in the expression of gratitude', *Royal Society Open Science* 5:5.

12   Cialdini, R. (2005), 'Don't throw in the towel: Use social influence research', *APS Observer* 18.

13   Lapinski, M. K. et al. (2013), 'Testing the effects of social norms and behavioral privacy on hand washing: A field experiment', *Human Communication Research* 39:1.

14   Cialdini, R. B. (2003), 'Crafting normative messages to protect the environment', *Current Directions in Psychological Science* 12:4.

15   Reynolds, K. J., Subašić, E. and Tindall, K. (2015), 'The problem of behaviour change: From social norms to an ingroup focus', *Social and Personality Psychology Compass* 9:1.

16   Nolan, J. M. et al. (2008), 'Normative social influence is underdetected', *Personality and Social Psychology Bulletin* 34:7.

17   Norms can also get in the way – illustrating, though, the pathway to change: Sparkman, G., Howe, L. and Walton, G. (2021), 'How social norms are often a barrier to addressing climate change but can be part of the solution', *Behavioural Public Policy* 5:4.

18   Yamin, P. et al. (2019), 'Using social norms to change behavior and increase sustainability in the real world: A systematic review of the literature', *Sustainability* 11:20.

19   Some interesting articles here that hint at some of the complexities: Culiberg, B. and Elgaaied-Gambier, L. (2016), 'Going green to fit in – Understanding the impact of social norms on pro-environmental behaviour, a cross-cultural approach',

International Journal of Consumer Studies 40:2; Park, H. S. et al. (2020), 'Temporal distance and descriptive norms on environmental behaviors: A cross-cultural examination of construal-level theory', *Sage Open* 10:1.

20   Beckerman, S. and Valentine, P. (2002), *Cultures of Multiple Fathers: The Theory and Practice of Partible Paternity in South America*; Beckerman, A. et al. (2002), 'Population dynamic consequences of delayed life-history effects', *Trends in Ecology & Evolution* 17:6; Crocker, J. (2002), 'The costs of seeking self-esteem', *Journal of Social Issues* 58:3; Hill, K. and Hurtado, A. M. (2017), *Ache Life History: The Ecology and Demography of a Foraging People*; Walker, R. S., Flinn, M. V. and Hill, K. R. (2010), 'Evolutionary history of partible paternity in lowland South America', *Proceedings of the National Academy of Sciences* 107:45.

21   Manguvo, A. and Mafuvadze, B. (2015), 'The impact of traditional and religious practices on the spread of Ebola in West Africa: Time for a strategic shift', *The Pan African Medical Journal* 22.

22   See for example: Richerson, P. J. and Boyd, R. (1998), *The Evolution of Human Ultra-sociality, Indoctrinability, Ideology, and Warfare: Evolutionary Perspectives.*

23   See for example: Schwartz, S. H. (2012), 'An overview of the Schwartz theory of basic values', *Online Readings in Psychology and Culture* 2:1.

24   Bateson, M., Nettle, D. and Roberts, G. (2006), 'Cues of being watched enhance cooperation in a real-world setting', *Biology Letters* 2:3; Francey, D. and Bergmuller, R. (2012), 'Images of eyes enhance investment in a real-life public good', *PLoS ONE* 7.

25   Schmidt, M. F., Rakoczy, H. and Tomasello, M. (2012), 'Young children enforce social norms selectively depending on the violator's group affiliation', *Cognition* 124:3; Schmidt, M. F. and Tomasello, M. (2012), 'Young children enforce social norms', *Current Directions in Psychological Science* 21:4; Rakoczy, H. and Tomasello, M. (2009), 'Done wrong or said wrong? Young children understand the normative directions of fit of different speech acts', *Cognition* 113:2; Rakoczy, H., Warneken, F. and Tomasello, M. (2009), 'Young children's selective learning of rule games from reliable and unreliable models', *Cognitive Development* 24:1.

26   Gestures key too: Cataldo, D. M., Migliano, A. B. and Vinicius, L. (2018), 'Speech, stone tool-making and the evolution of language', *PLoS ONE* 13:1; Lieberman, P. (2006, June), 'The FOXP2 gene, human cognition and language', *International Congress Series* 1296; Fitch, W. T. (2011), 'The evolution of syntax: An exaptationist perspective', *Frontiers in Evolutionary Neuroscience* 3:9.

27   Dunbar, R. I. (2004), 'Gossip in evolutionary perspective', *Review of General Psychology* 8:2.

28   Social proof and authority may be particularly useful influence tactics in a collectivist culture –provoking shame when norms are not lived up to (i.e. 'Look how you did not act the same way as everyone else' may be more effective than guilt: 'Look how you failed to live up to that commitment you made'). On the other hand, in an individualist context, using tactics relating to consistency/commitment may work especially well.

29   Beaulieu, C. (2004), 'Intercultural study of personal space: A case study', *Journal of Applied Social Psychology* 34:4.

30   Copeland, L. and Griggs, L. (1985), *Going International.*

31   Rozin, P., Haidt, J. and Fincher, K. (2009), 'From oral to moral', *Science* 323:5918.

32   Billig, M. and Tajfel, H. (1973), 'Social categorization and similarity in intergroup behaviour', *European Journal of Social Psychology* 3:1; Yang, X. and Dunham, Y. (2019), 'Minimal but meaningful: Probing the limits of randomly assigned social identities', *Journal of Experimental Child Psychology* 185.

33   Cunningham, W. A. et al. (2012), 'Rapid social perception is flexible: Approach and avoidance motivational states shape P100 responses to other-race faces', *Frontiers in Human Neuroscience* 6.

34   Navarrete, C. D. et al. (2009), 'Fear extinction to an out-group face: The role of target gender', *Psychological Science* 20:2.

35   Hertel, G. and Kerr, N. L. (2001), 'Priming in-group favoritism: The impact of normative scripts in the minimal group paradigm', *Journal of Experimental Social Psychology* 37:4.

36   Galinsky, A. D. and Moskowitz, G. B. (2000), 'Perspective-taking: Decreasing stereotype expression, stereotype accessibility, and in-group favoritism', *Journal of Personality and Social Psychology* 78:4.

37   Patané, I. et al. (2020), 'Exploring the effect of cooperation in reducing implicit racial bias and its relationship with dispositional empathy and political attitudes', *Frontiers in Psychology* 11.

38   Scholars such as David Beereby are critical of contact theory, not least because it seems to assume fixed identities and identity features, rather than fluid flexible ones. However human identity is subject to wider structures no matter how fluid. In the Israeli-Palestinian example, even if manipulating identity features could be used to bring these individuals together under the specified conditions, once they returned to their respective home environments the social structures there appeared to make the more entrenched, antagonistic aspects of identity salient once more.

39   Leiserowitz, A. et al. (2021), 'Global warming's six Americas: A review and recommendations for climate change communication', *Current Opinion in Behavioral Sciences* 42.

40   Bliuc, A. M. et al. (2015), 'Public division about climate change rooted in conflicting socio-political identities', *Nature Climate Change* 5(3), 226–9.

41   See, for instance: Markov, A. V. and Markov, M. A. (2020), 'Runaway brain-culture coevolution as a reason for larger brains: Exploring the "cultural drive" hypothesis by computer modeling', *Ecology and Evolution* 10(12), 6059–77.

4. Identity

1   *The Bible*, Genesis 3:7, New International Version.

2   Anderson, J. R. (1984), 'Monkeys with mirrors: Some questions for primate psychology', *International Journal of Primatology* 5:1.

3   But some fascinating new research suggests a range of other animals may be able to do so. See: Buehler, J. (2018), 'This tiny fish can recognize itself in a mirror. Is it self-aware?', *National Geographic*.

4   Casonova, J. (1797) *History of My Life Until the Year 1797*.

5   Barrick, M. R. and Mount, M. K. (1991), 'The big five personality dimensions and job performance: A meta-analysis', *Personnel Psychology* 44:1.

6   Cobb-Clark, D. A. and Tan, M. (2011), 'Noncognitive skills, occupational attainment, and relative wages', *Labour Economics* 18:1.

7   Cialdini, R. B. (2006), *Influence: The Psychology of Persuasion*.

8   Shih, M., Pittinsky, T. L. and Ambady, N. (1999), 'Stereotype susceptibility: Identity salience and shifts in quantitative performance', *Psychological Science*, 10:1.

9   Snyder, M. (1974), 'Self-monitoring of expressive behavior', *Journal of Personality and Social Psychology* 30:4. See also: Snyder, M. and Tanke, E. D. (1976), 'Behavior and attitude: Some people are more consistent than others', *Journal of Personality*, 44:3; Gangestad, S. W. and Snyder, M. (2000), 'Self-monitoring: Appraisal and reappraisal', *Psychological Bulletin* 126:4; Shavitt, S. (1992), 'Evidence for predicting the effectiveness of value-expressive versus utilitarian appeals: A reply to Johar and Sirgy', *Journal of Advertising* 21:2.

10   DeBono, K. G. and Telesca, C. (1990), 'The influence of source physical attractiveness on advertising effectiveness: A functional perspective 1', *Journal of Applied Social Psychology* 20:17.

11   Baca-Motes, K. et al. (2013), 'Commitment and behavior change: Evidence from the field', *Journal of Consumer Research* 39:5.

12   Catmull, E. (2008), *How Pixar Fosters Collective Creativity*.

13   Stenner, K. (2005), *The Authoritarian Dynamic*, vol. 10. See also: Schnelle, C. et al. (2021), 'Authoritarianism beyond disposition: A literature review of research on contextual antecedents', *Frontiers in Psychology* 1843.

14   Though we also share around 99 per cent of our DNA with chimps, 70 per cent of our DNA with deep sea worms, and 60 per cent with bananas.

5. Power

1   Nietzsche, F. (1883), *Thus Spoke Zarathustra*.

2   De Waal, F. (1995), 'Bonobo sex and society', *Scientific American* 272:3.

3   Ungar, L. et al. (2012), 'The good judgment project: A large-scale test', *AAAI Technical Report* FS-12-06, Machine Aggregation of Human Judgment; Tetlock, P. E. and Gardner, D. (2016), *Superforecasting: The Art and Science of Prediction*; Tetlock, P. (2017), *Expert Political Judgement: How Good Is It? How Can We Know?*

4   Penned by English author Edward Bulwer-Lytton in Bulwer-Lytton, E. (1839), *Richelieu, or the Conspiracy*.

5   Bachrach, P. and Baratz, M. S. (2012), 'Two faces of power', *American Political Science Review* 56:4.

6   Lukes, S. (1974), *Power: A Radical View*.

7   Marmot, M. (2004), 'Status syndrome', *Significance* 1:4.

8   Rule, N. O. et al. (2012), 'Perceptions of dominance following glimpses of faces and bodies', *Perception* 41:687.

9   Thomsen, L. et al. (2011), 'Big and mighty: Preverbal infants mentally represent social dominance', *Science* 331:477.

10   Boehm, C. (1993), 'Egalitarian behavior and reverse dominance hierarchy', *Current Anthropology* 34:3, 227–54.

11   Goodall, J. (1971), *In the Shadow of Man*.

12   Sandman, M. (1938), Texts from the Time of Akhenaten.

13   Shariff, A. and Norenzayan, A. (2007), 'God is watching you: Priming God concepts

increases prosocial behavior in an anonymous economic game', *Psychological Science* 18:803; Gervais, W. (2012), 'Like a camera in the sky? Thinking about God increases public self-awareness and socially desirable responding', *Journal of Experimental Social Psychology* 48:298.

14   Norenzayan, A. and Shariff, A. (2008), 'The origin and evolution of religious prosociality', *Science* 422:58.

15   'AP EXPLAINS: What we know about S. Korean political scandal', *Associated Press*, 26 October 2016, retrieved 31 October 2016.

16   Raven, B. H. (1999), 'Kurt Lewin address: Influence, power, religion, and the mechanisms of social control', *Journal of Social Issues* 55:1.

17   Foucault, M. (1978), *History of Sexuality*.

18   Lord Acton (1887), found in Acton-Creighton correspondence (available to the public).

6. The Stage

1   Exodus 24:4

2   https://blog.britishnewspaperarchive.co.uk/2014/10/27/11-unusual-tales-of-terror-from-historical-newspapers/

3   The *New York Sun*, 3 September 1833.

4   Hancock, J. T., Thom-Santelli, J. and Ritchie, T. (2004), 'Deception and design: The Impact of communication technology on lying behavior', CHI '04: Proceedings of the SIGCHI Conference on Human Factors in Computing Systems, pp. 129–134.

5   https://www.scmp.com/news/world/article/1691364/russian-woodpecker-depicts-moscow-ordering-1986-cernobyl-nuclear-meltdown; or see this for detail of the 'woodpecker': https://www.bbc.com/reel/video/p0864g3p/the-secret-soviet-radar-hidden-in-chernobyl-s-shadow ; and on the 'black bird': https://www.news.com.au/technology/environment/the-frightening-supernatural-story-of-the-black-bird-of-chernobyl/news-story/74ea2f417564e6ca1a289e0813d09341

6   https://www.wired.com/2002/06/lech-walesa-tech-freedom-fighter/

7   Pomerantsev, P. (2017), *Nothing is True and Everything Is Possible*, p. 269.

8   A great summary of these can be found here: Mathur, A., et al. (2019), 'Dark patterns at scale: Findings from a crawl of 11k shopping websites', *Proceedings of the ACM on Human-Computer Interaction* 31, CSCW, article no. 81, pp. 1–32, https://doi.org/10.1145/3359183

9   Kramer, A. D. I., Guillory, J. E. and Hancock, J. T. (2014), 'Experimental evidence of massive-scale emotional contagion through social networks', PNAS, 111:24, pp. 8788–90

10   Berger, K. and Milkman, K. L. (2011), 'What makes online content viral?', *Journal of Marketing Research* 49:2.

11   https://www.theguardian.com/commentisfree/2021/may/30/big-tech-cat-video-artists-tips-musicians-spotify-donation

12   Bond, R. M. et al. (2012), 'A 61-million-person experiment in social influence and political mobilization', *Nature* 489.

13   Goel, S., Watts, D. J. and Goldstein, D. G. (2012), 'The structure of online diffusion networks', *Proceedings of the 13th ACM Conference on Electronic Commerce*; Tatar, A. et al. (2014), 'A survey on predicting the popularity of web content', *Journal of Internet Services and Applications* 5:8.

14 https://www.hindustantimes.com/india-news/he-looked-like-a-terrorist-how-a-drive-in-rural-india-ended-in-a-mob-attack-and-a-lynching/story-48MpOGGkqjbDwgv3eigOwJ.html

15 https://www.wired.co.uk/article/5g-health-risks-concerns

16 Shahsavari, S. et al. (2020), 'Conspiracy in the time of corona: Automatic detection of emerging Covid-19 conspiracy theories in social media and the news', *Journal of Computational Social Science 3:2*.

17 https://www.reuters.com/article/uk-britain-election-debate-twitter-idUSKBN1XT2U6

18 https://www.bellingcat.com/news/uk-and-europe/2018/01/05/kremlins-shifting-self-contradicting-narratives-mh17/

19 Ramsay, G. and Robertshaw, S. (2019), 'Weaponising news: RT, Sputnik and targeted disinformation', Kings College London, https://www.kcl.ac.uk/news/how-russian-state-media-weaponises-news

20 https://www.polygraph.info/a/classic-formula-russia-spins-multiple-navalny-poisoning-narratives/30821607.html

21 For example see: https://www.eeas.europa.eu/delegations/azerbaijan/pro-kremlin-disinformation-covid-19-vaccines_en?s=217 or https://www.rferl.org/a/russian-state-tv-repeats-bizarre-baseless-claims-about-bill-gates-and-covid-19/30585799.html

22 Most spectacularly, in the case of lead pastor of New Life Church and President George W Bush confidante, Ted Haggard. See also the travails of evangelical pastor Jerry Falwell Junior.

23 Stop the steal deep roots: https://www.bbc.co.uk/news/blogs-trending-55009950

24 https://www.foxnews.com/politics/trump-claims-mail-in-ballots-will-be-printed-by-foreign-countries https://www.breitbart.com/europe/2020/11/10/britains-sordid-history-mail-in-voting-fraud/

25 https://www.bbc.co.uk/news/election-us-2020-54874120

26 https://www.washingtonpost.com/lifestyle/style/kraken-trump-election-powell-giuliani/2020/12/09/6f6944ea-381e-11eb-bc68-96af0daae728_story.html

27 https://www.npr.org/2020/11/10/933112418/the-trump-campaign-has-had-almost-no-legal-success-this-month-heres-what-they-ve?t=1658248069948

28 https://www.propublica.org/article/election-fraud-ballot-mules-facebook-tiktok-memes

29 https://www.independent.co.uk/news/world/americas/us-politics/trump-china-thermostats-jeffrey-clark-b1898785.html

30 https://www.reuters.com/article/uk-fact-check-debunking-italy-gate-idUSKBN29K2N8

31 https://www.foxnews.com/opinion/tucker-carlson-government-agents-helped-organize-capitol-riot

32 https://fivethirtyeight.com/features/at-least-120-republicans-who-deny-the-2020-election-results-will-be-on-the-ballot-in-november/

33 https://www.theatlantic.com/ideas/archive/2020/09/future-propaganda-will-be-computer-generated/616400/

34 https://twitter.com/dileeplearning/status/1598959545229115392?s=20&t=NRPR88KBbdcsd3Rbui2HMQ

35 https://twitter.com/Bumblebor/status/1598723667608879105?s=20&t=5jB0ouzaB8z88LG3VA3pgg

36   https://www.newsguardtech.com/misinformation-monitor/march-2023/

37   Kozyreva, A. et al. (2022), 'Critical ignoring as a core competence for digital citizens', *Current Directions in Psychological Science* 32:1.

38   Allcott, H. et al. (2020), 'The Welfare effects of social media', *American Economic Review* 110:3.

7. The Cast

1   https://medium.com/@ushadrons/this-is-space-is-a-repository-for-content-from-the-russian-twitter-account-jenna-abrams-c1570b468b86

2   https://www.thedailybeast.com/jenna-abrams-russias-clown-troll-princess-duped-the-mainstream-media-and-the-world

3   https://gizmodo.com/here-are-the-microsoft-twitter-bot-s-craziest-racist-ra-1766820160

4   See for example: https://www.theguardian.com/technology/2021/apr/09/facebook-removes-over-16000-groups-trading-fake-reviews or https://www.ft.com/content/bb03ba1c-add3-4440-9bf2-2a65566aef4a

5   See: https://www.wired.com/2016/05/twitterbots-2/; https://www.mediaite.com/online/these-latino-twitter-accounts-all-have-suspiciously-identical-praise-of-trump/; https://www.pastemagazine.com/articles/2017/06/how-the-trump-russia-data-machine-games-google-to.html or deeper analysis in Howard, P. N., Woolley, S. and Calo, R. (2016), 'Algorithms, bots, and political communication in the US 2016 election: The challenge of automated political communication for election law and administration', *Journal of Information Technology and Politics* 15:2.

6   https://venturebeat.com/2016/09/05/this-is-the-first-chatbot-to-be-arrested/

7   https://www.globalbankingandfinance.com/the-growth-in-click-fraud-and-the-telling-signs-to-look-out-for-when-running-ad-campaigns/ and https://cheq.ai/biggest-ad-fraud-cases-in-2020/

8   https://www.newscientist.com/article/mg23130851-300-troll-hunters-the-twitterbots-that-fight-against-online-abuse/

9   https://www.cloudflare.com/en-gb/learning/bots/what-is-a-social-media-bot/

10 Howard, P. N. (2020), *Lie Machines: How to Save Democracy from Troll Armies, Deceitful Robots, Junk News Operations, and Political Operatives*, p. 74.

11 https://www.cs.cmu.edu/news/nearly-half-twitter-accounts-discussing-reopening-america-may-be-bots

12 https://medium.com/dfrlab/patriotic-astroturfing-in-the-azerbaijan-armenia-twitter-war-9d234206cdd7

13 https://www.washingtonpost.com/news/monkey-cage/wp/2016/05/19/the-chinese-government-fakes-nearly-450-million-social-media-comments-a-year-this-is-why/

14 https://www.cosmopolitan.com/uk/reports/a12013334/how-to-build-successful-instagram-influencer-accounts-fake/

15 https://www.dailymail.co.uk/news/article-2772489/I-complete-fool-admits-Tory-minister-Brooks-Newmark-forced-quit-sending-explicit-photos-Paisley-pyjamas.html; https://www.buzzfeed.com/jimwaterson/brooks-newmark-resignation; https://graziadaily.co.uk/life/real-life/tweets-brought-brooks-newmark-far-20-something-activist-really-behave/

16 Joinson, A. N. (2004), 'Self-esteem, interpersonal risk, and preference for e-mail to face-to-face communication', *Cyberpsychology and Behaviour* 7:4, pp. 472–8, http://dx.doi.org/10.1089/cpb.2004.7.472

17 Originally outlined in Walther, J. B. (1996), 'Computer-mediated communication: Impersonal, interpersonal, and hyperpersonal interaction', *Communication Research* 23:1; for a more recent view see Scott, G. G. and Fullwood, C. (2020), 'Does recent research evidence support the hyperpersonal model of online impression management?', *Current Opinion in Psychology* 36, https://pubmed.ncbi.nlm.nih.gov/32615509/

18 https://www.hsbc.co.uk/help/security-centre/romance-scams-case-study/

19 https://www.theguardian.com/us-news/2022/feb/15/tinder-swindler-americans-romance-scam-con-fbi

20 https://threatpost.com/investment-scammers-dating-app-interpol/163179/

21 https://www.independent.co.uk/news/world/americas/gaming-violence-white-nationalists-online-b2051956.html

22 Here's one overview: https://www.axios.com/2022/04/27/video-games-extremism

23 Guadagno, R. E. et al. (2010), 'Social influence in the online recruitment of terrorists and terrorist sympathizers: Implications for social psychology research', *Revue internationale de psychologie sociale* 1:23.

24 https://www.nytimes.com/2019/08/27/world/asia/china-linkedin-spies.html; see also the case of 'Mia Ash' https://www.secureworks.com/research/the-curious-case-of-mia-ash and advice from the Canadian Security Intelligence Service https://twitter.com/csiscanada/status/1671224330359799817

25 https://earthweb.com/how-many-phishing-emails-are-sent-daily/#:~:text=Email%20Statistics%202022-,1.,that's%20quite%20massive%20and%20scary!

26 https://threatcop.com/blog/russian-spear-phishing-campaign-hits-ukraine/

27 https://www.nature.com/articles/d41586-019-03759-y; https://www.interacademies.org/sites/default/files/2022-03/1.%20Full%20report%20-%20English%20FINAL.pdf; https://www.technologynetworks.com/tn/articles/inside-a-fake-conference-a-journey-into-predatory-science-321619; https://www.nature.com/articles/495433a

28 See Estonian Foreign Intelligence Service (2012) Security Environment Assessment, https://www.valisluureamet.ee/doc/raport/2021-en.pdf

29 https://carnegiemoscow.org/2008/09/16/valdai-voodoo-pub-22124

30 House of commons select committee (2018) 'Disinformation and 'fake news': Interim Report' https://publications.parliament.uk/pa/cm201719/cmselect/cmcumeds/363/36308.htm
Kirkpatrick, D. D. and Rosenberg, M. (2018) Russians Offered Business Deals to Brexit's Biggest Backer, *New York Times* https://www.nytimes.com/2018/06/29/world/europe/russia-britain-brexit-arron-banks.html

31 https://www.newsweek.com/chinas-trojan-horse-confucius-institutes-persist-campuses-opinion-1725085; https://www.heritage.org/homeland-security/commentary/confucius-institutes-chinas-trojan-horse; https://inews.co.uk/news/education/banning-china-confucius-institutes-uk-mandarin-teaching-1703186

32 https://www.independent.co.uk/voices/donald-trump-theresa-may-white-house-meeting-us-russia-relations-fight-terror-together-a7550486.html; https://www.independent.co.uk/news/business/analysis-and-features/russia-and-the-west-need-a-compromise-over-the-crimea-9848221.html

33 Johnson later admitted to having met there the former intelligence officer and father, Alexander Lebedev. Yevgeny Lebedev was later ennobled on the direction of Johnson, becoming Lord Lebedev of Siberia – a process that included Johnson overruling the House of Lords Appointments Commission as well as the advice of MI5, which once believed Lebedev represented 'a national security risk'.

34 See for example: https://www.state.gov/wp-content/uploads/2020/08/Pillars-of-Russia%E2%80%99s-Disinformation-and-Propaganda-Ecosystem_08-04-20.pdf

35 https://www.wired.co.uk/article/dnc-hack-proof-russia-democrats

36 https://firstmonday.org/ojs/index.php/fm/article/view/7090/5653

37 DiResta, R. et al. (2019), *The tactics & tropes of the Internet Research Agency*. New Knowledge.

38 Here is a useful study on the lack of provable direct impact (but remember, that's not necessarily the point): Eady, G. et al. (2023), 'Exposure to the Russian Internet Research Agency foreign influence campaign on Twitter in the 2016 US election and its relationship to attitudes and voting behavior', *Nature Communications* 14, https://www.nature.com/articles/s41467-022-35576-9

39 CIA, FBI and NSA (2017), 'Assessing Russian activities and intentions in recent US elections', Intelligence Community Assessment.

40 See it for yourself: https://thispersondoesnotexist.com/

41 https://www.sixthtone.com/news/1006531/the-ai-girlfriend-seducing-chinas-lonely-men

42 Balliet, D. (2010), 'Communication and cooperation in social dilemmas: A meta-analytic view'. *Journal of Conflict Resolution* 54:1

43 https://www.buzzfeed.com/craigsilverman/facebook-account-rental-ad-laundering-scam

44 https://www.nortonlifelock.com/blogs/norton-labs/identifying-sockpuppet-accounts-social-media

8. Who Are We?

1 https://www.nytimes.com/2020/11/23/technology/election-misinformation-facebook-twitter.html

2 See: Lawson, R. (2006), 'The science of cycology: Failures to understand how everyday objects work', *Memory and Cognition* 34; or Rozenblit, L. and Keil, F. (2002), 'The misunderstood limits of folk science: An illusion of explanatory depth', *Cognitive Science* 26:5.

3 Festinger, L., Riecken, R. and Schachter, S. (1956), *When Prophecy Fails: A Social and Psychological Study of a Modern Group That Predicted the Destruction of the World*.

4 Sunstein, C. and Vermeule, A. (2008), *Conspiracy Theories*.

5 McLuhan, M. (1967), *The Medium is the Massage: An Inventory of Effects*.

6 Investigated at length in Stenner, K. (2005), *The Authoritarian Dynamic*.

7 https://www.csis.org/blogs/examining-extremism/examining-extremism-qanon; see also the excellent BBC podcast on same topic, 'The coming storm', https://www.bbc.co.uk/programmes/m001324r

8 For a good discussion on this see: Atkinson, M. D. and Dewitt, D. (2019), 'The politics of disruption: Social choice theory and conspiracy theory politics', in

J. E. Uscinski (ed.), *Conspiracy Theories and the People Who Believe in Them*.

9   https://www.pressgazette.co.uk/uk-local-newspaper-closures-at-least-265-local-newspaper-titles-gone-since-2005-but-pace-of-decline-has-slowed/

10   https://www.usnewsdeserts.com/reports/news-deserts-and-ghost-newspapers-will-local-news-survive/the-news-landscape-in-2020-transformed-and-diminished/vanishing-newspapers/#:~:text=Since%202004%2C%20the%20United%20States,from%20almost%209%2C000%20in%202004.

11   See: https://www.cjr.org/analysis/breitbart-media-trump-harvard-study.php or related book: Benkler, Y., Faris, R. and Roberts, H. (2018), *Network Propaganda: Manipulation, Disinformation, and Radicalization in American Politics*.

12   Hassell, H. J. G., Holbein, J. B. and Miles, M.R. (2020), 'There is no liberal media bias in which news stories political journalists choose to cover', *Science Advances* 6:14, https://www.ncbi.nlm.nih.gov/pmc/articles/PMC7112764/

13   Mosleh, M. et al. (2023), 'Trade-offs between reducing misinformation and politically-balanced enforcement on social media', currently unpublished, https://psyarxiv.com/ay9q5

14   Reidl, M. J. et al. (2021), 'Reverse-engineering political protest: The Russian Internet Research Agency in the heart of Texas', *Information, Communication and Society* 25:15.

15   Benkler, Faris and Roberts, *Network Propaganda*, pp. 77–9.

16   This is represented in the Social Identification of Deindividuation Effects (SIDE) model – see Postmes, T., Spears, R. and Lea, M. (1998), 'Breaching or building social boundaries? SIDE-effects of computer-mediated communication', *Communication Research* 25(6), pp. 689–715, https://doi.org/10.1177/00936509802 5006006

17   A number of studies support these findings including Eleuteri, S., Saladino, V. and Verrastro, V. (2017), 'Identity, relationships, sexuality, and risky behaviors of adolescents in the context of social media', *Sexual and Relationship Therapy* 32:3-4; Landry, M. et al. (2017), 'Social media and sexual behavior among adolescents: Is there a link?', *Public Health and Surveillance* 3:2; and this meta-analysis, Vannucci, A. and Simpson, E. G. (2020), 'Social media use and risky behaviors in adolescents: A meta-analysis', *Journal of Adolescence* 79:1.

18   Lea, M., Spears, R. and de Groot, D. (2001), 'Knowing me, knowing you: Anonymity effects on social identity processes within groups', *Personality and Social Psychology Bulletin* 27(5), pp. 526–37, https://doi.org/10.1177/0146167 201275002

19   https://twitter.com/merrydevo/status/1261097380625121282

20   De Vries, A. (2015), 'The use of social media for shaming strangers: Young people's views', 48th Hawaii International Conference on System Sciences, https://ieeexplore.ieee.org/abstract/document/7070057

21   https://www.mic.com/articles/146335/donald-trump-supporters-on-twitter-got-tricked-into-arguing-with-an-assbott ; https://www.newscientist.com/article/mg23130851-300-troll-hunters-the-twitterbots-that-fight-against-online-abuse/

22   https://www.npr.org/2021/10/22/1048543513/facebook-groups-jan-6-insurrection

23   See https://www.wired.com/story/opinion-platforms-must-pay-for-their-role-in-the-insurrection/ and https://www.bostonglobe.com/2021/01/08/opinion/move-fast-break-things/

24   https://www.npr.org/2021/10/22/1048543513/facebook-groups-jan-6-insurrection

25 Bossetta, M., Segesten, A. D. and Trenz, H. (2017), 'Political participation on Facebook during Brexit: Does user engagement on media pages stimulate engagement with campaigns?', *Journal of Language and Politics* 17:2; Bossetta, M. et al. (2018), 'Shouting at the wall: Does negativity drive ideological cross-posting in Brexit Facebook comments?', SMSociety'18: Proceedings of the 9th International Conference on Social Media and Society.

26 Bail, C. A. et al. (2018), 'Exposure to opposing views on social media can increase political polarization', *PNAS* 115:37, https://www.pnas.org/content/115/37/9216.full

27 Broockman, D. E. and Kalla, J. L. (2022), 'The manifold effects of partisan media on viewers' beliefs and attitudes: A field experiment with Fox News viewers'. OSF Preprint.

28 https://pressgazette.co.uk/news/times-telegraph-trust/

9. Who Am I?

1 https://www.bbc.co.uk/news/uk-england-merseyside-61247774

2 https://www.theguardian.com/politics/2022/aug/03/revealed-uk-children-ensnared-far-right-ecosystem-online

3 See: https://www.nytimes.com/2018/03/10/opinion/sunday/youtube-politics-radical.html; or https://www.wired.com/story/youtube-algorithm-silence-conspiracy-theories/

4 Ribeiro, M. H. et al. (2020), 'Auditing radicalization pathways on YouTube', FAT* '20: Proceedings of the 2020 Conference on Fairness, Accountability, and Transparency.

5 Cho, J. et al. (2020), 'Do search algorithms endanger democracy? An experimental investigation of algorithm effects on political polarization', *Journal of Broadcasting & Electronic Media* 64, pp. 150–72.

6 Coroner as quoted here: https://www.theguardian.com/commentisfree/2022/oct/01/molly-russell-was-trapped-by-the-cruel-algorithms-of-pinterest-and-instagram

7 Pariser, E. (2011) *The Filter Bubble: What the Internet Is Hiding From You.*

8 Bakshy, E., Messing, S. and Adamic, L. A. (2015), 'Exposure to ideologically diverse news and opinion on Facebook', *Science* 348:6239.

9 Talamanca, G. F. and Arfini, S. (2020), 'Through the newsfeed glass: Rethinking filter bubbles and echo chambers', *Philosophy and Technology* 35:20, https://link.springer.com/article/10.1007/s13347-021-00494-z; also see this review of filter bubble and bias in information consumption: Arguedas, A. R. et al. (2022), 'Echo chambers, filter bubbles, and polarisation: A literature review', University of Oxford Reuters Institute https://reutersinstitute.politics.ox.ac.uk/echo-chambers-filter-bubbles-and-polarisation-literature-review

10 Mølmen, G. N. and Ravndal, J. A. (2021), 'Mechanisms of online radicalisation: How the internet affects the radicalisation of extreme-right lone actor terrorists', *Behavioral Sciences of Terrorism and Political Aggression.* https://doi.org/10.1080/19434472.2021.1993302

11 https://www.theguardian.com/technology/2022/mar/21/tiktok-algorithm-directs-users-to-fake-news-about-ukraine-war-study-says

12 Encapsulated in Edward Bernays' seminal book *Propaganda,* published in 1928.

13 https://www.mirror.co.uk/news/uk-news/gavin-barwell-conservative-mp-

blunder-1772319 or https://www.theguardian.com/technology/2013/mar/17/gavin-barwell-date-arab-girls-twitter

14 https://www.forbes.com/sites/kashmirhill/2012/02/16/how-target-figured-out-a-teen-girl-was-pregnant-before-her-father-did/

15 https://moonshotteam.com/the-redirect-method/

16 https://www.theguardian.com/world/2023/feb/25/google-adverts-direct-pregnant-women-anti-abortion-groups

17 https://www.nytimes.com/2013/06/23/magazine/the-obama-campaigns-digital-masterminds-cash-in.html

18 https://www.parliament.uk/globalassets/documents/commons-committees/culture-media-and-sport/Fake_news_evidence/Vote-Leave-50-Million-Ads.pdf

19 https://www.theguardian.com/news/2018/may/06/cambridge-analytica-how-turn-clicks-into-votes-christopher-wylie

20 Kosinski, M., Stillwell, D. and Graepel, T. (2012), Private traits and attributes are predictable from digital records of human behavior, *PNAS* 110:15, pp. 5802-5805. https://doi.org/10.1073/pnas.1218772110

21 Park, G. et al. (2014), 'Automatic personality assessment through social media language', *Journal of Personality and Social Psychology*, http://dx.doi.org/10.1037/pspp0000020 and Bachrach, Y. et al. (2012), 'Personality and patterns of Facebook usage', *WebSci '12: Proceedings of the 4th Annual ACM Web Science Conference*.

22 On images see: Segalin, C. et al. (2017), 'The pictures we like are our image: Continuous mapping of favorite pictures into self-assessed and attributed personality traits', *IEEE Transactions on Affective Computing* 8:2; on music see Nave, G. et al. (2018), 'Musical preferences predict personality: Evidence from active listening and Facebook likes', *Psychological Science* 29:7.

23 Youyu Wu, Y., Kosinski, M. and Stillwell, D. (2015), 'Comupter-based judgements are more accurate than those of people', *PNAS* 112:4.

24 See: https://soccermatics.medium.com/my-interview-with-aleksander-kogan-what-cambridge-analytica-were-trying-to-do-and-why-their-f869ef65d945; or https://www.wired.com/story/the-noisy-fallacies-of-psychographic-targeting/

25 Matz, S. C. et al. (2017), 'Psychological targeting as an effective approach to digital mass persuasion', *PNAS* 114:48.

26 This is supported too by this more recent study: Zarouali, B. et al. (2020), 'Using a personality-profiling algorithm to investigate political microtargeting: Assessing the persuasion effects of personality-tailored ads on social media', *Communication Research* 49:8.

27 https://www.globalwitness.org/en/blog/who-micro-targeted-political-ads-more-trump-or-biden-campaign/

28 https://www.globalwitness.org/en/campaigns/digital-threats/damaging-democracy-us-voters-uneasy-about-online-targeted-political-ads/

29 Many in the UK, at least, agree: https://yougov.co.uk/topics/technology/articles-reports/2020/10/15/most-brits-think-targeted-ads-are-creepy

30 https://www.digitaltrends.com/social-media/seriously-internet-online-ads-can-trail-you-across-devices/ or https://www.technologyreview.com/2015/07/01/167251/how-ads-follow-you-from-phone-to-desktop-to-tablet/

31 https://www.digitaltrends.com/computing/how-do-advertisers-track-you-online-we-found-out/

32   https://intelligence.house.gov/social-media-content/
33   Kosinski, M. (2021), 'Facial recognition technology can expose political orientation from naturalistic facial images', *Scientific Reports* 11:100, https://www.nature.com/articles/s41598-020-79310-1
34   Calo, R. (2014), 'Digital market manipulation', University of Washington School of Law UW Law Digital Commons
35   See: https://www.forbes.com/sites/ywang/2017/07/11/how-china-is-quickly-embracing-facial-recognition-tech-for-better-and-worse/ or https://www.scmp.com/tech/innovation/article/2174564/facial-recognition-catches-chinas-air-con-queen-dong-mingzhu
36   Yee, N. and Bailensen, J. (2007), 'The Proteus Effect: The effect of transformed self-representation on behavior', *Human Communication Research* 33:3.
37   https://slate.com/transcripts/WWpTZ0EzMktsdm1UWktiT2RGZXpNN1liVDl6czVJbWVBcXU4MXFZaHlVND0=
38   https://fullfact.org/health/maajid-nawaz-joe-rogan-covid/
39   https://www.thejc.com/lets-talk/all/how-maajid-nawaz-went-from-hero-to-conspiracy-theorist-7uMoIzMTT32E9ozWyfox9b
40   https://www.nbcnews.com/feature/nbc-out/meet-brandon-straka-gay-former-liberal-encouraging-others-walkaway-democrats-n902316
41   https://edition.cnn.com/2018/07/17/opinions/russian-bots-2018-midterm-elections-opinion-love/index.html; https://www.salon.com/2018/07/09/russian-bots-are-back-walkaway-attack-on-democrats-is-a-likely-kremlin-operation/; https://www.thedailybeast.com/the-rights-new-viral-star-is-red-pilled-hair-stylist-from-new-york
42   https://www.washingtonpost.com/politics/2019/08/02/hours-after-an-fbi-warning-about-qanon-is-published-qanon-slogan-turns-up-trumps-rally/
43   https://www.independent.co.uk/news/world/americas/us-politics/capitol-rioter-jan-6-cpac-fake-cell-b2142577.html
44   Just in case you are not convinced: https://www.npr.org/transcripts/1089530038 – 'Ukraine war: Fact-checking Russia's biological weapons claims', BBC News, 15 March 2022. Wong, Edward, 'U.S. fights bioweapons disinformation pushed by Russia and China', the *New York Times*, ISSN 0362-4331, retrieved 13 March 2022. 'In Ukraine, US-military-linked labs could provide fodder for Russian disinformation', *Bulletin of the Atomic Scientists*, retrieved 2022-03-21. Landay, Jonathan, Pamuk, Humeyra and Lewis, Simon, 'U.N. says no evidence to back Russian claim of Ukraine biological weapons program', Reuter, retrieved 21 March. 'China pushes conspiracy theory about U.S. labs in Ukraine', Bloomberg, 8 March 2022. Rising, David, 'China amplifies unsupported Russian claim of Ukraine biolabs', Associated Pres, retrieved 11 March 2022. McCarthy, Simone, 'China's promotion of Russian disinformation indicates where its loyalties lie', CNN, retrieved 11 March 12022.
45   See more here: https://www.armscontrol.org/factsheets/timeline-chemical-biological-weapons-developments-during-russias-2022-invasion-ukraine; also https://foreignpolicy.com/2022/03/02/ukraine-biolabs-conspiracy-theory-qanon/ Or on Chinese claims directly see: https://www.globaltimes.cn/page/202105/1223060.shtml
46   https://www.nytimes.com/2022/12/15/technology/russia-state-tv-ukraine-war.html
47   Zuboff, S. (2018), *The Age of Surveillance Capitalism*.

10. The Play

1   Pomerantsev, P. (2015), *Nothing Is True and Everything Is Possible*, p. 272.
2   I.e. Fukuyama, F. (1992), *The End of History and the Last Man.*
3   Rhode, D. L. (2019), Currie-Kenan Distinguished Lecture #METOO: WHY NOW? WHAT NEXT? https://scholarship.law.duke.edu/cgi/viewcontent.cgi?article=3997 &context=dlj
4   https://www.susanjfowler.com/blog/2017/2/19/reflecting-on-one-very-strange-year-at-uber
5   Epstein, R. and Robertson, R. E. (2015), 'The search engine manipulation effect (SEME) and its possible impact on the outcomes of elections', *PNAS* 112:33, https://www.pnas.org/doi/10.1073/pnas.1419828112
6   https://qz.com/1530831/an-obituary-for-baidu-argues-chinas-vast-internet-has-no-search-engine/
7   https://restofworld.org/2023/musk-twitter-right-wing-safe-space-brazil/
8   https://twitter.com/marcowenjones/status/1621226052159668227
9   https://op.europa.eu/en/publicationdetail/-/publication/c1d645d0-42f5-11ee-a8b8-01aa75ed71a1/language-de
10 https://www.platformer.news/p/yes-elon-musk-created-a-special-system
11 https://www.theguardian.com/technology/2022/oct/30/elon-musk-twitter-baseless-conspiracy-theory-paul-pelosi-attack
12 https://twitter.com/elonmusk/status/1622461270573125632?lang=en https://www.independent.co.uk/news/world/americas/elon-musk-fake-story-nato-ukraine-b2276877.html
13 https://dfrlab.org/2023/04/21/state-controlled-media-experience-sudden-twitter-gains-after-unannounced-platform-policy-change/
14 Barrett, P. M. (2022), 'Spreading the Big Lie: How social media sites have amplified false claims of US election fraud', NYU Stern, https://bhr.stern.nyu.edu/tech-big-lie; King, G., Pan, J. and Roberts, M. E. (2017), 'How the Chinese government fabricates social media posts for strategic distraction, not engaged arguments'.
15 Zuboff, *The Age of Surveillance Capitalism*, p. 413.
16 https://www.cnbc.com/2017/09/27/mark-zuckerberg-says-facebook-impact-on-2016-election-went-beyond-ads.html
17 https://www.wsj.com/articles/facebook-knows-it-encourages-division-top-executives-nixed-solutions-11590507499
18 Reported in 'Andrew Anglin: The making of an American Nazi', the *Atlantic*, https://www.theatlantic.com/magazine/archive/2017/12/the-making-of-an-american-nazi/544119/
19 Barrett, P. M. and Sims, G. (2021), 'False Accusation: The unfounded claim that social media companies censor conservatives', NYU Stern, https://bhr.stern.nyu.edu/bias-report-release-page
20 On or https://washingtonmonthly.com/2021/03/13/facebook-is-killing-journalism-and-democracy-we-should-do-something-about-it/
21 https://www.wsj.com/articles/facebook-hate-speech-india-politics-muslim-hindu-modi-zuckerberg-11597423346
22 https://freedomhouse.org/country/india/freedom-world/2022
23 https://twitter.com/mehdirhasan/status/1651590080283267074

24   https://twitter.com/UrielEpshtein/status/1657493383743406081 or https://twitter.com/JuddLegum/status/1658135845642072065

25   Here is one useful summary: https://twitter.com/badiucao/status/1586179778821836800

26   https://www.theguardian.com/us-news/2023/feb/28/fbi-director-endorses-china-lab-leak-covid-theory

27   See: https://www.hrw.org/news/2023/08/29/saudi-arabia-man-sentenced-death-tweets

28   See: https://www.theguardian.com/world/2023/sep/04/twitter-saudi-arabia-human-rights-abuses

29   https://www.ft.com/content/9ef9f592-e2bd-11e7-97e2-916d4fbac0da

30   https://www.reuters.com/world/german-spy-chief-russia-is-storm-china-is-climate-change-2022-10-17/

31   https://www.theguardian.com/commentisfree/2022/nov/27/xis-iron-grip-country-stopping-covid-uturn-desperately-needs

32   https://www.bellingcat.com/tag/crowdsourcing/

33   Benkler, Y. et al. (2020), 'Mail-in voter fraud: Anatomy of a disinformation campaign', Berkman Center Research Publication no. 2020-6, SSRN.

34   https://www.salon.com/2019/01/28/fox-news-host-julie-banderas-slams-donald-trump-bullying-journalists-is-not-presidential/

35   https://edition.cnn.com/2020/01/22/india/india-women-politicians-trolling-amnesty-asequals-intl/index.html

36   https://www.huffingtonpost.co.uk/entry/deepfake-porn_uk_5bf2c126e4b0f32bd58ba316

37   https://medium.com/cybersecurity-for-democracy/far-right-news-sources-on-facebook-more-engaging-e04a01efae90

11. Conclusion

1   Democracy leads to more stable economic growth, less corruption, and more nuanced and moderate policies – Halperin, Siegle and Weinstein (2010), https://gsdrc.org/document-library/the-democracy-advantage-how-democracies-promote-prosperity-and-peace/

2   Health policy interventions and life expectancy seem to be 'conditionally correlated with' democracy – Besley and Kudamatsu (2006), http://eprints.lse.ac.uk/33708/1/Health_and_democracy(lsero).pdf; https://www.researchgate.net/profile/Marilyn-Wise/publication/5650707_Democracy_the_forgotten_determinant_of_mental_health/links/54627cea0cf2c0c6aec1b37c/Democracy-the-forgotten-determinant-of-mental-health.pdf

3   This outlines the Capability, Opportunity, Motivation Behaviour Change model (COM-B), part of the UCL School of Behaviour Change's Behaviour Change Wheel model.

Index

Notes are indicated by the use of 'n'